THE SUCCESSFUL MIDDLE SCHOOL LEADER

CEDRICK GRAY, ED.D.

Association for Middle Level Education

Copyright © 2023 by the Association for Middle Level Education. All rights reserved.

Permission is hereby granted to the purchaser of one copy of *The Successful Middle School Leader* to reproduce pages in sufficient quantity only for meeting the purchaser's own non-commercial educational needs.

No part of this publication may be transmitted in any form or by any means, electronic or mechanical, without permission in writing from the publisher except in the case of brief quotations embodied in reviews or articles.

AMLE, The Successful Middle School, and This We Believe are registered trademarks of the Association for Middle Level Education.

ISBN: 978-1-56090-012-2
Library of Congress Control Number: 2023949636

Acknowledgements

No one that I know has succeeded without a teacher, guide, cheerleader, or mentor. And I'm sure that nobody anywhere thrives without support. I am deeply grateful for the good fortune that has been mine to have wise and caring influences in my life—people who have believed in me, challenged me, told me the truth, and stood by me.

First, I acknowledge the giver of every good and perfect gift I have by thanking God for the grace to experience the stories in the book and the ability to write them. I am living proof that with God, all things are possible.

In addition, I give warm and high tribute to the anchor and cornerstone of my life, my wife Karen, and to the sunshine of my life, my daughter Peyton. They are both in the Hall of Fame of supportive and loving family members.

For every school and school district to which I have been connected—JPS, FCS, and Legacy MCS—and every educator and staff member and person in those settings who helped me grow, learn, and develop as a leader and as a person—I am profoundly thankful.

Thank you to my mentors: Carol R. Johnson-Dean, Brenda Cassellius, James Pughsley, and Terry L. Brown, who all saw something in me that I didn't see in myself. Thank you to the "get fresh crew" who followed me from pillar to post and loved me, in spite of me: Lorene Essex, Vonda Beaty, and Elder Andrew Perpener.

Thank you, as well, to Creative Leadership Solutions led by Douglass Reeves; the Association for Middle Level Education led by Stephanie Simpson; and the Tennessee Association of Middle Schools led by Danny Trent in the legacy of Paul Williams—for allowing me the grace to lead in my unique way.

And then there's Marj Frank: thank you for answering emails at 2 am in preparation of this manuscript—patiently guiding me through long retellings of stories of triumph and trouble.

And finally, to my mom and dad, who sacrificed their dreams so that I could one day live mine—how blessed I am to be your son.

Foreword by Dr. Dru Tomlin

This book started on a mountain. Imagine being asked to drive a van up an imposing mountain with tremendous inclines, sudden switchbacks, and no guardrails on either side of the narrow passes. Imagine doing so while also carrying nervous passengers (other school and district leaders) up that precarious peak. That was how I first met Dr. Cedrick Gray and experienced firsthand his confident, personable, unflappable brand of leadership.

It was summer 2007, and Dr. Gray and I were both new faculty members of the AMLE Institute for Middle Level Leadership, a stellar gathering of school leaders from around the world dedicated to improving the educational lives of young adolescents. At the time, I was an assistant principal working outside of Atlanta, Georgia, and Dr. Gray was a principal in Memphis, Tennessee. We were both trying to feel our way around this new leadership journey with AMLE. We had new people to know. We had new questions to ask. We had new answers to discover. And we had new mountains to climb—both figurative and literal mountains. As part of a team-building activity in Colorado Springs, the AMLE Leadership Institute faculty decided to take the long, soaring journey up Pikes Peak one brisk afternoon before the Institute officially started.

Our journey began with a question: How are we going to get up there? We had neither the skills nor endurance to climb. But as school leaders, we had the ability to rent a van, which we did in no time. With van in hand, we were faced with another leadership conundrum: Who is going to drive this thing up there? Standing at the bottom of Pikes Peak, we scanned each other's faces for a courageous, willing person to answer the call. We were nervous and cautious, but then it happened. With a calm confidence and no mountain-driving experience, Cedrick stepped up, got the keys to the van, took the wheel, and drove us 14,115 feet to the summit. That was the first time I saw Cedrick's leadership in action—and I knew it was not going to be the last.

The Successful Middle School Leader

That mountainous journey in Colorado Springs taught me that anyone ascending the tricky terrain of education should learn from Cedrick's exceptional leadership outlook. We are all working and climbing through tough challenges at our schools and districts, and educational improvement needs someone who is willing to take the wheel and help others on the difficult road forward.

Fortunately, that first meeting with Cedrick grew into a friendship. I encouraged him to ponder writing about his leadership experiences, and we continued that conversation (and many others!) for several years as he gathered content for his book. And I'm thrilled to see the fruition of that work here in *The Successful Middle School Leader*.

There are two key elements that set this book apart. First, Cedrick's thoughts about leadership and learning are built on a solid foundation of bona fide experience: as a substitute teacher, teacher, school administrator, district superintendent, coach for administrators, and a student himself. While other educational authors write from theory and abstract notions about leadership, Cedrick comes from a place of authenticity. The stories he tells are genuine, honest, and filled with lessons that are like handholds on the mountain of educational change: They contain moments of challenge as well as triumph. Controversy as well as victory. And consternation as well as celebration.

The second key aspect that separates this book from others is that it is a true body of work: the heart, the head, and the hand of educational leadership. By framing his ideas within an extended metaphor of human anatomy, Cedrick has taken the abstract notion of leadership and has made it something we can see, understand, and grow from. He has created a book that is both artful and instructional.

For these reasons, I am excited for you as a reader. By opening this book, you are getting ready to experience what I did when I stood with Cedrick at the base of Pikes Peak. Through the heart, the head, and the hand—and from his years of true experience in the field—he will help you ascend the mountain of educational leadership and change.

Dr. Dru Tomlin
Principal, Heritage Middle School
Faculty, AMLE Institute for Middle Level Leadership
2nd chair tuba player, Lynnhaven Jr. High Marching Band (7th & 8th grades)
Author, *The Middle Grades Mindset* (2021, AMLE)

Words from the Author

An interesting exchange brought me to the place of writing this book. Yes, it took place on a mountain. You've already had an introduction to that by Dr. Dru Tomlin. "You have a way of putting things that anyone can relate to," he'd said after some discussions that began atop Pikes Peak. "You should write a book." I paused in disbelief for only one millisecond; his words planted a seed that kept pushing its way up through the soil of my experiences.

Several years later, we were deep into a discussion about leading schools during challenging times. Schools across the country had suddenly been closed due to the threat of a novel coronavirus. As a former superintendent, my district leadership wheels started turning at breakneck speed. All I could think about was what I would be doing if I were in the superintendent's seat again. I immediately began to blurt out dozens of thoughts, stream-of-consciousness style. As I pontificated on the predicament, he took notes feverishly. According to Dru, my "regurgitation" was overwhelming, and he suggested I take some time to write it all down for him. And so, I thought that I would write it down for everyone.

Like many other career educators, I got into teaching because I loved kids and wanted to have some positive impact on their lives. I enjoyed engaging in a pedagogical process that produced both productive struggle and electrifying enlightenment. I spent literally thousands of hours writing lesson plans, planning educational activities, and mastering instructional standards, while attending students' ballgames, spelling bees, and, unfortunately, funerals. Not unlike many teachers, I did these things because I genuinely cared about the students I taught. My students would respond to this attention by applying themselves in rigorous ways so that they achieved success—because I showed them that they could and worked to set a climate and give the support that fostered the success.

The Successful Middle School Leader

As a teacher, I couldn't help but wonder what kind of impact I might have over a school full of students. I decided, after five years in the classroom, that I would try my hand at being a school principal. As a middle school principal of 1,100 students, the role was all that I imagined and more. It was an enormous honor. I was assigned to the school with an objective to "get it off the list." We were falling in the accountability ratings and needed a solid plan to start the climb back into good standing. I felt I was the person for the job, so I rolled up my sleeves and went to work. But, of course, I wondered: What do I do first? How do I lead a "school turnaround"? This was the beginning of a long journey of asking questions and investigating the tenets of effective school leadership. And looking back, I now realize how fortuitous it was for me as a learner that I got the chance to begin the journey as a middle school leader.

At the time of this writing, I have been in the field of education for 27 years. Within that time, I have had the blessing of leading two school districts as superintendent and three schools as assistant principal or principal; I also served as teacher, lead teacher, or grade chair in the middle grades. I have twice been president of our state middle school association, as well as facilitator for a premier national organization's middle school leadership conference for 15 years. And it has been a high honor for me to participate on an advisory council for a former president regarding education and mentoring of our young African American males.

Across my career and in my current role as a leadership consultant and trainer, I have coached school districts and their leaders on multiple aspects of leadership, including turnaround practices. I have also trained school boards on developing vision and mission statements and passing balanced budgets. Additionally, I served as director of education for county government representing the educational vision and interests of the county's seven school districts and county government administration and agencies.

In all these roles, starting with that middle school principalship, I continue to explore, question, and learn about the keys to effective school leadership.

Acting on the spark ignited by Dru Tomlin, on energy and ideas from our continuing conversation, and on insights from my ongoing coaching and advising, I

Words from the Author

dove into writing. I gathered my real-time reflections and compiled the thoughts, lessons, and experiences I could recall from the last two decades. (Thank goodness I have kept journals, coaching summaries, voice memos of meetings, and close connections with many former colleagues, students, and their families!) In this book, I have the opportunity to present what I have learned for current and future middle school leaders.

Dr. Cedrick Gray

Contents

	Acknowledgements	iii
	Foreword by Dru Tomlin	v
	Words from the Author	vii
	Anatomy of a Middle School Leader (Introduction)	xiii

PART 1
Leading from the Heart — 1

1	What Does It Mean to Lead from the Heart?	3
2	Traits of Heart-Centered Leadership	11
3	Heart-Centered Leadership Strategies	49

PART 2
Leading from the Head — 89

4	What Does It Mean to Lead from the Head?	91
5	Traits of Head-Centered Leadership	103
6	Head-Centered Leadership Strategies	151

PART 3
Leading from the Hand — 191

7	What Does It Mean to Lead from the Hand?	193
8	Traits of Hand-Centered Leadership	201
9	Hand-Centered Leadership Strategies	243

Middle School Leader, You Are Built for This!
(Final Thoughts) — 273

Anatomy of a Middle School Leader

What an energizing and dynamic experience it is to be a part of a middle school! It's a place bustling with young adolescents experiencing physical, social, and emotional transitions and challenges unlike any other school group. They transform before our eyes from the first day of school to the last, and even from the opening bell to the final bell of a single day. The same young adolescent may seem like a second grader or a young adult, depending on the time of day and situation. They may be groggy one minute and bursting with energy the next; switch from a stance of "know-nothing" to "know-it-all" in a heartbeat; and fluctuate between ultra-dependence and striking independence several times a day. They can surprise you with their brilliance and innovation and delight you with their sense of humor. There's nothing quite like the rewards of helping these young people navigate the complex challenges and stresses of their lives—and doing whatever it takes to see them thrive.

This awesome group of scholars—diverse in every imaginable way—is joined by a league of courageous, creative, and diverse adults who understand and love the uniqueness of this age group. Everyone in a middle school learns and lives within the sphere of the colossal realities of change and transition, as well as among the enormous influences and pressures of the society in which they live. There is an obvious need to see and embrace the broad number of attributes and needs—academic and far beyond—of the whole person that is each of our scholars!

That's why middle school leaders must lead as whole persons. *School leader* is not a job description with a checklist of actions or skills. It is a way of being. Now more than ever, each school, classroom, and team needs a living organism at the helm—one with all its parts strong, healthy, and functioning together. As I see it, the successful school leader has a distinct anatomy that enables them to join with others in working relationships to produce the results our scholars deserve. That is, I believe that leaders are most successful when they develop and use **leadership from the**

> **Heart**—tapping into deep knowledge of themselves, their scholars, and others in the school community; attending to the emotional and personal aspects of leadership, building relationships, and inspiring and motivating those they lead.
>
> **Head**—leading with intentional thoughtfulness and reflection to consider every angle and possibility, sharpening discernment and decision making, building collaborative systems to make action plans, and acting only after serious contemplation.
>
> **Hands**—leading by visibly **doing**—demonstrating expected behaviors, setting a tone of accountability, establishing protocols that make it easy for things to get done, and leading with a can-do spirit.

These sources of leadership are highly interdependent; they're needed equally and work in harmony with one another. Each leadership source is also robustly supported by other parts of the anatomy: **the eyes**, for constant and keen observation; **the ears**, for open and active listening; and **the mouth**, carefully monitored and used to inform clearly and support positively.

ABOUT THIS BOOK

The Successful Middle School: This We Believe

Since the inception of *This We Believe*, the Association for Middle Level Education's (AMLE) landmark position statement first published in 1982, middle level educators have been reading and studying the characteristics of effective middle grades schools. The document was born from a collective group of educators passionate about the concept that the learning needs of young adolescents were different than high school and elementary students. *This We Believe* quickly became an essential resource for schools that had been trying to implement the middle school model since the 1960s. It provided a true definition of the young adolescent and detailed their unique programming needs. Over the past four decades, we have seen the original 10 Characteristics of *This We Believe* evolve into the 18 Characteristics outlined in the 2021 fifth edition, *The Successful Middle School: This We Believe*, as we continue to define how to meet the needs of young adolescents.

This companion guide to *The Successful Middle School: This We Believe* will help school leaders in various leadership roles to develop and sustain effective, visionary leadership. The descriptions of the heart, head, and hand sources of leadership, as well as the leadership traits, practices, and strategies in this book are tied to *The Successful Middle School: This We Believe* and linked to research and best practice.

The Successful Middle School Leader

In this book, I use an anatomy metaphor to present a picture of the effective middle school leader as one who leads from the heart, head, and hand. The term *school leader*, as I see it, is not limited to the principal but can include any professional educator who leads a classroom, a set of classrooms, a team or club, a school or set of schools, or who leads another school leader or group of school leaders or district leaders.

The book is presented in three parts:

- Leading from the Heart
- Leading from the Head
- Leading from the Hand

Each part contains:

- A chapter that explains what it means to lead from the heart (or head or hand) and beneficial outcomes that flow from that leadership source.
- A chapter that describes visible leadership traits or behaviors resulting from the leadership source.
- A chapter that provides hands-on leadership strategies with practices to develop and use that leadership source.

In addition, the concepts and traits are enhanced with real-life stories from my experiences that bring flavor and power to the information as well as a sprinkling of "Gray Matter" comments. These are nuggets of wisdom—bits of personal beliefs or advice that provide additional thoughts for navigating your leadership journey.

The conclusion reminds readers of the interdependence of all the leadership sources and approaches. It also encourages all middle school leaders to believe that they are built for the job—that they have the anatomy to succeed and thrive in this lively, life-changing role of a middle school leader.

Note: You'll notice in this book that I have sometimes referred to *students* as *scholars*. Years ago, I began using *scholars* as a way to refer to our students as people being laser-focused on education and learning. It was a way to let them know that I expected more from them, and that to me, each represented a true pursuer of knowledge. I found that this elevated their own self-belief and expectations of themselves as thinkers and learners.

PART 1

LEADING FROM THE HEART

Chapter 1   **What Does It Mean to Lead from the Heart?**
Chapter 2   **Traits of Heart-Centered Leadership**
Chapter 3   **Heart-Centered Leadership Strategies**

The Successful Middle School: This We Believe
Characteristics Crossover

- Educators respect and value young adolescents.
- The school environment is welcoming, inclusive, and affirming for all.
- Every student's academic and personal development is guided by an adult advocate.
- Comprehensive counseling and support services meet the needs of young adolescents.
- The school engages families as valued partners.
- The school collaborates with community and business partners.
- Health, wellness, and social-emotional competence are supported in curricula, school-wide programs, and related policies.
- Policies and practices are student-centered, unbiased, and fairly implemented.
- Leaders are committed to and knowledgeable about young adolescents, equitable practices, and educational research.
- Leaders demonstrate courage and collaboration.
- Professional learning for staff is relevant, long term, and job embedded.
- Organizational structures foster purposeful learning and meaningful relationships

Chapter 1

What Does It Mean to Lead from the Heart?

A Challenge for the New Principal

Three months after a horrifying event in the neighborhood, I was assigned as the principal at Lester Demonstration School. The murders of several members of a local family (including children) had left the Binghampton community and city of Memphis reeling. Some family members survived but were severely traumatized. People were terrified. Our hearts were broken. In this neighborhood, starting school was the very last thing on anyone's mind. Except mine.

Several of the surviving students attended Lester. Teachers were apprehensive, to say the least. District officials said they needed someone who could "walk on water." That was supposed to be me! It was just my second experience as a principal. I felt the only way to push forward was to inspire first, then support.

The weather was hot and oppressive. I was frustrated. It was about two weeks from the opening of school, and no one was looking forward to it—not the school staff, not the community.

Most educators know about those before-the-school-year preparation weeks. Usually, the leader welcomes everyone and gives a pep talk. In addition to getting classrooms ready, teachers attend meetings to review procedures, look over data and information about incoming students, and take care of various "housekeeping" chores. I knew these kinds of activities would deaden us further. I had to think of a way to uplift the teachers and inspire the neighborhood around the opening of school.

I designed and printed some attractive flyers that gave an upbeat back-to-school welcome, the schedule for the opening of school, and an outline of the registration process. When the teachers arrived on the first day of their contract, I greeted them with this: "No meetings today, folks. Instead, you're invited to accompany me on a field trip." We grabbed piles of flyers and headed out for a walk around the neighborhood.

As we walked, teachers began to notice that the streets were named after Ivy League schools: Harvard, Yale, and Princeton, to name a few. I was inspired to stop at the corner of Harvard and Carpenter Street. We stood in solemn silence for a few minutes as we looked around the neighborhood with its blighted houses and overgrown weeded lots. Then I began to speak to the group (all of them new to me) about the hope that we as educators can instill in our scholars. "In the middle of the Binghampton community of Memphis," I told them, "if we do our jobs right, we can send these scholars from the heart of Binghampton straight to Harvard, Yale, and Princeton. We are their hope. They have us. And we have each other. Together, we can do this."

It was right there that we derived our mantra, which stood for years after I left Lester Demonstration School: "The heart of Binghampton—around the corner from Harvard!"

The teachers were energized. They continued the walk around the community, passing out flyers and talking to neighbors. Their inspiration and enthusiasm grew as they connected and shared with parents and caregivers. (And so did mine!) We could see faces brighten as community members engaged in conversations about the opening of school.

H**eart-centered leadership** is heart-to-heart connection. It happens when the leader's heart speaks to someone else's heart. When you lead from the heart, all the communications and actions of leadership derive from the source of human-to-human connection.

Heart leadership does not always come in the form of a speech to a group or even a conversation with an individual. Sometimes it's just a few words, or only one whispered word. Or no words. The connection might be just a look, a smile, a thumbs-up, or a high five. It can be a touch on the shoulder, a hug (or "air" hug), a positive nod, a few tears. Heart-to-heart communication happens with an extended hand, a quickly passed note, an unexpected gift of a cup of coffee, opening a car door for a student arriving at school, or grabbing someone's load of books and carrying it in through the doors. Keeping your office door open is also a dynamic act of leadership from the heart.

One of the most powerful forms of heart leadership is **just being there**. This is something that, as a leader, you have an opportunity to do hundreds of times throughout your week, on and off the school campus. From spending the first hour of the school day popping in and out of classrooms to "showing your face" at sporting events and birthday parties, your engaged presence reaches deeply into hearts.

You lead from **your heart** when the people you lead sense these messages in **their hearts**: "The leader sees me, knows something about me, knows what I need. The leader believes I am an important part of this school. The leader wants me here. The leader values me and what I do. The leader is interested in what I feel and what I have to say."

THE FRUITS OF HEART-CENTERED LEADERSHIP

When the heart is a source of leadership, such results as these naturally follow:

Inspiration and Motivation

Inspire means to awaken and enliven in someone the urge to do or accomplish something. Heart-centered leadership is profoundly inspirational. Something that the leader says, does, or shows influences others in a way that brings to life all kinds of talents, passions, and possibilities. It affects someone in a way that stimulates them **to realize** something they want to do, **to notice** the abilities they already possess that can make it possible, **to believe** that they can do it, and **to go for it**!

Notice that the definition does not say that the inspirer **gives** life to the other person, or **transfers to them** the urge or the ability to do something. You can't give it to someone else. No, the actual inspiration comes from within. An outside person or event can light the spark or sound an alarm, but the passion and the will to go after a goal or fulfill a purpose were already there, waiting to be ignited. And when they're ignited, watch out! The inspiration combustion releases all kinds of energy, growth, and accomplishments.

Motivate means to offer a reason or need for doing something. Usually, we're motivated by external circumstances to act or perform. Often there is an incentive or reward associated with the motivation. Many things can motivate: a person, a group, a positive or negative circumstance, an urgent need or crisis. (The events of 9/11, for example, motivated thousands of U.S. citizens to enlist in military service.) When the leader motivates, they stimulate or encourage someone in a direction—maybe even providing ideas for what the person can try. Something the leader says or shows turns on a light, illuminating a reason for others to act.

Though *inspiration* and *motivation* are commonly confused or used interchangeably, there is a difference. *Motivation* is a **push**. *Inspiration*, on the other hand, is intrinsic, even divine. It **pulls** us to act even when we might rather not or when doing so might create adverse consequences or difficulties for us personally. Rev. Dr. Martin Luther King, Jr. was *motivated* to participate in the Civil Rights Movement because of his experience as a Black man. He had plenty of reasons to want to change the culture. He was *inspired from within*, ignited by his faith, to sacrifice time with his family and even his own life to help make the world a better place for all people, specifically Black and Brown people. This inspiration stirred up and emboldened the passions and gifts that were already his.

Motivation can get you started, but *inspiration* will keep you going because it draws from your deepest resources. When you are inspired from the fire within, you will continue to get up each morning to put in the work to accomplish your goals. Inspiration drives you through challenges that arise during your journey; it becomes your keystone of hope. Truly inspired educators touch the lives of hundreds of students and their families, regardless of where that student comes from. A leader is called on to both motivate and inspire. Leadership from the heart develops and spreads each of these gifts.

Passion

When a trusted leader speaks from their heart to yours, it helps you unearth what you really care about—what's important to you. This breeds enthusiasm to work hard. It triggers your drive to make something happen. A heart-centered leader taps into their own passions, showing and speaking them freely. The leader models the zeal and intensity that helps make a difference with dedication to something that matters. Passion is inspiration on steroids! It is from the heart-leadership source that you share your passion for your job and all its facets. Most importantly, the heart-centered leader exudes deep passion and care for all of those folks in their sphere.

Honor for Others

Strong and healthy heart-centered leadership acts on deep beliefs in the equal and undisputable value of everyone. In all actions and interactions, the leader outwardly acknowledges this value—so that every individual feels a sense of belonging. This regard for others includes high esteem and gratitude for all members of the school community. The leader's reverence for the worth of each person is evident in their interactions, in school policies and procedures, in school curriculum, and throughout the school culture.

No matter what important explanation or wisdom is communicated, the heart-centered leader is aware that their listeners and watchers are also picking up messages about their own place and importance in the school community. These messages get passed on through many behaviors and actions—everything from the way the event is organized to the words and body language of the speaker.

Connection

You cannot speak from your own heart without a deep connection to yourself. And you can only speak to the hearts of others when you have somehow connected to what is in theirs. Heart-centered leadership naturally fosters connections of all sorts. This leader is aware of the need for people to talk to each other, listen to each other, learn about each other, work together, struggle together, make decisions together, and celebrate together.

Part of leading from the heart is a heightened awareness of your own and other people's emotions. Keen perceptions of emotions further the processes of knowing and honoring others. And that's what authentic human connection is: *a sense of closeness or trust that involves people feeling seen, heard, and valued by one another*.

Empathy, Compassion, and Comfort

Empathy is the action of being aware of and experiencing the feelings or experiences of another person. Empathy flows from heart-centered leadership. When leading from the heart, you come to know members of your school community and be known by them. You learn about their joys and hopes and heartaches. These processes breed empathy—understanding, kindness, tenderness—into your interactions with those you lead.

Compassion gives importance and value to the pain of others and vitalizes us to want to help alleviate the pain. Literally, *compassion* means *to suffer with*. You cannot always feel (empathize with) someone else's feelings because you may not have had the same experiences. But your compassion enables you to be with them in their pain. It galvanizes you to act in ways that give some help or comfort to the other—to be kind and gentle, to listen, and most importantly, to be present.

Comfort is consolation or relief, especially in difficult times. Within any human community, there will be many scary moments, uncontrollable situations, crises, issues, disappointments, and wounds in the life of that group. These happen on small scales daily, but too often on large scales as well. It can be anything from a broken wrist on the playground to a broken heart leaving someone crying in the bathroom (or faculty room) to murder in the neighborhood. Any leader frequently finds themselves in the role of comforter. Only heart-centered leadership can begin to reach the souls of those who are hurting.

Security

Leadership that comes from the heart embraces the understanding that everyone's deepest needs, feelings, hopes, and fears are part of the landscape of any school situation. A member of the school community senses this and feels: "I can trust that this leader intends to protect and support us and that they care about our needs. I see that the leader values all of us as individuals and wants to know our viewpoints and feelings as part of discussions and decisions about school programs and policies. It is safe to listen to and communicate with this leader."

Hope

These components and outcomes of heart-centered leadership beget something else extraordinary and powerful. It's that uplifting four-letter word: HOPE. The inspiration, swell of passion, and connection generated by heart-to-heart connection nourishes elements that add up to hope. Optimism rises. The leader's inspiration and confidence spreads to teachers, staff, students, and others beyond the school. People begin to believe that they **do** have the ability to get things done, that challenges **will** be met, and that things **can** get better. They see prospects as possible. The future looks brighter.

A Challenge for the New Principal, continued

During the darkest hours in the Binghampton community, amid depressing surroundings and the discouraging history of failure, we educators went together onto the streets to be with the people. We connected to their hearts by reaching out with ours. With every minute and hour that passed, our confidence and optimism grew. Street by street and block by block, passions awoke. The teachers got an infusion of hope—hope that they could do a good job of teaching these students, that the young people could reach great heights. The community members experienced the school staff coming to them right where they live and showing care for them and their families. This spread hope to folks in our neighborhood—hope for their children and the success of the school and hope of recovery from aching, broken hearts. Everyone found new energy for the venture of a new school year.

I'm thrilled to report that this fresh enthusiasm carried through the school year and beyond. Over that year and the following year of my leadership, Lester Demonstration School recorded the greatest academic growth it had experienced in a decade. This took plenty of hard work, a lot of mutual support among leaders, staff, parents, students, and the wider community—plus large doses of hope.

DEVELOPING HEART-CENTERED LEADERSHIP

Without heart-centered attitudes and actions, a critical piece of leadership is missing. The most brilliant policies, initiatives, procedures, or decisions don't stand a chance. They'll just be words and flowcharts on paper or screens. Without heart, they'll be empty of connection and inspiration. This is why I began the book with leadership from the heart. Yes, we need strategic leadership from a sharp mind and leadership where hands get moving to get things done well. But it's imperative to fortify head and hand leadership with heart leadership.

My descriptions of leadership from the heart assume some things that may not be true at all times of every leader's heart. To be an effective heart-centered leader, your heart must be open and welcoming. It must contain care and kindness. If the heart is closed, hostile, self-sufficient, overly protected, arrogant, or biased, you won't be able to connect with other hearts. If what's in your heart is fearful, suspicious, bitter, or pessimistic, it is unlikely to inspire other hearts. So part of heart leadership development is examining your own heart, noticing how it affects you and others, and working to keep a healthy, caring heart.

Your heart is not the only "part of the anatomy" that must be open. To understand what is in your heart and the hearts of others, you will need to stay finely tuned to your senses—your eyes developing a keen observation and your ears becoming skilled listeners. This is how we learn about ourselves and others. Eyes and ears are part of leadership. So is the mouth. In speaking to the hearts of others, a leader must be highly alert to what they say *and* how they say it.

There are deliberate steps you can take to develop the habits of heart-centered leadership. Chapter 2 describes the leadership traits that flow from the heart, and Chapter 3 offers hands-on strategies that leaders can use to put heart-centered leadership into practice.

Once you understand what heart-centered leadership means and get a picture of how you can further develop it, you can attend to the heart in your views and practices. You can grow your healthy heart-to-heart communications. You can enjoy the fruits of heart-centered leadership as you watch such miracles as inspiration, connection, passion, and hope blossom.

Chapter 2

Traits of Heart-Centered Leadership

How does heart-centered leadership evidence itself? How can the leader tell when heart is a major source of their own leadership inspiration and action? How do others recognize and experience leadership from the heart? What follows are some of the key **observable** characteristics or behaviors that flow from the heart source. As leaders develop such traits, they grow further in their abilities to lead from the heart.

The Successful Middle School Leader
Heart-Centered Leadership Traits
The Heart-Centered Leader...

Heart Trait 1	Attends to what is in their own heart.
Heart Trait 2	Consistently examines their own behavior and how it affects others.
Heart Trait 3	Notices what is in others' hearts.
Heart Trait 4	Welcomes inspiration from others.
Heart Trait 5	Stays alert to their possible impact.
Heart Trait 6	Allows no student to flounder.
Heart Trait 7	Speaks with care.
Heart Trait 8	Radiates passion for their job and their people.
Heart Trait 9	Puts relationships at the heart of everything they do.
Heart Trait 10	Is keenly aware that they are always "on duty."

Heart Trait 11	Seeks and listens to all input and feedback.
Heart Trait 12	Adds heart to their discernment.
Heart Trait 13	Is real.
Heart Trait 14	Taps into their own empathy and compassion.
Heart Trait 15	Regularly debriefs and reflects after key events.
Heart Trait 16	Develops heart-centered leadership as a team.
Heart Trait 17	Shows up (and shows their heart) during crises.
Heart Trait 18	Affirms and celebrates all stakeholders.
Heart Trait 19	Is brave.

Heart Leadership Trait 1: The heart-centered leader attends to what is in their own heart.

The leader works hard to know and understand what is in their own heart. As part of building healthy school cultures, educators give serious attention to the state of relationships among the various members of school communities. We strive to develop trusting, healthy teacher-student relationships, peer relationships, staff relationships, school-family relationships, and school-community relationships. But frequently, we neglect to attend to a relationship that is foundational to the others: **our relationships with ourselves**. When a leader reaches out from the heart to touch the hearts of others, they absolutely must do so with awareness of the status of their own heart—that is, their own personal emotions and drives.

This means that a focus on the heart is a priority for any leader. Knowing your heart means paying attention to your deepest goals, feelings, passions, fears, joys, motivations, hopes, and your level of belonging. It means digging into these to notice underlying attitudes, agendas, and biases, as well as what triggers, pleases, energizes, or threatens you. And it means honest inspection of your behaviors (often automatic or unplanned) that result from these.

Traits of Heart-Centered Leadership

American psychologist and science journalist Daniel Goleman, who first coined the term *emotional intelligence*, defines self-awareness as "having a deep understanding of one's strengths, limitations, values, feelings, and motives. People with high self-awareness are honest with themselves about themselves. They are realistic, neither overly self-critical nor excessively optimistic."[1] Goleman also notes that self-awareness is a core component of emotional intelligence—the necessary foundation for other components such as empathy.[2]

The intentional practice of self-awareness (deliberate delving into facets of your "heart matters") increases the leader's own positive self-development and self-control. In addition, it leads to better decision making, better communication, greater job satisfaction, and more authentic, satisfying relationships with others.[3,4,5,6]

Research also shows that self-awareness allows leaders to see things from the perspective of others and become more compassionate, inspirational leaders.[7,8,9] Albert Bandura, Stanford psychologist and author of the self-efficacy theory, pointed to another benefit of intentional self-awareness. He found that enhanced self-awareness increases self-efficacy, which is the belief or confidence that one can handle a situation or do a job well.[10]

As you develop your heart-centered leadership, learn more about self-awareness. Practice stepping back to notice and examine your thoughts and emotions. When you do this diligently, you can be more certain that the messages going from your heart to the hearts of others are what you want them to be: loving, comforting, inspiring, and energizing.

In Chapter 3, see **Heart Leadership Strategy 1: Leader's Heart Check-Up, Part 1: Looking Inward** on page 50, for practice in attending to what is in the leader's heart.

HEART LEADERSHIP TRAIT 2: THE HEART-CENTERED LEADER CONSISTENTLY EXAMINES THEIR OWN BEHAVIOR AND HOW IT AFFECTS OTHERS.

Part of self-awareness is understanding how one's emotions and thoughts influence their behavior. As a leader, you can learn plenty about what's in your own heart by:

Scrutinizing your behavior. If you reflect on your patterns of responses and actions in various situations, you can find clues. For example, pay attention to your level of patience or irritation. Think about how you speak, how quickly you speak, and what you say. Consider how your responses link to your values or biases. Notice your nonverbal reactions. When do you laugh? Smile? Scowl? Pull away? Tense up? Ask yourself: "What situations or incidents trigger such feelings as fear? Anxiety? Compassion? Insecurity? Confidence? Talking too much? Hyper-control?"

Noticing the effects of your behavior on others. People often see a leader differently from the way a leader sees themselves. Keep your ears and eyes open to learn from others. When someone freely asks you questions, chats easily, or shares ideas readily, you get a message that they're comfortable with you or feel respected. If their questions dry up after your first answer, their responses are short, or they don't readily approach or engage you, you get a different message. Few people will respond to a leader's behavior by telling them how it comes across (especially if the effect is unpleasant). The leader will have to read the body language. Does the other person smile? Laugh? Scowl? Blush? Cry? Get red in the face? Cringe? Shake your hand? Move closer? Shrink away? Walk away? Shrug?

Practicing analysis of your own behavior. Frequently and intentionally, dig deep to name and understand emotions and how you act upon them. Practice close observation and active listening to pick up clues from others. Then take time to reflect on what you learn about your own behavior and the underlying feelings and motivations.

In Chapter 3, see **Heart Leadership Strategy 2: Leader's Heart Check-Up, Part 2: Looking Outward On Behavior** on page 54, for practice in examining a leader's behavior and the way it affects others.

HEART LEADERSHIP TRAIT 3: THE HEART-CENTERED LEADER NOTICES WHAT IS IN OTHERS' HEARTS.

In order for a leader's heart to connect with the hearts of others, the leader must know something about those hearts.

Students—The heart-centered leader takes the time and puts in the work to learn the hearts of their students. At the middle school level, this means knowing and giving special attention to the developmental needs and characteristics of young adolescents. It means intentionally setting practices to get to know students and listening to them closely. The goal is to get to the matters of their hearts: their wants, hopes, needs, fears, interests, quirks, struggles, passions, and challenges. Understand well their deepest primary needs for safety, acceptance, belonging, community, and personal value. Understand well what their hearts need from you and other leaders.

Plan ways to be responsive to every aspect of the particular developmental characteristics of young adolescents—characteristics in each student as well as those that widely apply to the age group. For an overview of young adolescent developmental characteristics and implications for educators, see AMLE's *The Successful Middle School: This We Believe*.[11] It also includes a discussion of why these should be noted as generalized traits and why educators must understand each student's unique developmental characteristics.

School staff, parents and caregivers, and community members—The heart-centered leader also seeks to know what is in the hearts of other adults in the school community (other leaders, school staff, parents and caregivers, volunteers, community members beyond the school, neighbors, etc.). Whatever someone's connection to the school, you can speak to their heart only if you know something about them. To know them better, get to the matters of their hearts, too: their hopes, wants, needs, and fears. Learn about the jobs they do and what their roles involve. Learn about their past experiences with the school as well as the talents and ideas they wish to contribute to the school. Find out what the school means to them. Understand their deepest needs—such needs as safety, connection, value, esteem, appreciation, and meaningful involvement. Understand well what their hearts need from you and other leaders.

How does a leader learn about others' hearts? You work at getting to know people. You show up, meet, chat, greet, and engage students and families, staff members, community members. You tune in all your senses to individuals and groups. You watch. You listen. You pick up emotional signals. And, mostly, you ask them! (Here we have the eyes, ears, and mouth as parts of your leadership again!) Plan multiple ways to find out what they have to tell you about their hearts. You can best inspire, motivate, reassure, calm, comfort, and work effectively with others when they trust that you want to know them.

In Chapter 3, use these Heart Leadership Strategies to deepen knowledge of young adolescent students: **Strategy 3: Know Your Middle Level Students** on page 59 and **Strategy 8: Hearing Student Voices** on page 73.

Also in Chapter 3, see

- **Heart Leadership Strategy 4: Know Your Colleagues** for help learning more about the adults in the school on page 64.
- **Heart Leadership Strategy 5: Empowering Families** for ways the leader and school staff can learn about students' families and invite them to participate meaningfully in school decisions on page 66.
- **Heart Leadership Strategy 6: Value Community Partners** for strategies to help the school make connections with the wider community beyond the school on page 69.

HEART LEADERSHIP TRAIT 4: THE HEART-CENTERED LEADER WELCOMES INSPIRATION FROM OTHERS.

An Unexpected Gift

"There's absolutely no way that I'm coming back," I said to myself as I wrapped up my first substitute teaching assignment at Wooddale Heights Middle School. I thought that teaching at the very school I had attended a decade earlier would be an easy experience. But I was exhausted and overwhelmed as I placed stray wads of paper in the trash can and cleaned the board late that Friday afternoon. I had chosen the week-long assignment to gain some experience as I worked to earn my

teacher's license. The teacher preparation program at the University of Memphis was rigorous; but my instructors did not prepare me to manage the energy of a roomful of middle schoolers. After working with antsy and inquisitive young adolescents for just five days, I wondered if I wanted to spend the rest of my life trying to survive the hormonal impulses of these preteen "knuckleheads."

As I straightened up the last desk in the classroom, I noticed a student waiting in the doorway. All of five feet tall, Sonya stood with her hand on her hip and a funny smirk on her face. She looked as if she wanted to say something but could not find the words. I asked, "Sonya, right? What's up? Did you forget something?"

In typical middle school fashion, she bounced into the room in a panic. "Hey, Mr. Gray, have you seen my glasses?" She was frantic as she nearly turned over two desks looking for the treasured spectacles. "My mom is going to strangle me if I lose another pair."

"You mean this pair?" I held up the red-rimmed glasses and gave her the "you should keep them on your face, young lady" look. You would have thought that I saved the world from a zombie apocalypse as she sprinted toward me, grabbed the glasses, and hugged me.

"Thank you, Mr. Gray! You've saved my life!" With glasses in one hand, she gave me a high five with the other one. Then she was off to enjoy her now stress-free weekend.

Just as she passed through the doorway, she paused and turned back. Her next statement changed the course of my career: "Mr. Gray, I hope you are coming back next week. You're the best teacher we've ever had."

Sonya didn't know it, but she had just flipped the switch from "Off" to "On" for what would become a lifelong career in education. Out of the blue, a pair of glasses—of all things—inspired me. Though I never wore them, those glasses cleared up my vision. Her enthusiastic affirmation was the spark that reignited the passion for teaching that had filled me at the beginning of the week. I had allowed numerous distractions and frustrations to fizzle my flame. That moment inspired me to continue teaching students and, later, to lead teachers, administrators, and other district-level leaders.

As a leader, it's likely you'll find yourself in the role of the grand "inspirer." This is a core of heart-centered leadership. It's what those around you need. It's what spurs passion and the desire to get on board and get things done! But the wise leader has their eyes, ears, and heart open to **receive** inspiration as well. Don't assume that your inspiration is only triggered by "experts" or celebrated books or speeches. Your greatest inspiration will likely sneak up on you from surprising sources in places and at times that you'd never anticipate. Don't miss these gifts. You might have to practice watching for inspiration from unexpected sources so that you don't miss it when it shows up.

> **Gray Matter**
>
> *Inspiration is the alarm clock to your passion.*
>
>

See **Heart Leadership Strategy 7: Inspiration Inspection** on page 71 for an activity that increases awareness of and appreciation for moments and sources of inspiration.

HEART LEADERSHIP TRAIT 5: *THE HEART-CENTERED LEADER STAYS ALERT TO THEIR POSSIBLE IMPACT.*

The Student Superintendent

During a visit to an elementary school in my district, I joined the principal on a visit to a classroom of special needs students. I noticed one student working with several others; he appeared to be "teaching" his students a math lesson. I paused just within range so as not to disturb his process. A moment passed before he noticed me. Then suddenly, he jumped up and hurried toward me. What he said next brought tears to my eyes: "Good morning, Dr. Gray! My name is Cedrick too. Because of you, I am the 'superintendent!'"

Later, I asked the teacher what this student meant. The teacher explained that Cedrick had seen me on TV describing ways we help students succeed in our schools. This inspired him to help his fellow students in their classwork. He would bring snacks for the class and extra pencils and paper for his "students." To follow me as a model, he decided to call himself the "student superintendent." I was so humbled and moved to learn that he had been inspired by me, especially when I didn't even know or intend it.

What an astonishing cycle of inspiration: The "student superintendent" had heard my words but, more importantly, he had felt what I said. It came from my heart to his. This energized him to help others. Undoubtedly, his leadership inspired his fellow students. And watching and listening to him in action inspired me.

You may sometimes feel powerless as a school leader, but your example in and of itself sets the tone for the entire school, class, or team and can impact others in ways you've not imagined. This happens when you lead from the heart. Often, a teacher, assistant principal, student, or lunch server, for example, may say something like: "I'm just a teacher" or "I'm just the assistant" or "I'm only a lunch lady" or "I'm just a kid, not a principal!" In these instances, I'll gently correct them with, "Nobody is 'Just a . . .'! You are a leader."

When you have young, impressionable eyes watching you, you suddenly grow to a highly important person in their lives. The actions of all the adults in the school leave impressions on others. All of us can inspire and be inspired.

Heart Leadership Trait 6: The heart-centered leader allows no student to flounder.

Heart-centered leadership for young adolescent students starts with knowing who they are as a group and what they need. This knowing extends to noticing, listening, and talking to them as individuals. The leader makes sure that no student gets lost or overlooked. Each one is seen.

When you lead from the heart, you do your absolute best to build and sustain practices that will offer opportunities to speak from your heart to the heart of every student. This entire book is about leadership connections, approaches, and actions that address all of a student's needs, academic and otherwise. In this chapter, I want to emphasize the need to deliberately follow practices that nurture this matter of reaching students' hearts. This includes instituting programs or practices that involve the following:

- Curriculum and policies that support overall health and wellness, including social-emotional competence
- Structures, such as professional learning communities (PLCs), that foster purposeful relationships
- Frequent academic success checks on every student
- Consistent and targeted advisory activities
- Establishment of a welcoming, inclusive, and affirming environment for everyone
- Building a culture of belonging; monitoring the status of belonging
- Intentional teaching of specific SEL skills
- Multiple opportunities to invite, highlight, and affirm student voices
- Processes for each student to have an assigned adult advocate
- Regular, positive, and supportive contact with families
- System for informing parents and caregivers of school schedules and activities
- Training staff in trauma-informed practices and restorative practices

- Teacher expectations that show equal belief in the capabilities of all students
- Comprehensive counseling and student support services
- Commitment to addressing and eradicating bias in relating to students
- Training for staff members to identify students in need of support around adverse childhood experiences and events
- School-wide expectations that teach positive behaviors paired with an incentive program that notices and rewards students "caught being kind"
- Focus on nurturing healthy, positive relationships (teacher-student, peer, other staff-student)

I'm sure you can add to this list as you ponder what school practices strengthen leadership from the heart. Indeed, as leaders, we can all try to include heart leadership in the school's programs and practices. And, most of the items listed above apply to others in the school community. Such "attention" is due to staff members, students' family members, and community members.

In Chapter 3, see **Heart Leadership Strategy 8: Hearing Student Voices** on page 73 for questions to help leaders examine their openness to and practices for hearing from all students. Also see **Heart Leadership Strategy 9: An Advocate for Every Student** on page 74 for a way to match individual students to adult advocates.

HEART LEADERSHIP TRAIT 7: THE HEART-CENTERED LEADER SPEAKS WITH CARE.

Death and life are in the power of the tongue and those that love it shall eat the fruit thereof.[12]

Words have great power. They can encourage, bless, uplift, teach, praise, console, and inspire. They can also criticize, gossip, mislead, lie, demean, or discourage. I'm reminded of the above quote almost daily, and I frequently see its truth: we **will** "eat the fruit" of our words. And that fruit may be sweet and nourishing, or it may be bitter—even deadly.

When words are positive, they'll brighten spirits and be remembered. When they're vague, they will confuse or bore the listener. And sadly, when they're negative, they can devastate. Critical, harsh, or derogatory words will be remembered far longer than the positive ones, and their hurtful effects can last a lifetime. Sometimes even the best intentions in speaking falter because of faulty language choice, words and messages not properly tuned to the audience, or choice of the wrong time or place for the speech, discussion, or advice.

The heart-centered leader takes seriously the power of words. They are keenly aware of the effects of what they say and how, when, and where they say it. They don't assume that whenever they open their mouth, they will be heard and understood and that their message will be accepted. Whenever a leader speaks, some impact is made. The heart-centered leader is aware that the impact may be different from or beyond what they intend.

When you lead from the heart, you know that what you say and how you say it will affect the hearts of the listeners. This helps you develop the habit of using language mindfully—whether it is spoken or written. You are intentionally thoughtful about word choice, the audience, the setting and time, and the context. You take time to focus beforehand on how you will communicate. You attend to your demeanor, tone of voice, and nonverbal expressions.

> **Gray Matter**
>
> *Another thing about words is that you can't take them back.*
>
> $%#@

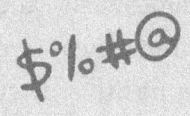

HEART LEADERSHIP TRAIT 8: THE HEART-CENTERED LEADER RADIATES PASSION FOR THEIR JOB AND THEIR PEOPLE.

Heart leadership fuels a leader's passion—for their job, their responsibilities, and their opportunities and possibilities. It also feeds the leader's passion for the students, families, staff members, and others in the school community.

Passion is that powerful, compelling desire to persevere—sometimes even in the face of frustration, fear, or pain. Whether you're a teacher, leader of teachers, or any other leader, your job requires every ounce of energy you can muster. There are probably even days when you just want to give up and throw in the towel. On those days, the strong zeal for your work and for your people will propel you to keep going despite difficulties. Real passion helps you overcome obstacles and break down barriers.

> **Gray Matter**
>
> *Motivation sets your alarm clock. Inspiration starts it ringing. PASSION is what wakes you up and gets you moving.*

The adage "when the going gets tough, the tough get going" leaves out an important point: the tough must have a reason to get going in the first place (even before it gets tough)! Passion arises from the deep belief in what you are doing, in the urgency to make a difference. It flows from the depths of your heart. Drive, grit, and determination are outcomes of passion.

The heart-centered leader exudes passion. Everyone who shares the school space or works with them can feel this fervor. Enthusiastic love of their job and their students, staff, and school community is evident. It shows even (or especially) in the most demanding or troublesome situations. It shows up through the leader's energy, actions, shared hard work, and shared tears, hugs, or celebrations.

The leader honors the passions of others. As a leader, it's likely that you are often in a position where you want to share and promote ideas about which you are very passionate. You want others to endorse your crusade! But they must concretely observe and experience you, the leader, genuinely opening **your** heart to **their passions** before you ask them to open their hearts to receive and embrace **your passions**.

The leader knows how to refuel their own passion. Once passion is awakened—alarms blaring and ringing—keep it on full blast. But passion is not endless. Knowing passion is central to moving forward and motivating others, the heart-centered leader is intentional about refueling passion.

We've Got that Feeling!

There is really nothing like the first day of school with students! These first-day feelings were on full display one summer when we launched a student internship program in my county. As county director of education, I was tasked with developing and managing a summer program for high school students. We needed a format that would offer students an enriching summer experience while providing professional development to prepare them for the real world after high school. I tapped my aspiring education leader to assist with the details. She was kind, energetic, and a masterful project manager.

"I'm so excited!" Melissa announced as she bounced into the room with a broad smile. She had been working for weeks to launch the program and was particularly excited about the young people who'd been selected. The project kickoff was

scheduled to begin in 45 minutes, and she could hardly contain her anticipation. "This feels like the first day of school all over again," she quipped.

I had to admit, I was excited too. But Melissa's energy was heightened. She'd been an intern in my office for two months and the grind of running a government office was taking its toll on us both. Working for government on behalf of education didn't get us in front of students as often as we would have liked. So actually working with the youth over the summer was a highlight for us, and her enthusiasm was infectious. It reminded me how passion brings out the best in us, how one person's passion spreads to others, and especially, how there is nothing that accelerates my passion quite like being with students!

In the story above, passion for both of us was ignited just by the prospect of spending time with students! My passion was also refreshed by being in the presence of Melissa's renewed energy. As you lead from the heart, be alert to ways you can form habits for boosting your passions for your work, your mission, and for the students and others in your school community.

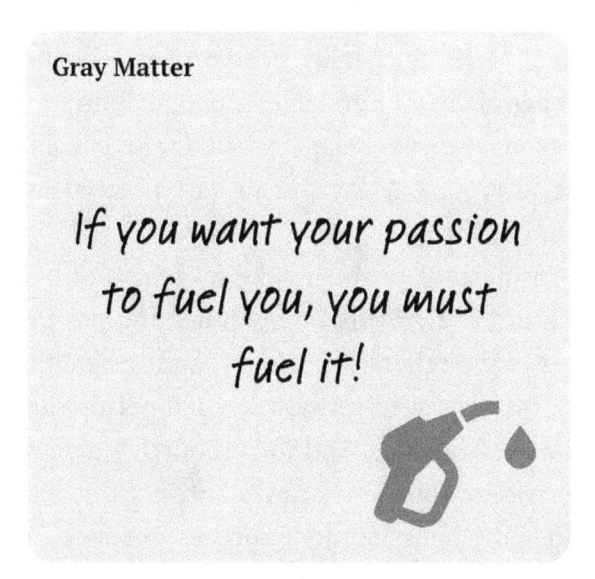

Gray Matter

If you want your passion to fuel you, you must fuel it!

See **Heart Leadership Strategy 10: Keep the Alarm Clock Ringing** on page 76 for more ways leaders can refuel their passion for their work and for the people they lead.

> **HEART LEADERSHIP TRAIT 9: THE HEART-CENTERED LEADER PUTS RELATIONSHIPS AT THE HEART OF EVERYTHING THEY DO.**

Though specific definitions of the word *relationship* differ, it's generally agreed that relationships involve connection (often some sort of emotional connection), attachment or interdependence, and level of regard for one another (this could be a high or low level or anything in between). In short, a relationship is a heart matter. In the process of relating, our hearts speak to one another in some way.

When I look back over any school day or week, I realize that in virtually every moment, I am connected in one or more relationships. Relationships are part of every meeting, contact, discussion, greeting, decision, phone call, classroom visit, announcement, digital communication, and situation in which I find myself. They follow me into the hallways, cafeteria, boardroom, classroom, playground, and parking lot. Even if I'm alone in my office, some relationship is connected to the issue, task, or program that has my attention.

And that's just me! Multiply that by everyone else in the school, and you'll realize that the number of encounters among people in the school on a given day tallies into the thousands. Relationships flow all day long in all directions between individuals and among groups. Many people are affected by each relationship, even some not present at the interaction.

Discussions of relationships in the school fill reams of books, articles, blogs, and speeches. Educators know of the many powerful, positive effects of caring, trusting relationships in the school. We've learned the benefits for students' connection and success, for employee satisfaction and performance, for comfort and involvement for students' families, and for productive community partnerships. We've seen healthy relationships break down barriers and biases, increase school connection and belonging, boost student success in school, and uplift students, families, and staff. We also know firsthand of the devastating effects to individuals and the school culture when relationships are uncaring, strained, downright toxic, or absent.

Traits of Heart-Centered Leadership

> **Gray Matter**
>
> *Every day, value the fact that everything a leader does starts with relationships. There is simply nothing a leader does that does not involve relationships.*

Simply put, we lead through relationships. A heart-centered leader serves as a model of caring relationships. In all communications, decisions, and actions, they tend to their relationships. They are alert to the relationships among the others in the group. This leader also challenges and guides the other adults in the school to foster positive peer relationships and to build trusting, quality relationships themselves with students, colleagues, and students' families. This leader knows that when the people who work and learn together do not clearly treat each other with kindness and value, the hearts won't connect to inspire one another.

In Chapter 3, see **Heart Leadership Strategy 11: Picture That Relationship!** on page 80 for an activity that captures good relationships in action.

Heart Leadership Trait 10: The heart-centered leader is keenly aware that they are always "on duty."

A school leader is always in the public eye. As one of my mentors constantly reminds me, "You are never off duty when you're outside of your home." Throughout my career, I have been in high profile positions from principal to superintendent to mayoral appointee. Each role required that I be aware of my surroundings, being mindful of who was in the room or area, where they were coming from, and what their intentions might be. (Oh, and always avoiding the hot mic!)

You're a Leader to Them Even After They Leave

A favorite Friday afternoon activity in my years as an administrator was walking students home from school to their nearby neighborhood. I really enjoyed doing this; it felt like a perfect way to end a very busy week. One hot Friday, we noticed a large crowd at the convenience store across the street from the school. I knew that the students in my group would need to pass that store to get to their neighborhood, so I went to investigate. The crowd had gathered to witness a large fight that had just broken out. As I approached the scene, one of the students who was involved ran past me. He ran so fast that, had I not been paying attention, I would not have recognized him as one of my former students.

"Bobby?! What are you doing?" He looked at me in disbelief. His anger clouded his vision as it took him a moment to recognize me.

"Dr. Gray? Man, I'm sorry, but you need to get out of here." I looked at him more closely and realized that he was holding a knife in his right hand.

"Boy, what are you doing?" I have always maintained great relationships with my students. The term "boy" was one of endearment for him and he knew it.

"You need to go, Dr. Gray. It's going down today, and you'll be hurt if you don't get out of here!"

Just then, in that moment, I noticed something else: Bobby's countenance changed. A very angry, uncontrollable teen suddenly became Bobby, that fifth grader I once knew. My awareness of his change also altered my response to the emergency. Instead of shouting at the top of my lungs to get his attention, I asked him to come closer for just a moment and whispered into his ear five words that a former teacher of mine once said to me in a similar, yet less violent, situation: "You know better than that."

Wait, what? How could I tell an enraged, trauma-triggered teen that he knows better than what he's conditioned to do? It is because I am the one who taught him better.

Here's a quick side note on the intangible impact of leadership: When you have built the right relationship, the right response during crisis emerges at the right time. As you grow in leadership, you will value how you lead more than who you lead. The "how" is wrapped in relationship building. To be an effective school leader, you must be intentional about how you engage with people. Those with whom you have relationships will respect your decisions even when they don't agree with them. This is leadership from the heart.

Now, I wish I could tell you that I talked him out of participating in the big fight. I did not. What I was able to do, because I was aware of my surroundings, was to get him to drop the knife. I also realized that it was the best he was able to do. I was aware of my surroundings and his situation. In that moment, surrounded by his "boys," he had some reputation to uphold—and I knew that. I likely saved his life, and he saved face. This was an early leadership lesson that has kept me in good graces with many students and colleagues alike: be aware that everyone has a cross to bear.

Whatever leadership position you hold—teacher, counselor, principal, bus driver—you know that you are noticed and recognized beyond the school grounds. You also know that your connections with students, staff, and students' families have history that follows you and them wherever you are, even many years later.

Yes, we leaders all know this in theory. But the heart-centered leader goes beyond the theory to the heart, holding onto this awareness and holding onto the connections. The leader is ready for these unplanned encounters. Their eyes and ears are wide open, along with their heart.

They remember to tune into what they know about the other person(s) and to the nuances of the current situation, setting, and audience. They are alert to the underlying human needs, and they respond with heart wisdom.

Heart Leadership Trait 11: The heart-centered leader seeks and listens to all input and feedback.

Feedback is part of every leader's life. You'll get it whether you ask for it or not! Warm feedback is supportive. Cold feedback feels negative and critical. Any leader is likely to get both.

Many of us are uncomfortable with feedback. Even if we ask for it, we cringe a bit when we read or listen to it. Facing the reactions of others to your programs, decisions, or treasured ideas may be threatening. The picture changes when you envision feedback and other input as coming from someone's heart, and see yourself opening your heart to receive it. This view allows a leader to embrace the other's thoughts without resisting their responses. The heart-centered leader develops this habit of viewing input and feedback as honest communication that comes from the heart of whomever offered it.

When you consider these messages as coming from someone's heart to yours, you might think of them differently than if you consider them as "purely objective" ideas. If the feedback is warm, you might take time to think about the source of the warmth: "Why did your speech or action help that person feel good?" If the feedback is cold, you might think about what's beneath the criticism or resistance: "What has caused the person to be uncomfortable, threatened, or angry?"

When you lead from the heart, you actually **welcome** ideas and insights from students, teachers and all other staff members, parents or caregivers, other leaders, board members, and members of the wider community. You find many ways to elicit their input in conversations, Q&A sessions, social media, emails, notes, and formal surveys. You make this a regular part of your leadership.

As you receive the input or feedback with an open heart and mind, you hear **all the words** (even the ones you don't want to hear) and value them. You go beyond listening and receiving feedback. You learn from what people tell you. You take what is helpful and make use of it to change something, improve something, or start something new. Furthermore, you let your audiences know that you have heard their opinions by showing them exactly how their ideas or responses are being put into action. This shows them that you respect them for honoring you with their ideas and that you have high regard for their input.

As you get in the habit of requesting, receiving, and using input and feedback from others, the habit gets easier and more useful. It also becomes less threatening. And in the process, you build history and relationships with folks, setting a foundation that will serve you well when you tackle tough topics and decisions together later on. The process also breeds trust that will foster more honest and productive input and feedback in the future.

HEART LEADERSHIP TRAIT 12: THE HEART-CENTERED LEADER ADDS HEART TO THEIR DISCERNMENT.

Discernment is the ability to distinguish something with the senses. Most definitions of discernment also include the idea that the process includes some difficulty—that it is a quality of being able to grasp and comprehend what is obscure. It is often about seeing beneath the surface to determine if something is good or bad, sincere or fake. Discernment is a powerful tool for leaders. It is a gift; use it wisely.

Discerning how someone really feels about you or discerning the truth about someone else's feelings or motives can be beneficial. But you also have the burden of deciding how to react, given that information. At some point, you must **do** something about what you have discerned, be it true or false. For me, the step of discerning what is true (when the truth may be obscure) and what to do about it is something like feeling "a disturbance in the Force" or a tingling "Spidey-sense" (*a powerful intuition*).

We all may think of discernment as a process that only comes from the head—a use of reason. But situations that need careful examination and evaluation are rarely black-and-white matters of reason. Hearts are inevitably connected to the components of the situation, the people involved, and the outcome of your discernment. Thus, when you practice heart-centered leadership, speaking from your heart to another's heart is part of the discerning process.

Here's an example in which I paid attention to my "Spidey-sense" and combined heart discernment with "head" (cognitive) discernment.

Getting to the Bottom of the Rumor Mill

"I don't know, sir, but I didn't say it." I had called Mr. Walters into my office that day to confront the source of a harmful rumor. My newly inherited deputy superintendent had more than 30 years of service in our school system and the unfettered respect of its 4,000 employees. Mr. Walters had been a teacher, an award-winning principal, and the right-hand man of the former superintendent.

Three weeks into my tenure, I had received word that he was spreading terrible rumors about me. I had to get to the truth, so I called him into my office. (Note: Courageous conversations like this should not be delegated to a designee or subordinate. Leaders know how to "put on their big person pants" and address these matters personally. Do not let others do your dirty work; you will abdicate your authority and lose respect from others.)

I had been told that the deputy superintendent was telling others that I was using this new opportunity to pad my resume and that I would be gone in a year to my next gig. It was early in the year, so we had talked only a few times before, and I didn't know him well yet. But my heart was telling me something was not quite right here; I was not fully convinced that the rumor was true.

I attended to my heart and let it speak to him by being honest about what I had heard, sharing it with him in open-hearted tones and terms. Then I listened respectfully. Ten minutes into the conversation, I began to sense that Mr. Walters was not being disloyal to me. Instead, he was showing loyalty to the district that he loved so dearly. He was respectful, honest, clear, and precise in responding to my questions. He suggested that a source of the rumors might be another former cabinet-level employee who had wanted Mr. Walters to be the superintendent instead of me. This person looked at my resume and background, saw that I had risen through the ranks quickly, and surmised that I would only be around a short while.

Through this frank conversation I discerned that Mr. Walters was telling the truth. Even in the face of termination, he was willing to protect and defend his district. His commitment was inspirational for me. He became a trusted colleague and a dear friend. He continued to be my deputy superintendent throughout my entire tenure.

HEART LEADERSHIP TRAIT 13: THE HEART-CENTERED LEADER IS REAL.

You can't fake heart leadership. You can't fake passion or regard for others (or any of the other fruits of leading from the heart described in Chapter 1.) NBA legend Shaquille O'Neal is known to have said, "Don't fake the funk on a nasty dunk."[13] Even if you don't get the basketball lingo, you can see that this has to do with presenting yourself as something you are not or showing off to mislead others about something you can't really do well. Middle schoolers can spot a pretender a mile away. Your colleagues know disingenuousness when they see it. So do students' parents and caregivers. These people may not tell you if they sense fakery, but if you carefully watch their responses to you, you can read the signs. To truly lead from the heart, you must be real.

You certainly can't fake inspiring others. When you are truly inspiring someone, you feel an indescribable sense of humility. It is "me" (the giver) being sincere about the inspiration of others and "you" (the receiver) being aware that there is genuine inspiration to be gleaned. If you are only "being inspirational" to impress someone, then you are feeding a dead animal. Others will (or should) call you out on it. Your students and staff know you; they see your daily actions and interactions; they can tell when you are authentic.

Inauthenticity is not heart connecting. It's the opposite. It gets in the way of leadership from the heart. It puts up barriers, breaks trust, derails plans, fractures relationships, and triggers setbacks in success. When a leader's fakery disconnects people in these ways, it can take a long time to recover. Some breaches of trust may never heal.

Developing heart-centered leadership helps a leader to be authentic, even when it's scary. Speaking from an open heart with the clear awareness of touching the hearts of others keeps one more humble, more truthful, more real.

Heart Leadership Trait 14: The heart-centered leader taps into their own empathy and compassion.

Every decision, conversation, confrontation, or issue facing a leader needs heart as part of the leadership. Heart-centered leaders grow the habit of consulting their hearts and tuning into the hearts of others many times a day. This means that the leader brings to any circumstance—planned or unplanned—mindfulness about what they say, along with wide-open eyes, ears, and heart.

When leading from the heart, you draw on the honor you have for others and the connections you have with them. This allows you to meet each person and situation with empathy and compassion.

The Superintendent's Dilemma

Three hundred bus drivers gathered in the school auditorium, ready to strike if they didn't like what I had to say when I entered to speak to them. (This was to happen in a few minutes.) Having heard that the teachers would receive a raise that year, but that they would not, the drivers were upset (to say the least). As I prepared to meet them, I knew I had to draw on my heart leadership, for there was no way that a raise was possible and explaining that fact would only foment division.

I'd had calls from the school board, the mayor, city councilors, and state senators—so to say the situation had escalated is an understatement. But I knew there wasn't enough money in the budget to provide raises for both groups. I quieted myself and began to reflect on how each of the stakeholders impacted by this decision might feel. I consciously drew on my empathy and compassion for these groups and tried to walk for a few moments in each of their shoes. Parents and caregivers wanted their children safely transported to school. The community wanted a harmonious school system. The bus drivers wanted more pay and to know the district respected and appreciated them as much as the teachers. They wanted to be heard.

Holding these reflections in my heart, I entered the room and spoke only briefly. Then, for three and a half hours, I listened and responded to every one of their questions, transparently addressing the limitations of our budget. And by the end, we had an agreement. A raise would be carved out for the following year. In the meantime, their time off would be increased. They would enjoy an immediate benefit, while trusting that I would address their main concern as soon as I was able. I also committed to creating a focus group of support staff so I could regularly check in with them and hear concerns before they bubbled up, as this one had.

At the end of the meeting, I stood at the door and shook each bus driver's hand as they left the auditorium. I even got a couple of hugs. One particularly passionate driver noted, "I know we won't get a raise today, but I appreciate your listening to us!"

While we did eventually adjust the drivers' salaries, we also changed the culture of the transportation department. This included staff restructuring, route adjustments, and providing families, drivers, and school leaders with support and back-up plans when buses did occasionally run behind. Making these changes was not easy. It took a team that agreed to leave egos at the door and focus on the goal of getting our students to school and back home, safely and on time.

The very anxious moment had turned into a teachable moment for me. Leading with my heart was a great first step in achieving an overall goal of becoming a compassionate and accountable school leader.

> **Gray Matter**
>
> *As one of my mentors once told me, it's better to under-promise and over-deliver than to over-promise and under-deliver.*

HEART LEADERSHIP TRAIT 15: THE HEART-CENTERED LEADER REGULARLY DEBRIEFS AND REFLECTS AFTER KEY EVENTS.

The Superintendent's Dilemma, continued

After spending hours with the bus drivers (see story with Trait 14), it was time to be with my team. I needed to decompress, and we all needed to reflect. How did we get to this point? What promises did I make during the meeting? Which items needed immediate follow-through to build on the trust we'd just established? Which matters needed more collaborative processing—that is, which matters required additional input and voices?

On this occasion, the process included me, the deputy superintendent, and the director of finance. Our debrief was informally conducted on the ride back to the office. The deputy superintendent was famous for taking advantage of every possible moment to be productive. He led the discussion by asking multiple questions *about the process; many of these I never would have thought to ask: Did we space out the participants in the right way, leaving the malcontents separate from one another? Is it more effective to pass the microphone or collect written questions to be read by a moderator? Is it better to have the administrative team enter after the participants are seated or should the team be seated as the participants arrive? Or should the team enter at the same time as the participants, so as to mingle with them? Questions such as these would guide our decisions for future meetings of this type.*

The reflection didn't end when the three of us parted ways that day. Our discussion ignited more questions that I needed to personally explore. (This often happens when you reflect with others!) These questions were less about process and more about impact. I wanted to be sure that each time I spoke with any group of folks I led, that my leadership acts and decisions were coming from the heart. So I cross-examined myself: Did I leave the group motivated or enraged? Was there another way to reach the disenfranchised? Were my opening words straightforward but fair enough that folks didn't completely shut me out? Did I reach their hearts with clarity and inspiration?

And of course, we knew that there were more "wrap-up" tasks to do. Though we felt the meeting went well enough to call it a victory, we knew there were still important next steps. These also drew on our heart-centered leadership, because there were many others (not present at the meeting or the debriefing) who had strong feelings about the situation and needed to know what happened. As a leadership team, we wanted to control the narrative: we wanted to talk about the meeting in such a way that gave facts, shined a light on the positive results, and dispelled rumors or misunderstandings. And we knew that there were some folks (school board and school principals, for example) who needed to hear details of the meeting directly from one of us and others that could read about it in a wider general announcement later.

A post-meeting or post-scenario debrief with key stakeholders is a critical action for a leader. Be sure to use this reflection practice often—after meetings, major events, crises, or other key moments in school life. This process not only reviews what happened and helps create a record of next steps needed in order to carry out decisions. It also develops your reflection abilities—skills that enable you to dig in to understand what happened and why, what worked and didn't, what else is needed, and what to do differently next time. Tailor the approach to fit your situation. Be sure to keep notes of what you discover and what you intend to do from what you learn.

Reflective debriefing is a key part of heart-centered leadership. When you ask and answer reflective questions (such as those in the story above) together, you get to the broader personal and emotional effects of the meeting or situation. Your insights help you to add other elements on your "to-do" list—elements that have to do with how you attend to heart needs now and in future situations. Remember: Debriefing only works well if you have actually led from your eyes, ears, and mouth as well as your heart! You need to have carefully observed, listened, and asked the right questions in order to have gained insights about what happened!

The process also nurtures growth and connection among your team (those present at the debriefing). All of you learn about yourselves and the others. The debriefing process invites others to tap into their strengths and suggest solutions; it inspires you all to value and trust each other more deeply. It boosts connection and is amazingly uplifting. And it is comforting, because you know you are all in it together (whatever the current "it" may be)! Our situation with the bus drivers worked out, but not all meetings, discussions, issues, and such resolve so well. The leader must be ready to respond to both outcomes with heart leadership. It is easier to do this when you have a trusting, competent team working together.

> **Gray Matter**
>
> *Effective heart-centered school leaders seize every opportunity. In some situations, you can learn what to do better. In others, you can learn what not to do at all.*

Just as reflection with your team is a critical practice, it is also necessary for leaders to take time alone to reflect on their leadership practices. In Chapter 3, see **Heart Leadership Strategy 13: Journaling: Leading from the Heart** on page 85 for a guide to journaling your reflections on this aspect of your leadership.

HEART LEADERSHIP TRAIT 16: THE HEART-CENTERED LEADER DEVELOPS HEART-CENTERED LEADERSHIP AS A TEAM.

Leadership is not a solitary endeavor. If approached that way, a leader is destined to fail. Any style of leadership needs input, support, and collaboration with others. Because many, perhaps, do not intentionally include heart-centered leadership as part of their approach, this kind of leadership may need development more than other approaches.

THE SUCCESSFUL MIDDLE SCHOOL LEADER

Successful leaders encourage professional growth in heart leadership for all leaders, teachers, and other staff members. In each case, challenge colleagues to find and share ways to apply heart-centered leadership to their particular work situations, content areas, and types of interactions with students and each other. Teach the principles to parents, caregivers, and student leaders too. That way the effects of good leadership from the heart spread widely.

Here are a few topics and goals that relate to heart-centered leadership. Address any topics you choose in the context of heart-to-heart connections. Examine the concepts or current status at your school, search for strategies, or develop practices to address such matters as:

- Teacher relationships with administration, school board, community
- Leader relationships with one another and other staff
- Relationships among teaching and non-teaching staff
- Connections with students' families
- Increasing belonging for students, families, staff members
- Helping students name, accept, and manage feelings
- Fostering resilience (for students and for teachers)
- Helping students overcome trauma
- Erasing bias—explicit and unintentional
- Engaging the disengaged students
- Increasing SEL competencies
- Digital citizenship, safety, and self-control
- Restorative practices
- ACEs and trauma response
- Collaborative learning
- Student voice and choice
- Teacher and student mental health and morale
- Harassment of all forms
- Racial inequality and discrimination
- Addictions, including screen addiction
- Smartphone social media use, misuse, effects, benefits, and dangers
- Peer pressure

- Body image matters
- Influence of pop culture
- Drug or alcohol use
- Gender identity
- Risky sexual activity
- Feeling safe at school
- Effects of poverty
- Community violence

Consider and discuss how to apply heart leadership to:

- Classroom management and climate
- Discipline intervention strategies
- Use of digital commercial learning programs
- Assessment and grading processes

HEART LEADERSHIP TRAIT 17: THE HEART-CENTERED LEADER SHOWS UP (AND SHOWS THEIR HEART) DURING CRISES.

It's one thing to lead when everything is rosy. It's another thing altogether to lead when the roof is caving in. How you respond as a leader during a crisis reveals the shape of your leadership. Experiences of leading in crisis can derail or develop your leadership.

In educational leadership, crisis will come. One recent event was the COVID-19 pandemic that shuttered thousands of schools overnight and disrupted them for months. In recent years, wildfires have devastated some west coast towns, leaving children without schools and homes. Schools are affected all too often by human-caused dangers and natural disasters. School leaders encounter multiple other crisis-level challenges that shift the way they lead and manage schools. In the rush to do something to avert, relieve, or end the crisis, the heart-centered leader does not forget that any crisis strikes at hearts. This leader remembers to keep their heart open and speak to the hearts of others. Sometimes the leader's challenge is to do this even with a broken heart.

Our students, parents, fellow educators, and the community we serve need the school leader to be fully present and engaged in a crisis. And they need the leader to be calm and collected. When others panic, the wise school leader shifts into low gear, responds to the needs of the moment, and does not overreact or increase the level of anxiety for others. But how do you do that when the world is falling around you? Unfortunately, I was about to find out.

A Mother's Heart

"I'm sorry, Mom." I softly spoke those words as I sat next to a distraught mother of a second grader recently admitted to the emergency room. The child had sustained multiple injuries as a result of a school bus accident. The sobbing mom could barely hear me as I explained what happened. Her son was hit by the bus while bending over to tie his shoes. The driver didn't see the bent-over student. By the time the driver saw him, it was too late. The paramedics arrived quickly, but the injuries sustained by the child were severe and required more attention than they could provide on the scene.

A week later, when I heard his condition had worsened, I dropped what I was doing and rushed to the hospital. I knew that my presence was needed; it was not the time to send anyone else in my place. As a superintendent, I also knew the risks of talking to the mother in this situation. The bus driver and the school could be considered at fault for the accident, thereby opening the potential for a lawsuit. But as a parent, I knew that being there with a mother in pain was more important than any legal action that I would face. I decided that this was a time to lead with my heart.

As it turned out, it was the right decision. The situation took a dire turn, but because I followed my heart and remained sensitive to Mom's heart, she and I maintained a cordial relationship. The mother was grateful for the support of the district and for my presence during the ordeal. The heart of a mother or other parent is to be considered a precious commodity during times of crisis. Be sure to use yours when making decisions that involve theirs.

Traits of Heart-Centered Leadership

Effective school leaders find opportunity in confronting a crisis. By showing up in a way that calms stormy seas, the leader has an opportunity to give care, comfort, and security to students and others at their most vulnerable time. A crisis also provides a leader with opportunities to:

- Use experience and wisdom to make good decisions that help to alleviate the problem or the pain.
- Draw on their courage and push beyond their comfort zone.
- Gather people together and use the power of a group to take quick actions.
- Break down barriers and dispel stereotypes as people are drawn together to help one another.
- Learn and grow as a leader.
- Reflect later and discern what to do better in the future.

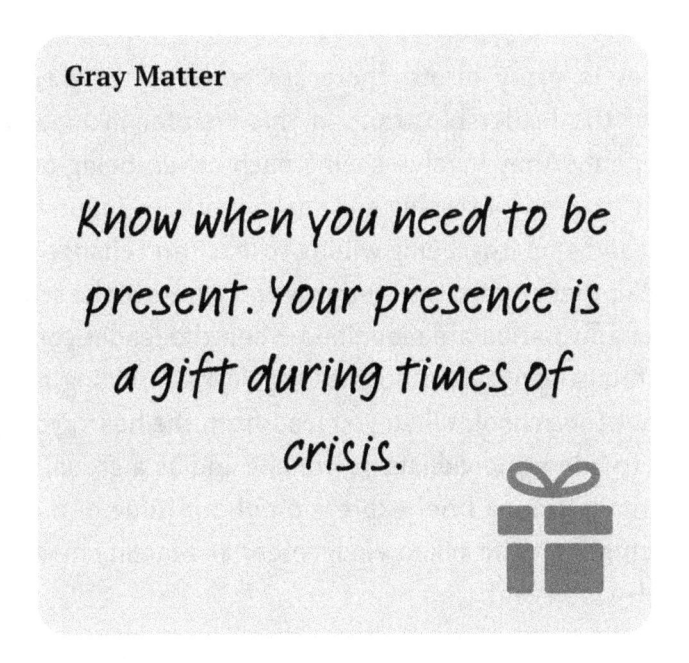

Gray Matter

Know when you need to be present. Your presence is a gift during times of crisis.

In Chapter 3, see **Heart Leadership Strategy 12: Taking Charge in A Crisis** on page 81 for more suggestions about heart leadership in a crisis.

> ***HEART LEADERSHIP TRAIT 18: THE HEART-CENTERED LEADER AFFIRMS AND CELEBRATES ALL STAKEHOLDERS.***

In the busy life of schools with so many moving pieces, programs, and people, it is easy to get stuck on the treadmill handling one task after another and keeping up with the schedule. The heart-centered leader remembers that all these moving pieces involve human beings—each one wanting to be noticed and feel important to the school and to others. Good leadership includes a focus on taking time to casually, formally, and frequently convey the value and appreciation each person needs and deserves. But first, of course, it takes watching, listening, and conversing to notice who and what to affirm and celebrate.

AFFIRM

Affirmation comes in many forms; there are hundreds of ways to pass it on. Basically, each of the leadership traits in this chapter includes an element of valuing others openly. They involve seeing each other, being open-hearted and honest, attending to needs, listening and seeking others' input, making decisions with compassion and empathy, being willing to learn and change, being authentic, and showing up. All these affirm the students and adults in the school community.

The benefits of affirmation are magnified when the leader consciously intends to affirm and establishes ways to do that regularly—building a climate of affirmation throughout the school. When you lead from the heart, you grab hundreds of opportunities to honor individuals personally and as a group, in private and in public. This can range from a brief expression of gratitude or a compliment on a skill or accomplishment, to an acknowledgement at a faculty meeting or a presentation at a school-wide event.

CELEBRATE

When you celebrate, you affirm. And when you affirm, you celebrate individuals, or a group, or the entire school! Celebration is a trademark of leadership from the heart. This is a hard behavior for me to embrace (and maybe for other school leaders). With the many responsibilities, I tend to spend far more time on what's not working than on what is. (Just ask my daughter, whose report card is full of As, about how it's the one B that we spend two days discussing.) And as a middle school principal, I found myself spending 90% of my time with the 10% of students who had the most behavioral issues and not enough time building relationships with the other 90% of students.

I now realize that if I'm leading from the heart, I will celebrate victories more than I lament defeats. There are so many reasons (and so many people) to celebrate in a classroom, on a team, with students' families, with the whole school, and with the wider community. These include but go far beyond the sports teams' hard work or victories. When you lead from the heart, you deliberately plan for all kinds of celebrations, and inspire your staff and students to do the same. Encourage students, families, and staff to generate the ideas and occasions! Sing, dance, smile, clap, rejoice together.

Celebrate . . .

- Individual breakthroughs and accomplishments
- Class accomplishments
- School-wide, PLC-wide, or team-wide goals met
- Lessons learned from setbacks
- School or group milestones
- Completing a unit
- Athletic events
- Nonathletic events
- Surviving standardized test week
- Making it through a pandemic! (or any other unexpected circumstance)
- Kindness

Celebrate . . .

- Students
- Staff members
- Leaders

- Volunteers
- Parents, caregivers, families
- Community members
- Holidays
- Birthdays
- Any special day or moment

Celebrate . . .
- In classrooms
- At PLC or team gatherings
- In assemblies
- On the playground
- In the lunchroom
- In the gymnasium
- In the auditorium
- In hallways

Celebrate with . . .
- Streamers and horns and confetti
- Words of acknowledgement and praise
- A congratulatory banner in the hall
- Speeches
- Slideshows
- Trophies and other rewards
- And, oh, yes—with food!

HEART LEADERSHIP TRAIT 19: THE HEART-CENTERED LEADER IS BRAVE.

All of the leadership traits in this chapter require an element of bravery. It takes courage to:

- Examine and name your own feelings, thoughts, and values and identify the behaviors that they spawn.
- Open your heart and be known and to work hard to know others.
- Look straight into the faces of those you lead and notice their responses to your ideas, passions, actions, speeches, interactions.
- Ask for feedback and embrace it and work to make use of it, rather than discount or run from it.
- Be transparent—to show your deepest beliefs and passions, even when they may differ from those of your fellow school community members.
- Keep your heart open to others, even when they might be closed to you.
- Go to the deep places in your heart to tap into your empathy and compassion.
- Share responsibility and trust others.
- Monitor what you say and how you say it and maybe make tough changes.
- Start school after a tragedy in the neighborhood.
- Show up in crises and tragedies that are beyond your control and where you can't fix everything (or anything, sometimes).
- Stay calm and centered in a crisis.
- Lead with a broken heart.
- Tell groups of employees that there is no money for what they ask and need.
- Show up at a student's funeral and stand by the family.
- Absorb the responsibility of inspiring others.
- Be "on duty" almost around the clock.
- Be authentic 24-7.
- Honestly reflect on your heart leadership and work hard to do better.

We can conclude that heart-centered leadership is not for the faint of heart! When you lead from the heart, you do so amid such hard stuff as these examples.

I find the following familiar quote true: "Courage is not the absence of fear. It's doing something important or necessary while you are afraid." Honesty about your fear is one aspect of leading from the heart. Attention to your own heart and the hearts of others actually enables you to do these difficult things and help other leaders do the same.

Chapter 3

Heart-Centered Leadership Strategies

Follow up your understanding of heart leadership traits (Chapter 2) with some concrete practices to develop those traits further. Strategies such as those in this chapter are designed to motivate leaders and challenge them to continue growth in heart-centered leadership by giving practical processes they can put into action right away. I'm confident these strategies will also ignite ideas that lead you and your staff to create other approaches to heart leadership.

Overview of Heart-Centered Leadership Strategies

Strategy #	Strategy	Referenced in Heart Leadership Trait #
Heart Strategy 1	Leader's Heart Check-Up, Part 1: Looking Inward	1
Heart Strategy 2	Leader's Heart Check-Up, Part 2: Looking Outward at Behavior	2
Heart Strategy 3	Know Your Middle Level Students	3
Heart Strategy 4	Know Your Colleagues	3
Heart Strategy 5	Empower Families	3
Heart Strategy 6	Value Community Partners	3
Heart Strategy 7	Inspiration Inspection	4
Heart Strategy 8	Hearing Student Voices	3, 6
Heart Strategy 9	An Advocate for Every Student	6
Heart Strategy 10	Keep the Alarm Clock Ringing	8
Heart Strategy 11	Picture That Relationship!	9
Heart Strategy 12	Taking Charge in a Crisis	17
Heart Strategy 13	Journaling: Leading from the Heart	15

Heart Leadership Strategy 1: Leader's Heart Check-Up, Part 1: Looking Inward

Purpose: Leaders assess the status of their self-awareness and follow steps to expand it.

When you lead from the heart to speak to others' hearts, it's critical to be alert to emotions involved in any interaction or situation. A foundation of heart leadership is practicing and sharpening awareness of your own personal moods and emotions—the sources, triggers, and attitudes and actions that flow from them. To be self-aware means to be consciously aware and understanding of your own personal character, values, emotions, assumptions, and motives.

How do you expand your self-awareness? You pay attention to yourself with close listening and observation. You're curious about your strong emotional experiences. You ask: "Oooo, what's going on here? Where is this coming from? What can I learn from this?" You notice actions that flow from your emotions. You ask for feedback from others you trust. You learn from watching the responses of others to your actions, moods, or attitudes.

Here are some steps to practice self-awareness, checking in on what's in your heart.

Step 1: Tune into your heart.

Answer each question below with "yes," "no," or "not sure." As you respond, think of yourself in your school leader role.

Are you able to:

- Identify some of your emotional characteristics?
- Name some of your deepest values or strongest beliefs?
- Name some of your most demanding challenges or personal limitations?
- Describe your level of emotional resilience (and tell how you know)?
- Name some of your greatest strengths (connected to heart leadership)?

- Regularly name and understand your feelings in an emotional situation?
- Write a phrase that describes your inner responses to distressful thoughts or situations?
- Write a phrase that describes how you manage negative emotions?
- Write a phrase that describes how you manage positive emotions?
- Identify some of your emotional triggers? (i.e., What contributes to you feeling satisfied? Angry? Emotionally safe? Intimidated? Valued? Fearful? Powerless? Powerful? Hostile? Appreciated? Unappreciated? Afraid? Hostile? Self-satisfied? Superior? Curious? Delighted? Gleeful? Accepted? Shy? Guilty? Ashamed? Disgusted? Self-doubting? Hopeful? Valued? Included? Excluded? Energized? Defeated or hopeless?)
- Notice any patterns in situations that trigger strong emotions for you—and briefly describe some of the patterns?
- Identify a personal characteristic that causes discomfort, embarrassment, or insecurity—and briefly describe your relationship to that characteristic? (i.e., How do you feel about that attribute? How does it affect your outlook or attitude?)

Step 2: Reflect on your answers.

Go back and skim over the answers that you've given.

- If the answer to a question is "yes," then do what the question suggests.
- For questions that you answered, "not sure," probe deeper. Take more time to reflect on these. Ask a trusted friend or colleague to give an honest appraisal of what they think the answer would be. Ask them to tell you what they've seen, heard, or felt that leads them to their answer. After you reflect longer and consider responses from others, decide whether you can change your answer.
- For questions with "no" answers, set some goals for some self-awareness practices to work on further.

Step 3: Practice with a specific situation.

Realize that feelings are messengers. When feelings are aroused, it is only with identifying, acknowledging, and accepting what you find in yourself that you can handle, release, or transform the inner experience. This enables you to learn about yourself; it also enables you to go forth from the emotional experience with much healthier responses and actions than might otherwise result.

- Select an actual school-related situation that stimulated strong feelings. This can be anything that instigates any emotion for you.

- Use the template on the next page, **A Deep Dive into Feelings**, to guide you in examining those feelings. Find a quiet place where you can be mindful about a situation and connect to the feelings it generated. Spend several minutes going through these steps. Record your responses on this form or something you create, or use this as an exercise for your journal. This process can be applied to any situation with powerful feelings involved. Use this guide again, preferably as soon as possible after a situation occurs, when the feelings are strongest.

Heart-Centered Leadership Strategies

A Deep Dive Into Feelings

Use this to guide you in a close exploration of an emotional situation. Select a specific situation that ignited strong feelings. Then...

1) Briefly describe the circumstance.	
2) Name one or two of the strongest feelings.	
3) Let yourself feel those feelings. *Notice sensations that come to you: images, thoughts, or memories that are part of the emotional experience. Sometimes you'll become aware of another, perhaps deeper or stronger, feeling associated with the one you chose to identify. Notice physical responses.* **Make some notes about what you sense as you let yourself feel.**	
4) Accept the feelings. *It can be hard to embrace some feelings. We often want to reject such painful feelings as fear, shame, guilt, or deep disappointment. Pushing away your emotions can rob you of some important information. Remember that feelings are messengers. Accepting your feelings means resisting the temptation to control them or get rid of them and realizing that they are helpful. Usually, a scary feeling loses some of its power when you name, examine, and accept it. You no longer have to put a lot of energy into avoiding the feeling.* **Make some notes about what you learn from acknowledging the feeling(s).**	

Heart Leadership Strategy 2: Leader's Heart Check-Up, Part 2: Looking Outward at Behavior (Follow up to Strategy 1)

Purpose: Leaders expand self-awareness by examining their emotion-triggered behaviors and watching the responses of others to their behaviors.

A leader's self-awareness begins with recognition and understanding of their emotional landscape. (See Strategy 1: Leader's Heart Check-Up, Part 1.) But self-awareness also includes traits that go beyond those mentioned in the previous strategy. They are: 1) the ability to identify the behaviors that result from your feelings and emotional triggers, and 2) the ability to notice the effects of your behaviors on others.

This strategy can help you become more intentional about noticing (in the moment and in reflection afterward) your outward actions and how they affect others. **Your self-awareness will grow by leaps and bounds as you practice this.** But I can guarantee that you'll learn far more from the second step than the first! These steps aren't meant to be sequential. They interconnect and deepen one another. Work at both simultaneously.

Step 1: Pay close attention to your reactions.

Notice what actions you take in response to incidents, conversations, crises, annoyances, interruptions, etc.—anything that has aroused some emotion. From practice in using Strategy 1, you've already increased your awareness of what those situations are. For example, what are your "go-to" behaviors when:

A student challenges you?
A leader appears to favor someone over you?
A leader shows gratitude to you for the work you do?
You see a situation differently than a colleague?
Higher authorities overrule something you think is important?
Someone doesn't listen to you or seem to take you seriously?
A decision that affects you was made without your input?

Heart-Centered Leadership Strategies

You have an inspiring work session with teammates or other colleagues?
You notice students bullying or disregarding, excluding, criticizing each other?
You pick up that a colleague is envious, annoyed, distrustful, or unhappy with you?
You are complimented by a student's parent or caregiver?
You are not supported by a teacher, your principal, team leader, or other leader?
Someone else gets credit for work that you've done?
(You can add any number of other scenarios as you ponder these!)

For example, do you:

- Quickly correct or dismiss what someone has said?
- Ask questions to learn more about someone else's viewpoint?
- Excuse yourself from the situation as soon as possible?
- Express gratitude to someone else in the situation?
- Ask about how others feel in the situation?
- Spring into action to fix a problem?
- Admit to your mistakes or misunderstandings?
- Blame someone else?
- Ask for input or feedback from others?
- (You can add any number of other responses as you ponder these!)

Detect not only what you **do**, but also such subtle actions as your tone of voice, how you listen, your eye contact, the kinds of things you say, the kinds of questions you ask, the level of interest you show in another, and your body expressions and movements.

For example, do you:

- Step away from the person?
- Cross your arms across your chest?
- Speak in a higher or lower volume?
- Tune out?
- Step closer to someone?
- Sulk?
- Avoid eye contact?

- *Tense up?*
- *Frown?*
- *Reassure someone with a handshake or shoulder touch?*

Step 2: Pay close attention to how others respond to your reactions.

For any feeling and responses of yours that are connected to the feeling, stay alert to catch signals from others. Use your eyes, ears, and other "inner" and outer senses. You'll gain revealing information about your behavior by noticing their responses.

Watch for body language: Notice a person's physical response. Do they look comfortable or uncomfortable, step backward or forward, seem relaxed or tense, smile or frown, listen closely or appear dazed or confused?

Listen to what they say: Do they answer confidently or seem insecure? Give short answers or comfortably express themselves thoroughly? Speak honestly or say what you might most want to hear? Clam up and say nothing?

Ask for feedback: Don't wait for people to be bold enough to let you know about your behavior and how it affected them. Ask. Find ways for staff members, students, other leaders, or others in the school community to tell you what they "read" in your responses. You can do this with a simple question: "Are you comfortable with how our discussion went? Tell me more about your answer."

Get in the habit of using these two steps. The more you do this, the easier it will become and the more you will learn about yourself. You'll begin to notice patterns in your behavior and patterns in the responses of others. As your own self-awareness grows, you'll also practice skills of social awareness with this strategy. You'll increase in ability to recognize and value others' strengths, increase care for others' feelings, understand the perspectives of others, and show compassion—all components of heart leadership. Be sure to practice with situations that are pleasant, uplifting, or successful as well as those that are challenging.

Heart-Centered Leadership Strategies

For some extra practice with this two-step strategy, focus on a few real-life situations that have actually happened for you in your leader role. Follow the process shown in the template on the next page, **Leader's Behavior Examination**. You can develop a routine of considering these aspects of any circumstance involving strong feelings.

Take stock of what you learn about yourself and others. See every encounter or incident as an opportunity for growth, for new possibilities, and often, for celebration. One cause for celebration in any situation is that you get better at understanding how your feelings affect your behavior and how that behavior affects others. More good news is this: You always have a choice as to how you respond to situations. Your choices are much healthier, caring, and productive when you understand your patterns of behavior.

Leader's Behavior Examination

Identify one or two school-related situations in which you experienced a strong emotional response. Write a sentence, phrase, or list for each prompt.

The circumstance	The circumstance
Emotion you felt	Emotion you felt
Your behavior(s), action(s) (that you were aware of; verbal and nonverbal)	Your behavior(s), action(s) (that you were aware of; verbal and nonverbal)
Responses from others (that you heard, observed, or sensed)	Responses from others (that you heard, observed, or sensed)
What you could or would do next	What you could or would do next
Something you learned	Something you learned

HEART LEADERSHIP STRATEGY 3: KNOW YOUR MIDDLE LEVEL STUDENTS

Purpose: Leaders increase understanding of middle level students as individuals and as a group.

Every school leader or leadership team must plan activities and practices that help all staff in a middle school build knowledge of the characteristics and needs of young adolescents. It's critical that all adults in the school get to know students as much as possible, to understand them as a group and as individuals. AMLE's landmark position statement, *The Successful Middle School: This We Believe*, is a great place to start.

This strategy guides a book study in part of the above book: the section on young adolescent development and its implications for middle level educators (pages 54-66). Studying this together brings everyone in the school onto the same page, providing deep, consistent understandings. It establishes a base for a collaborative process of making the school rich in its responses to its young adolescent students.

The following guide, **Young Adolescent Development and Implications for Educators**, leads your group through questions as they read, explore, and discuss this material. It will enable your group to:

- Gain an overview of developmental characteristics of the age group.
- Examine and discuss the implications for educators of the characteristics and realities of young adolescent development.
- Work to understand the individual development of each student, realizing that those may vary from the characteristics pertaining to the age group in general.
- Acknowledge and understand the limitations and dangers of dependence on a generalized perspective of young adolescent development.
- Apply what they learn to their own schools, students, and situations.

- Expand and share their own insights based on their experiences with young adolescents.
- Identify ways they are already using this information well to address needs and to establish what else they can do.
- Understand the interconnectedness of all the aspects of development.

Notes for using the study guide (for *The Successful Middle School: This We Believe, pages 54–66*)

- Since the point is to learn together, this will work best done in pairs or small groups (perhaps teams or other established PLCs)—even if individuals do some of the reading and pondering on their own. Consider a way to gather insights and suggested actions with a larger group.
- I've included this strategy in Part 1 of this book because the topic of developmentally responsive practice IS a heart matter. Addressing the facets of young adolescent development is an effective way to help the school staff grow as heart-centered adults and leaders. However, the knowledge gained from this strategy applies to the other parts of the book and sources of leadership: leadership from the head and heart.
- A study such as this need not be limited to the educators in the school. Be alert to situations where it is useful to share this information with parents or caregivers, school support staff, students, school board members, and other community members.
- A study of the age group in general is **just part of getting to know middle level students**. Take deliberate steps to develop tools and processes to "learn" (know and understand) each student, and to help each one to feel understood and valued. This includes such methods as student surveys, notes exchanged between teacher and student, a strong advocacy and advisory program, a system of regular academic checks, comprehensive counseling and support services, and well-implemented engagement with families.

YOUNG ADOLESCENT DEVELOPMENT AND IMPLICATIONS FOR EDUCATORS

A Guided Study for *The Successful Middle School: This We Believe*, Pages 54–66
Use these questions to guide you in a close reading of this text.

"I Am Poem," page 54

- What is the main message of the poem?
- Which lines or phrases are the most powerful? Why?
- How could we use this poem further?

Introduction, pages 55–57

- What is the key idea in each of the seven paragraphs?
- What stands out to us most?
- What ideas do we want to examine or discuss further?
- How can we relate this information to some of our own experiences?

Physical Development, pages 57–58

- What was new for us or some of us?
- What stands out in this list?
- What do we want to discuss further?
- What do we want to learn about in more depth?
- What do we observe about individual variations from this list?
- What examples come to mind from our own experiences?

Physical Development Implications for Educators, pages 58–59

- What implications would we highlight?
- What options or ideas are already in place? What are we already doing well?
- Which need more examination and learning from us?
- What outside resources can we access to learn more or implement these ideas?
- Which items need work? What shall we do about these?
- How can we involve students? What do we need to hear or learn from students?

- What else can we learn from students' families? How?
- How do we involve other staff members?
- How can we address individual variations from this list?
- What cautions do we need to exercise in use of these characteristics?
- What would we add to the list?

Cognitive Development, pages 59–60

- What was new for us or some of us?
- What stands out in this list?
- What do we want to discuss further?
- What do we want to learn about in more depth?
- What examples come to mind from our own experiences?
- What do we observe about individual variations from this list?

Cognitive Development Implications for Educators, page 60

- What implications would we highlight?
- What options or ideas are already in place? What are we already doing well?
- Which need more examination and learning from us?
- What outside resources can we access to learn more or implement these ideas?
- Which items need work? What shall we do about these?
- How can we involve students? What do we need to hear or learn from students?
- What else can we learn from students' families? How?
- How do we involve other staff members?
- How can we address individual variations from this list?
- What cautions do we need to exercise in use of these characteristics?
- What would we add to the list?

Social-Emotional Development, page 61

- What was new for us or some of us?
- What stands out in this list?
- What do we want to discuss further?
- What do we want to learn about in more depth?
- What examples come to mind from our own experiences?
- What do we observe about individual variations from this list?

Social-Emotional Development Implications for Educators, page 62

- What implications would we highlight?
- What options or ideas are already in place? What are we already doing well?
- Which need more examination and learning from us?
- What outside resources can we access to learn more or implement these ideas?
- Which items need work? What shall we do about these?
- How can we involve students? What do we need to hear or learn from students?
- What else can we learn from students' families? How?
- How do we involve other staff members?
- How can we address individual variations from this list?
- What cautions do we need to exercise in use of these characteristics?
- What would we add to the list?

Psychological Development, page 63

- What was new for us or some of us?
- What stands out in this list?
- What do we want to discuss further?
- What do we want to learn about in more depth?
- What examples come to mind from our own experiences?
- What do we observe about individual variations from this list?

Psychological Development Implications for Educators, page 64

- What implications would we highlight?
- What options or ideas are already in place? What are we already doing well?
- Which need more examination and learning from us?
- What outside resources can we access to learn more or implement these ideas?
- Which items need work? What shall we do about these?
- How can we involve students? What do we need to hear or learn from students?
- What else can we learn from students' families? How?

- How do we involve other staff members?
- How can we address individual variations from this list?
- What cautions do we need to exercise in use of these characteristics?
- What would we add to the list?

"*Untitled,*" Presentation (art and words), page 65

- Look at the image without reading the words.
- What do we especially note about the image? What does it tell us?
- What about the piece is most powerful? Why?
- How does the piece, art and words, affect each of us? What did we learn?
- How could we use this piece further?

"*Bobcat Pride,*" Presentation (art and words), page 66

- Look at the image without reading the words.
- What do we especially note about the image? What does it tell us?
- What about the piece is most powerful? Why?
- How does the piece, art and words, affect each of us? What did we learn?
- How could we use this piece further?

HEART LEADERSHIP STRATEGY 4: KNOW YOUR COLLEAGUES

Purpose: Leaders learn about the individuals who work in their school, intentionally connecting with and showing value to them and the work they do.

Human connection is only authentic and meaningful when the people involved feel seen, heard, and known. This happens best when there are clear efforts to get to know one another and to have open hearts of curiosity, emotional awareness, and sensitivity. Each member of the staff wants to be important; they want colleagues to know what they do, what their skills are, what they are passionate about. They want to be valued for their contributions and skills, as well as for who they are as persons. It's impossible to effectively lead if you have very little knowledge of those you lead who work with you every day.

Heart-Centered Leadership Strategies

Of course, it is difficult to have close knowledge of dozens, sometimes hundreds, of co-workers. There are some colleagues with whom you interact regularly, but many others you rarely see or may not know at all. Yet there are dozens of small, meaningful gestures that you can fit into any day to connect with colleagues.

Here's one strategy that works well:

1. Get a list of every staff member and their role in the school. Include all teaching, non-teaching, and support staff. Include part-timers and regular volunteers. Don't forget to include other leaders on your list. Add to the list the location where each person would be found in the school and their schedule, if relevant. If other non-confidential information is available, add it to your list.

2. Gather a collection of ideas for actions you can consciously initiate that make contact with colleagues. Start with in-person contacts, but you can always also send a note of gratitude, encouragement, or comfort by text, email, or written thank you note in their personal mailbox.

3. Make a commitment to have some kind of contact with each of these people as many times as possible throughout the year.

4. Begin by noting five (or so) names each week, along with their job or role and where you might find them in the school. Make a point to have a contact with those people during the week. Or you might choose a particular department or location in the school so that you can make a connection, for example, with media workers, in one time period.

5. For your first contact, make a visit in person. Learn about their job. Find out something personal about the person. Ask what they feel is important about their role. Perhaps ask what the school means to them.

6. Keep a spreadsheet of the names where you can note dates of your contacts. You'll probably also want to keep some notes about what you learn about them. Respect confidentiality by being careful what you put in writing that anyone else might see.

7. Continue contacts with the next five or so colleagues. Try to get to everyone, if possible, in the first few months of school. There are multiple ways for

contacts. Some may be as brief as a "Hello, Jack!" or a quick word of gratitude for something you noticed. Others may be a quick question: "How's that new baby doing?" or "Did we get that broken mixer in the kitchen fixed to your satisfaction?" or "What do you need today?" (Don't ask a question that you don't have ample time for listening to the answer.)

8. With more encounters, even brief, get to know more about each individual and their passions and needs, experiences and successes. Find out how they feel about the school and their jobs. Find out a bit about their families. Find out what they need from the leader. And especially, show interest, spread kindness, and share gratitude. Make sure the person knows that you see and appreciate the work they do for the school and its students. Refer to a specific act or incident where they have made a difference.

9. As often as possible, ask for input and feedback in your contacts. Again, these don't have to be long. Make a specific request of something on which you'd like their opinion or suggestions. This respects their mind and skills, and makes use of their knowledge in their field. **Remember—they know stuff or how to do stuff that you don't.** They hear and see and experience stuff that you don't! The next time you see the person, say something that acknowledges what you did or learned with their suggestion.

10. Don't underestimate, also, the value of a shout across the parking lot, a handwave or thumbs-up, or a kind gesture to one of their family members. Any kind of acknowledgement can be meaningful.

Finally, don't keep this practice all to yourself. Spread it to all staff members so that people can get to know and appreciate more about each other.

This is a straight-from-the heart strategy, for sure. It will boost the sense of pride and connection for your colleagues. It will enrich their hearts and yours.

HEART LEADERSHIP STRATEGY 5: EMPOWER FAMILIES

Purpose: Leaders and school staff invite students' parents and caregivers to be part of the school family by participating in meaningful decision making.

Heart-Centered Leadership Strategies

There are dozens of ways for teachers, coaches, principals, superintendents, and other leaders to put heart-leadership into practice with students' families. This strategy focuses on planning processes that invite students' parents and caregivers to participate in matters important to the heart of the school.

Such processes give parents and caregivers a greater voice in the school mission. You and other school personnel find out what the school means to the families and what they need from school leaders. You gain insights and ideas that only families can give. At the same time, they'll learn more about the school and the school leaders.

Create opportunities for listening to the hearts of families and gaining their valuable input.

1. Collaborate with other leaders, including teachers and staff members, to brainstorm about kinds of processes that will give family members true participation in making plans and decisions that make a difference in the school program. Include student and parent representatives in the brainstorming and planning.

2. Select some ideas that are possible to carry out during each school year. Remember that one of your key goals will be to gain insights and wisdom that students' families have to offer—viewpoints that are unique to families. Such processes also increase two-way communication and connection. Look for ways that will deepen understandings, share inspiration, and mutually support.

Here are a few ideas to get your thinking started:

- **Establish a "Blue-Ribbon Committee" for site-based decision making.**
  This is a collaborative teacher-parent group empowered to make some policy and process decisions for the school (a PTA with specialized powers). The committee can take on responsibilities related to curriculum, instruction, assessment, scheduling, or other matters that the school designates when forming such a group. Focus the responsibilities on policies and processes that will contribute to student success in gaining knowledge and

skills. The school can set a mission for the committee, or the committee can contribute to the forming of the committee's goals.

- **Engage families in envisioning a successful school.**

    Engage parent or caregiver representatives to contribute to a vision for what their school should be like. Invite a group from across the grade levels to participate (perhaps a total of 12 parent-caregiver representatives). To this group, add an equal number of school staff members: teachers, nonteaching staff, leaders. (You might include some students, as well.) Individually, each person writes five things they need to see that reflect a high-functioning successful middle school. Then each person meets with another and the pair combines their ideas to agree on a list of five. Each pair then joins with another pair; together they form a list of their strongest five ideas. The teams of four join with the entire group. They agree on a honed list of five. These final five things become an anchor for a school vision or mission statement, or set of core beliefs. This group can continue to work together to decide how to share the ideas with others in the school community or how to take further steps toward a vision, mission, or core belief statement.

- **Solicit family input through an interactive website.**

    School websites and other social media platforms are wonderful tools to communicate with families, share important information, and help families feel valued and welcome. They are also valuable vehicles for getting to know families better and connecting from the hearts of leaders to the hearts of families. Set up a process where you regularly solicit input and feedback from families. All members of the family can contribute to their family's response. Select a specific topic every two weeks (or other time period). You could offer a short survey on a topic (only a few items) or just one question. State clearly what you are looking for. It could be something like:

    > *What is the best thing teachers (or the school) can do to help your child feel connected to the school?*
    > *What does your family need most to help your child with homework?*

What does the school do that helps your child feel successful with schoolwork?

Suggest food choices that you'd like to see added to the school lunch menu.

What is your top goal for your child at school this year?

Give us two suggestions for building good relationships with families.

Encourage families to collaborate with all the family members to decide what their response will be. They'll be watching for this regular feature. It can be a great bonding event. (By the way, don't ask for any input that you don't intend to use!)

Once you solicit and receive feedback, be sure to follow through on it. Have someone tally and summarize what was learned from a question. Then decide what you can do about it. Communicate your plans back to the families. Send out a message: *Here's what we heard from you. Here's what we'll be doing with the feedback you gave.*

HEART LEADERSHIP STRATEGY 6: VALUE COMMUNITY PARTNERS

Purpose: Leaders find ways to offer community members meaningful chances to take part in events that show the heart of the school, showing that the school community values them, their support, and their feedback.

Plan events or situations that will help you and the rest of the school community get to know the neighbors, community leaders, district patrons, business leaders and workers, and any others of the wider community. Find out about what the school means to them and what they need from school leaders. At the same time, help them get to know more about the school and its leaders. Create opportunities for sharing the goals, passions, and hearts of students and of the adults that are responsible for school programs.

1. Collaborate with other leaders, including teachers and staff members, to brainstorm about kinds of events that would connect with community members. To expand your pool of ideas, include student and parent or caregiver representatives in the planning.

2. Select a few ideas that are possible to carry out during each school

year. Remember that one of your key goals will be to increase two-way communication and connection. Look for ways that will deepen understandings, share inspiration, and mutually support.

Here are a few events to get your thinking started:

- **Host an "academic project" show.** Like an art show, students display academic projects to be viewed by visitors. (The projects could also include visual and performing arts, if you choose. This might give an opportunity for students to create projects in pairs or groups.) Visitors can provide feedback on presentation and content. If you want to add an award feature to the event, business leaders or other community "experts" in an area can provide prizes or honorable mentions to presentations.

- **Host a "principal for the day" event.** Invite persons such as CEOs, company presidents, school board members, or even the mayor to be the principal for an entire school day. Plan a post-event session to discuss the day and how the attending "principal" can better support the school. Give a chance for the "principal" to tell what they learned, including what was the most exciting (or challenging, or surprising) part of the job!

- **Host a block party for engagement of staff, students, students' families, and community.** Share fun and food together for a few hours. Plan mini-events or demonstrations where members of the school community can show their passions and talents to the wider community and vice versa. Ask each person present to set a goal of learning something new about a person or group and also to share something of themselves with someone they did not know. (You can include this goal on the invitation.)

- **Take teachers on a community field trip or scavenger hunt.** During back-to-school Inservice for teachers, take a half-day field trip around the community. Stop at some public places, businesses, and community establishments for a quick meet and greet with workers, leaders, owners, and customers. Set a goal for each stop. This might be a hope or goal for the school year, an encouragement to the business leader for the upcoming year, or an idea about how the school and the other establishment can support one another. It might be a question for teachers to ask individuals they meet. As you arrange ahead of time for each stop, you might encourage the folks at the establishment to have a question or thought ready for the school visitors. With a little more creativity, you could turn this into a scavenger hunt. Note: Include other school staff members if possible, or do a separate trip for them.

HEART LEADERSHIP STRATEGY 7: INSPIRATION INSPECTION

Purpose: Leaders examine the concept of inspiration and personal experiences of being inspired by others.

Inspiration is a driving component of heart-centered leadership. Leaders want to inspire their students, colleagues, and other members of the school community. But as much as they need to inspire, they need to stay open to the sparks that ignite the inspiration within themselves. Sometimes inspiration comes along and gets missed because we're not noticing it! This strategy is designed for leaders to "meditate" on and reminisce about personal experiences of inspiration.

1. **Focus on what inspires you.**

    Take some time alone or with a group of colleagues to focus on what inspires you. Remember that inspiration may be triggered by something outside, but its source is inside of you. This will help sharpen your awareness of the multiple sources and instances of inspiration, many of them from unexpected places. (Re-read the section on inspiration in Chapter 1.) The following questions can guide your inspiration inspection, but add other questions as they come to you.

    A. **What inspires you?**
    - What is inspiration? Write your own definition of inspiration. (Remember that inspiration comes from within you.)
    - What inspires you or has inspired you to be a leader?
    - What inspires you to stay optimistic in your job?

B. **When have you been inspired?**
   List five occasions on which you have been inspired. Identify the things, persons, events, or situations that lit the sparks and fired up your passion and energy.

C. **How would you describe an experience of inspiration?**
   Choose an inspiration source or moment. Briefly describe what happened.
   - What were you inspired to do?
   - What are some things (skills, passions, thoughts, behaviors) that were awakened and energized in you when were inspired?
   - Where did the inspiration lead you?

2. **Share your discoveries and answers.**
   Find a way to encapsulate and present this inspiration experience. This can include any or all of these elements about the inspiration: where it came from, what it was, who played a part, where it took you. Here are a few ideas:
   - Write a news headline that captures the essence.
   - Make a collage of words and phrases (and images too, if you wish).
   - Write a letter to someone or something identifying the part they played in the inspiration and thanking them. (Yes, this can even be something other than a person!)
   - Use any art form to depict the inspiration, such as a paper, wire, clay, wood sculpture; a dance or other movement performance; a piece of music with some narration; a drawing; a color or light show, etc.
   - What did you learn about yourself?
   - Share your inspiration inspection with others (and discuss inspiration inspections, if you wish). As you do this, think about what you learned about yourself from examining your experiences of being inspired.

Heart Leadership Strategy 8: Hearing Student Voices

Purpose: Leaders oversee self-examination of what the school and the leader does to invite and respond to student voice.

One of the best ways to check the status of student voice practices is to ask the students. They're the ones who know if their ideas, opinions, and reflections are invited; if there are vehicles for those expressions; and if their voices matter. The leader works with teachers, teams, or other staff to create ways to gather feedback from students—as to whether, and how, the school makes possible—for all students—expressions of student voice such as these. Find out if students believe that:

- Their opinions and ideas are regularly invited, listened to, and valued.
- They regularly take part in decisions about classroom processes.
- There are many chances for them to take part in making decisions about school processes.
- They are invited to contribute perspectives and ideas to major plans such as vision and mission statements, school improvement plans, or strategic instructional plans.
- All students have ways to be heard without being afraid or uncomfortable.
- There are ample opportunities to give input to, or get questions answered by, school administrators, even the school board.
- Students are trusted with responsibilities in the school and classrooms.
- Student governing bodies, such as a student council or student school board, offer opportunities for all students to participate.
- Student governing groups make important school decisions that are put into place.
- There is a system for them to give feedback about school procedures and practices.
- Students have a say in their learning processes—in what they learn and how they learn it—including projects, assignments, and homework.

- There are regular processes for them to give feedback on class lessons.
- The opinions and suggestions that they give are used and visibly lead to action or change.

Notes:

- Educators often talk about "giving students greater voice." Be aware that we do not "give" voices to students. They already have voices. It's our job to invite, celebrate, and listen to those voices!
- A practice that invites student voice has little effect (or has negative effect) if nothing is done with the input or feedback they give.

HEART LEADERSHIP STRATEGY 9: AN ADVOCATE FOR EVERY STUDENT

Purpose: Leaders see that the school has a system, developed and administered through teams or other PLCs, where there is a workable process for matching each student to an adult advocate and a plan for what the adults do to advocate for the students.

In AMLE's *The Successful Middle School: This We Believe*, this is identified as one of the defining characteristics of a successful middle school: "Every student's academic and personal development is guided by an adult advocate."[14] This must be more than a goal, more than a platitude. It must be an intentional part of the school program—one that is sustained and supported. The heart-centered leader makes sure no student is left untended.

With a good advocacy plan, when a student has an issue or needs support, they feel safe and sure, knowing just where to turn for help. And with this security, they are more likely to seek help. Any student is far less likely to "fall through the cracks"—to become disheartened or disconnected or fall far behind with academic work.

Step 1 The task is to have a clear process for matching students and advocates and for identifying the nature of the ongoing advocacy. A strong middle school advocacy approach is for teams to choose advocates for students on their team. In cases where there is just one teacher for the grade, that teacher may be the advocate for all the students; or that teacher may call on some other staff in the school to take the advocate role for some of the students. If there is no teaming process or other PLCs, sometimes a homeroom teacher or advisory teacher takes on the role for students in their class. Think broadly about the adults in the school that can serve as advocates. Set some criteria and guidelines for making the best match for each student.

However the advocates are assigned, a dedicated process for doing this is a key function of heart-centered leadership. Consult AMLE's book, *Successful Middle School Teaming*, where author Jack Berckemeyer outlines one thoughtful and effective way to find the right adult to guide and monitor each student.

Step 2 Once advocates and students are matched, be sure that the adults understand what this role means and what they are to do. Have a process in place for this. In general, we want advocates to promote (and often times boost or even rescue!) students' academic success as well as social-emotional well-being and growth. To do this, advocates take on the role of ongoing contact, building meaningful relationships and taking a variety of actions.

These actions can include such things as the following. Adult advocates can work together to develop their own specific list of what they can do.

- Learning about the student, academically and personally: their individual interests, strengths, fears, passions, challenges, family, cultural background, successes, failures, learning styles, goals, and hopes.

- Keeping a close check on a student's academic progress (completed assignments, grades, work habits, challenges, roadblocks, etc.). The advocate attends to what and how the student is learning. They help ensure that the student clearly understands the expectations in each academic course and helps the students reach the expectations.

- Meeting often with the student individually, or in a small group, to hear from the student and monitor their social-emotional status. The advocate observes, listens, and gently probes to learn what's going on in the student's life, exploring such topics as school connectedness, peer relationships, social issues, feelings of safety or threat, self-confidence, views of self as a student, etc.

- Helping students with hurdles by clearly identifying academic, social, or emotional needs and finding resources to help meet those needs.
- Serving as a major liaison and collaborator with the student's teachers and PLC.
- Serving as major liaison and collaborator with the student's family.
- Consistently and concretely showing care, catching many opportunities to affirm the student—preferably with a daily or almost daily brief check-in.

Heart Leadership Strategy 10: Keep the Alarm Clock Ringing

Purpose: Leaders learn ways to keep passion alive in their leadership.

As stated in Chapter 2, Heart Leadership Trait 8, passion is not limitless. Most educators know that it can wane if not refreshed. The heart-centered leader makes intentional use of strategies to wake up those passions when they sense them dwindling.

Use this strategy to keep your passion alarm clock ringing. Repeat this as often as you need it. Use the guide found later in this strategy, **Passion Wake-Up Calls**, as you do this, or design a graphic of your own.

- Make a habit of pondering passion and attending to its level of intensity. Note times when your passion for your leadership, your job, your vision, the school's vision, and your people is sizzling and when it is fizzling.
- Identify an example of a time when your passion is sizzling. How can you tell when this is happening? Can you identify what it is that is firing up your passion? Jot down some notes or examples.
- Identify an example of a time when your passion is fizzling. How can you tell when this is happening? Can you identify what is behind the fizzle?
- Brainstorm other situations, factors, events, or influences that keep your passion alive.
- Brainstorm situations, factors, events, or influences that diminish your passion. (It's highly important to learn to be aware of these.)

- Share examples and ideas with a few other colleagues.
- Read the examples of some of my passion energizers below.
- Go back to your brainstormed lists. Add ideas that arise from your discussions or that you want to borrow from the list below. Make a list of the top 10 things that keep the spark in your work. Keep the list handy.
- Consciously draw on the passion revivers and avoid the passion deflaters!

12 Ways to Keep Your Passion Alarm Clock Ringing:

1. **Read daily.** This helps you learn something new each day, which inspires ideas and refreshes enthusiasm. I spend 10 minutes each day scanning articles from educational journals and reviewing the headlines from online periodicals. I look for articles on leadership and professional practice, then print and study those of interest. This keeps me informed of trends and new practices. Sometimes it confirms the magnificent work happening in our own district.
2. **Pause three minutes to start each morning.** As a busy dad and superintendent, each morning was a bustle of activity while helping my then middle school daughter get ready for school. By the time I dropped her off, my mind would be racing. I started a practice that I still continue: Before shifting gears from dad to superintendent, I pause for three minutes. This gives me a chance to think about my day; it creates some mental space for the tasks ahead and provides moments for my heart to open to my passions.
3. **Be with students; talk to students.** This always reminds me of what everything I do at school is all about. It centers my work, and adds purpose and credibility to my decisions. Any time you feel your passion slipping, I recommend that you get out of your office or finish your meeting and find some students to hang out with, listen to, and enjoy.
4. **Enjoy and lean on your co-workers.** My colleagues and I support and draw from each other. We remind each other that we're in this together and that we need each other. So work as a team on causes and projects that give you and your co-workers life.
5. **Draw energy from the passion of others.** Passion is contagious. It triggers other passions. Don't get closed off, buried in your own passions. I am greatly

electrified when I notice and ask students, colleagues, school families, and community leaders and members what "rings their alarm." Their power empowers my passions too!

6. **Laugh—often.** Laughter is regenerating. I relearn this every day! Taking myself too seriously as I work inhibits the flow of my passion. Always have a good sense of humor. This helps the impact of your passion flow to others, who then see the humanity in you and your leader position.

7. **Reflect on leadership practices.** Here's some advice I once received that I find gives "juice" to my passion: Never make the same mistake twice; always repeat good decisions. When you have a system in place for making decisions, you're more likely to avoid the distress that drains your passion. When you have good practices in place for teamwork, communication, and reflection, your passion will have more fire.

8. **Notice the outcomes of your zeal.** Results that work improve school life for many stakeholders. This brings satisfaction on many levels and adds fuel to my passions.

9. **Continue to grow.** Mentoring or coaching others and engaging in planned professional development and action research brings significant personal and professional growth.

10. **Change things up.** This is a way to keep work from becoming mundane and monotonous. It prevents relationships from languishing. When I try new practices and approaches, my passion takes leaps! Surprise yourself. Surprise your staff and students. Keep lighting new flames!

11. **Rest, relax, and meditate.** I intentionally plan time for these, and that habit is a lifesaver! Exhaustion—mental, physical, emotional, or spiritual—depletes passion. But self-care in all these areas replenishes it. Refresh yourself while away from school.

12. **Connect with those you love.** Leadership roles take massive amounts of time and energy, which eats into our personal time. I set aside times where I intentionally turn off the phone and become fully present with those people in my life who need me and who feed my soul. Don't neglect this. Take time to turn your passions to these people as well. When you keep strong connections there, your passions for everything important in your life will blossom.

Heart-Centered Leadership Strategies

Passion Wake-Up Calls

Identify what lights your passion and what extinguishes it. Use your discoveries to set goals for how you will keep your passion zinging.

Brainstorm **Passion Revivers**

Passion Deflaters *Brainstorm*

Set Goals
Keep my alarm clock ringing!

Practices I'll Use

Things I'll Avoid

Heart Leadership Strategy 11: Picture That Relationship!

Purpose: Leaders guide stakeholders to consider and share qualities or attributes of what they see as quality relationships.

Use this strategy to instigate lively but deep conversations about what good relationships in the school really look like in action. Challenge staff and students to identify observable characteristics of quality relationships and to seek out examples in everyday life at school and beyond.

Step 1 Hold a brainstorming session with your group. Take about five minutes in pairs or small groups to consider what a quality relationship looks like. This means the kinds of relationships that you want to find at school—relationships that are satisfying and good for you and others. You might narrow this to peer relationships, leader-colleague relationships, relationships between school staff members and students' families, colleague relationships, school staff-community member relationships, or other kind of relationship within the school.

Step 2 Spark ideas by asking participants such questions as:

- *What positive relationship actions have you experienced at school or do you wish to experience at school?*
- *Where and when have you observed positive relationships?*
- *What do you do to show care and value to someone else?*
- *How can you tell if an action shows a positive relationship?*
- *Can you close your eyes and picture or remember specific instances where you saw signs of a social contact in which you sensed that someone felt valued and safe?*

Step 3 Join the brainstormers together to share and collate lists. Form a group list, or pairs or individuals can keep their own lists. Make sure you, the leader, take part in this! Find some time for sharing the lists.

Step 4 Challenge participants to watch for and "catch" examples of someone **doing** good relationship behaviors. Tell them that they'll be capturing these in some sort of image. These images might be actual photos—even selfies, if they are part of the example—but remember that it is good etiquette to ask permission of the people before taking their picture. There are other ways to show the relationship interaction. Participants can:

- Draw a sketch or cartoon, or even a graphic diagram.
- Cut pictures from a magazine or newspaper.
- Catch a screenshot of something they see (such as an advertisement, poster, or internet image of a real event).
- Create a collage of images and words.

Ask them to label each image they capture or create.

Set a time frame for doing this (one day, a few days, a week).

Step 5 Find a way to print or project the results so that you can have great sharing session. Let each person, pair, or group have the floor for a minute or two to explain what they found and what they learned. You'll be amazed at the insights and examples that everyone will find and gain!

Step 6 Challenge them all (and yourself) to continue watching for such situations and to be proactive these good relationship behaviors that they have identified.

HEART LEADERSHIP STRATEGY 12: TAKING CHARGE IN A CRISIS

Purpose: Leaders consider and plan some actions and principles for their response in crisis situations.

Crises range in intensity, duration, causes, consequences, lessons learned, and ensuing changes. No two crises call for the same response from a school leader or other leaders. It's a time when leaders often have to think on their feet. But all crises need heart-centered leadership, and when you lead from the heart, you alter both the outcomes and the way a crisis is experienced by those involved. This strategy encourages you to make some general advance plans that can inform your overall approach to crisis response and management.

1. **Be there, or get there as quickly as you can.** First, remember that effective school leaders affect crisis and often change it into opportunity by just showing up. Their leadership can also make a difference in the severity of outcomes. This is not the time for delegation. Yes, you'll involve other leaders in action. But be there yourself.

2. **Whatever the crisis, own it.** You or the school may not be accountable legally, but you are responsible for your response. Keep this in mind: "When you sign up for the glitz, get ready for the blitz." There will be times when you or members of your administrative team will face very difficult decisions. Those decisions may not all end up in your favor. Own it. Don't blame others or pass the buck. I was told once that I should not apologize because it could make me legally liable for the results. "Well," I said, "I'd rather be legally liable than spiritually vulnerable." If you're the leader, then lead. Step up, own the results, apologize where necessary, then plan to fix it. It is disloyal to your heart and unfaithful to the hearts of others if a leader is not honest about what culpability lies with them or the school.

3. **Keep your heart open to other hearts as you respond.** In the case of an accident, a potentially dangerous situation, or any situation that demands urgent response, a leader must act. The strategic thinking, decision making, and putting hands and feet to work usually can't wait. But that doesn't mean that heart-centered leadership is put on the back burner; the physical and emotional needs of all involved must remain front and center. They must be integrated into the whole of crisis leadership. For example, when a fight breaks out, whatever leaders are present or nearby know that the first need is to stop the fight and keep everyone as safe as possible. Another urgent need might be to get statements from witnesses before they disperse. But getting to the bottom of the issues, reasons, and responsibility can come later when things have cooled off. Heart leadership helps with these next steps when the leader is present with the people involved in the fight.

4. **Be the leader that's needed.** In a crisis, people want a leader. They want to know someone is taking charge—someone wise and stable whom they can trust to take care of things. The heart-centered leader can offer courage and strength while being human and empathetic. Be aware of the

social-emotional needs of others. You can do this by staying calm in your voice and body language and not acting on impulse. Communicate clearly and frequently to those around you: ask questions, listen, and share appropriate information. Respond thoughtfully; take time to think before making decisions if time allows you to do this.

5. **Be prepared.** A leader or school's response to a crisis will be more effective when the leaders are as prepared as possible. It's far easier for a leader to be calm when they are prepared. Of course, we can't be prepared for everything that happens or might happen. But careful forethought and training can contribute to better—even lifesaving—responses.

- **Learn state policies regarding school operations.** I gained great insight and knowledge from studying carefully (before the school year began) the policies, both local and state, for every district for which I have served. And I was grateful for this knowledge on many occasions. Knowing the rules of the game informs your decisions. Your heart leadership in these decisions, then, will be more about compassion than raw emotion.

- **Know these policies early and well.** Don't wait until an event occurs to learn local and state policies. The better you know them, the easier it will be to act effectively when something happens. Clear understanding of policies will also enable you to be aware when someone's not following them but telling you that they are.

- **Anticipate crises and train for them.** All schools have safety policies and procedures for such events as fire and other natural disasters, accidents and injuries on school grounds or at school activities, responses to illegal behaviors, bullying, or violence targeted at schools from outsiders. Leaders can anticipate these crises and others not listed in the manuals, and identify them with the staff.

- **Train everyone.** Provide professional development to all school personnel, intentionally planning training on all policies. Teach policies to your staff early and review them regularly. Don't count on members already knowing them from last year or learning on their own from reading a manual. Don't expect them to clearly follow policies they have not been well taught. In the case of the driver in the school bus accident I described in Trait 17 (Chapter 2), a policy was not adhered to fully. This led to limited liability on the part of the district and, unfortunately, severe consequences for the driver.

- **Practice.** Prepare procedures and practice performing them. Take to heart the hard work of putting plans into place by practicing them regularly. There's a reason the local fire department requires fire drills and tornado drills in schools. If something happens, the response becomes almost automatic. This counts for all facets of the school organization. For example, bus drivers practice checking the back of the bus for sleeping passengers so they are not left on a hot bus. They also check their surroundings while moving in and out of traffic. Consistent practice becomes response instead of reaction.

- **Monitor the knowledge and use of policies and procedures.** After professional development sessions, require post-session evaluation and ongoing monitoring of policy adherence. This can come in the informal observations of practice or official inspection of procedures, practices, and recordkeeping. Teachers and other staff members will gain confidence and safety in feeling prepared. Take nothing for granted. Inspect what you expect.

- **Maintain a high level of preparedness.** There is blessing in working with a team. As a leader, you can trust the team to get the work done, even in your absence. Once the goals and processes are set and specific tasks assigned, a great team sets out to accomplish the mission and usually does so without delay. There is, however, also a burden in leading a team. After a period of time, momentum turns into monotony and teams begin to take actionable items for granted, including important steps in safety protocols. This is where the leader uses their presence to reignite the fire for excellence in operations. Once you have set the tone and expectations, visit the operation frequently. Perform formal and informal inspections to keep the operation functioning efficiently and the team performing effectively.

HEART LEADERSHIP STRATEGY 13: JOURNALING: LEADING FROM THE HEART

Purpose: Leaders follow a practice of journaling to examine their leadership practices and enhance abilities to lead from the heart.

Reflection is slowing down to think about yourself, your actions, and your experiences. It is critical to growth as a leader and to your self-care.

1. Intentionally set aside a regular time, maybe 15 to 30 minutes. Protect this time.
2. Select a quiet place. Turn off devices and avoid distractions.
3. Put down your thoughts in paragraphs, sentences, phrases, outlines, poetry, or a narrative format. There is no one right or best way.
4. Choose a theme to ponder, or a topic or prompt, and get started.
5. Be honest. Notice your feelings as you write. Note those as well.

Some ideas for a journal entry related to leading from the heart:

- An overview of the week, pondering what you learned about leading from the heart
- Strengths you used; strengths you see that you need to develop
- One thought or lesson learned from a short encounter
- Examples of heart-centered leadership you have done or witnessed
- Thoughts or conclusions on your whole leadership style or direction, or any facet of it
- Personal experience of any of the "fruits" of heart-centered leadership (see Chapter 1)
- Best heart leadership moment or experience this week
- Gratitude observations—names of people who have reached your heart this week
- Reflections on any of the traits in Chapter 2 as they relate to the status of your heart-centered leadership
- A look at an important value of yours and how it connects to your leadership
- Heart-centered leadership strategies (Chapter 3) you consciously used and how they worked
- Or many other reflections. Ideas will come to you!

The journal guide template on the next page, **Journaling Heart-Centered Leadership**, is an example of a tool you might create to record your thoughts. This particular sample could be used for a general overview of your week. You might put blank template pages into a notebook, use an actual book-like journal, or capture your thoughts in a digital format as if you were preparing to write a book.

Journaling Heart-Centered Leadership

Use this to guide in your reflection. Add other ideas if needed.

Theme, event, or topic for reflection today	
My best heart-leadership moment	
Another example of heart-centered leadership that I observed in myself	
A heart-centered leadership trait that I needed but didn't use	
Feelings I noticed (my own) and how they manifested	
Feelings I noticed in someone else and what I learned	
An important value of mine and how it connected to this	

PART 2

LEADING FROM THE HEAD

Chapter 4   What Does It Mean to Lead from the Head?
Chapter 5   Traits of Head-Centered Leadership
Chapter 6   Head-Centered Leadership Strategies

The Successful Middle School: This We Believe
Characteristics Crossover

- Educators respect and value young adolescents.
- The school environment is welcoming, inclusive, and affirming for all.
- The school engages families as valued partners.
- The school collaborates with community and business partners.
- A shared vision developed by all stakeholders guides every decision.
- Policies and practices are student-centered, unbiased, and fairly implemented.
- Leaders are committed to and knowledgeable about young adolescents, equitable practices, and educational research.
- Leaders demonstrate courage and collaboration.
- Professional learning for staff is relevant, long term, and job embedded.
- Organizational structures foster purposeful learning and meaningful relationships.

Chapter 4

What Does It Mean to Lead from the Head?

The New Superintendent Between a Rock and a Hard Place

Each summer for more than a decade, our district's high school alumni association sponsored a basketball tournament at the local high school. Only a few days into my job as new district superintendent and just as planning for this event was underway, I was diving into my initial review of the policies related to the use of school facilities. Policy review is a standard practice of school leaders as we assume new positions. But I had been specifically charged to straighten out inconsistencies within the procedures for use of facilities, which had been administered unfairly and inequitably. As part of my review of this, I reminded our director of facilities not to allow use of any building without the proper paperwork on file.

Two days before the tournament was to begin, as Murphy's Law would have it, we discovered that the alumni association representative had failed to submit the proper paperwork for the event. The result was that we could not allow the association to use the high school gymnasium.

*Upon hearing this, the alumni association representative called me to ask how I could "lock him out of his school!" Later, he marched into my office, insisting that the principal normally just let him use the gym, but could not this year because, "**You** said that I couldn't use the building." He reiterated that it was not the principal's choice; the principal's hands were tied, he claimed, "because the superintendent said so." I was stuck between the needs of the alumni association, the loyalty of the principal to the basketball coach, and the realities of the district's rules and policies.*

My head for leadership signaled me that this was a moment to put everything on pause. I politely asked for time. Under less emotional conditions, saying no to the event might have seemed the proper response; obviously, procedures had not been followed. However, on this day, I needed to get to the bottom of some things. I was accused of being incompetent, insensitive, and gravely misinformed about "how we do things around here!" I needed to step back for a bit, gather information, and think in order to make an enlightened, well-considered decision.

One task was to investigate whether the principal was blaming me for enforcing the policy to save face with the alumni association. I was unsure of the principal's motives but did not assume the worst. To fully understand the situation, I needed a conversation with the principal. I had already reviewed all the district's rules and policies; but I wanted clarity on how this snafu had come about.

It turned out that the alumni association representative had insisted on the date but had never completed the proper paperwork, even after being asked to do so by the principal. While it was true that I said he could not use the building, what was left out of the conversation was that the principal had told him he needed the proper paperwork.

I had discerned that the group requesting to use the facility knew the procedures and had been reminded of them, but failed to follow through. This was not just about paperwork. These policies had been carefully crafted and were in place for important reasons of fairness, cost, safety, and impact on the school program. There was history of favoritism and erratic, arbitrary decisions about who received permission to use a facility and who didn't. The district management and finances at the time were under scrutiny from the state department. Things were messy. District morale was at a low, partly due to the disregard for rules, haphazard following of procedures, and general lack of structure.

As the new district leader, it was my responsibility to see that department heads were held accountable for operations. In addition, I saw that the basketball tournament required a great commitment of district funds and other resources such as staff time, maintenance, and matters of safety, security, and liability—not all of it covered by the rental fees. And there were so many needs for our resources for other values and purposes the district had already set.

What Does It Mean to Lead from the Head?

This brought me to the decision that the school campus and facilities would not be used this year for the tournament. I could have held to this without taking time to research and think. I could have just let the mistakes pass and said, "Let's see that it's done right next time." Either of these would have taken less time. The second option would have made some people happy (though would have continued the chaos). But leading mindfully—keeping the bigger picture in mind—brought me to the harder choice. I knew it was the right choice.

Head-centered leadership is leadership from a deep foundation of thoughtfulness—thinking that comes before action. This doesn't mean that there is no thinking during or after action. Head-centered leadership is founded, however, on the idea of not acting without intentional consideration.

The emphasis on thinking before acting applies to **all** actions, starting with the big picture of who you are and the sum of what you do as a leader and why you do it, and extending to the full scope of the attitudes, beliefs, and motivations that underpin your leadership. This emphasis applies, as well, to such actions as planning and launching an initiative, program, or procedure. It also includes the many actions you take in specific situations dozens of times a day—situations such as my dilemma above with the basketball tournament. In all cases of action within circumstances large or small, leading effectively from the head means considering the purpose, implications, and consequences of your decisions as a leader **before** (and even while) acting on those decisions.

In my training to become a school leader, I was told (and always believed) that leadership was defined as **action**. I was conditioned to the idea that leaders lead by doing the work that they expect those following them to do. In fact, much of what I saw and heard about leadership indicated that leaders who fail to **do** first must surely be nonresponsive or incompetent. From many sources, I picked up the message that if you needed to contemplate before making a decision or consult others before moving forward, you would be seen as unfit for the job, doubted as a leader, and eventually replaced.

Experience working in schools with hundreds of colleagues, students, and students' families, along with mentoring and soaking up sage advice, taught me differently. I now see that my earlier view was backwards. Acting first (before thinking) is the opposite of smart leadership. And smart (or strategic) leadership is not just a series of actions, no matter how well planned.

Now, *strategic* means plotting a well-thought-out plan for achieving a particular goal. However, the definition of *strategic* doesn't tell what **kind** of thought is needed. Usually those many hours of thought are spent grappling with such questions as: *What shall we do? Where are we headed? What do we want the outcomes to be? How will we do it? Where do we begin? Where and when will it happen? For how long? What is our timeline? Who needs to be involved? What are the steps? Who's responsible for each part? How much will it cost? What is Plan B?*

Now, don't get me wrong—these are all important questions. All are critical to an overall plan, be it a leader's plan for their own leadership in general, a plan of action for a long-term, school-wide change, or steps for development of one initiative. And all are parts of good head-centered leadership. Sharp cognitive skills are desired in a school leader, as are the technical abilities of organizing, planning, and designing systems.

Here's the problem: Something is missing from that model, even when we take time to think first. Leading from the head, as I want to share it, takes a step that comes before the traditional strategic thinking. There is one question at the core of good head-centered leadership, and it's the one to ask first. That question is **Why?** (I.e., *Why do I do what I do? Why am I a leader here, with young adolescent students? Why would we do what you are proposing? Why does our school, or this program, or this department, policy, etc. exist? Why does this matter? Why do we come to this school every day? Why would we change this procedure? Why would we try something different?*)

Simon Sinek, leadership expert and author of *Start with Why* (2009), says that most leaders and organizations begin by deciding on the "what" and the "how." But inspired leaders and organizations, he argues, "all think, act, and communicate from the inside out."[15] They start by knowing their beliefs and vision: why they exist or why they would take on some venture. Then they move outward to the questions of how and what.[16]

What Does It Mean to Lead from the Head?

In his TED Talk "How Great Leaders Inspire Action," Sinek noted that Martin Luther King's great speech was not an "I have a plan" speech. It was an "I have a dream" speech.[17] He also noted that King repeatedly used the words, "I believe." Having this speech on the wall of my office, I look at it daily. Indeed, King was an example of one who led from the why—the purpose. Yes, the speech certainly inspired and motivated actions with his dream of what could or should be. But primarily, it painted a vivid, powerful picture of his reasons for the struggle for justice that he led.[18]

So successful head-centered leadership is characterized by a combination of:

- **Knowing why**—a well-defined sense of purpose with actions that flow from the leader knowing who they are, why they lead, and how they lead. By "well-defined," I mean that the leader has worked to actually craft, write, and articulate in public their purpose and the specific actions that result from that base of belief.

- **Thinking before acting**—ongoing habits of thinking first in all situations. Gathering and analyzing background information and facts; considering possible outcomes and consequences for any action, including impacts on people involved. This is about making time for whatever kinds of pondering and discernment are appropriate to the situation and **then** taking well-informed, mindful actions.

- **Delegating and collaborating**—clear understanding by the leader that they do not have to (and shouldn't) do everything on their own; that they cannot think, decide, act without the benefit of the insights and assistance from others. Part of head-centered leadership is collaborating with other minds and trusting others to lead in accordance with their abilities and gifts.

- **Reflecting**—intentional, consistent reflection **after** actions. Examining what happened and why, and what is to be learned. The habit of thinking before acting naturally breeds reflection because when you think before you act, part of your information-gathering process will usually trigger revisiting past experiences and lessons learned.

THE FRUITS OF HEAD-CENTERED LEADERSHIP

When a leader operates from a thoughtful and well-articulated Theory of Action and develops the practice of thinking before acting in all situations, such outcomes as these naturally follow:

Clarity and Confidence

The leader has clarity and confidence about their own actions. There is no confusion or ambiguity about where the actions originated. The leader knows the source. So do colleagues and others affected by the action—because the leader has shared the purpose clearly. This helps others feel confident about what's happening in the school. Beyond that, leadership from the head breeds confidence for others in themselves and in their own part in supporting the purpose.

Shared Sense of Purpose

When the leader knows why they do what they do—has a thoughtful and well-shared purpose and Theory of Action—colleagues, parents, students, and others in the school community understand the big picture. Telling why for any venture or policy gives meaning to the plans and actions. Others see the cause and can join in to support it. When properly communicated, the leader's own understanding of why spreads to everyone.

In addition, the rest of the school community watches the leader making daily decisions thoughtfully and fairly and then reflecting back on those decisions. They see the leader keeping the why of leadership and of the school in the forefront in daily matters as well as big programs and policies. When they're asked to participate in individual situations or decisions, they can see the purpose. In turn, others start to pick up the leader's habits of examining purposes, delving into why something matters, and thinking first in specific situations. They grow as head-centered leaders too.

Order and Stability

There's a certainty in knowing that the leader has given this much forethought to their own purpose and processes for leadership. The leader's careful thinking about the whole of their leadership, as well as the habits of thinking first in specific situations, provides an order to the way issues are handled and decisions are made. As members of the school community watch such a leader practice this thoughtful leadership, over time they come to count on it continuing. Seeing the leader's thought-and-action plans gives a stability about how things will be done and how actions will generate. The staff members, students, and families all benefit from a consistent way of doing things.

Safety and Comfort
There's an aura of safety and comfort when school community members know the why of a leader's actions, when the effective head-centered leader has communicated the cause that is the core of their leadership. People feel safe in knowing that their leader is not going to make impulsive decisions or take erratic actions, but that the leader considers actions carefully before doing them. They've been shown what the leader believes, they've joined in on the purpose, and they can count on the leader not to take wild, unexpected detours. They can trust that the hard work they do on one initiative won't be dumped tomorrow for something different.

Belonging
Good leadership from the head boosts connectedness to the school and to one another. When people in the school community understand the purpose behind the leadership and the leader's vision of how that translates into action, they can see themselves fitting into the picture. They see why and how they are needed as well. They begin to envision how they can help to make the vision work. They experience themselves as part of a team working alongside the leader on things that matter to everyone rather than as someone who is "bossed" or "controlled" by the leader to do what the leader wants.

Productivity and Creativity
In an environment where individuals are part of a larger, well-considered purpose and feel that their skills and abilities are valued, people are better at their jobs! Productivity, creativity, innovation, and job satisfaction blossom.

This is true for teachers, non-teaching staff, students, family members, volunteers, and other school supporters. This includes school and district leaders, administrators and directors, and even district board members.

Communication and Collaboration
All aspects of thoughtful head-leadership are intertwined with communication, which begins with the leader's explanation of why they do what they do. Good communication is a built-in component of the thoughtful approach of good head leadership. So are cooperation and collaboration. All these are inspired by and flow out of effective head leadership. When people take part in a shared purpose, they energetically join in on the give-and-take of making decisions and solving problems together.

Buy-In
Every leader knows they are only effective as a leader to the extent that others join in their purpose. We leaders work hard to convince school stakeholders of the importance or promise of our visions. We take great pains to say the right words or take the right steps to motivate people to be as eager for a program or plan as we are.

When people know and share in the leader's purpose and experience such outcomes of thoughtful head leadership as clarity, confidence, order, stability, safety, and belonging, they want to get on board! As they find that their talents and contributions are not only used, but celebrated, not only do they buy into the cause—their buy-in is sustained. And their support and endorsements inspire others to join in.

Transparency
A leader who creates and publicizes an honest and thoughtful Theory of Action puts themselves out there! It's a kickoff for transparency in the leadership. This head-centered leader has taken the risk to publicize their deepest beliefs—their reason for being where they are. This sets a stage for the continued transparency of their leadership, and it inspires others to dig

deep into the why of their roles and how that translates into action. Putting forth their beliefs in this way holds the leader accountable too. Everyone will be watching. This motivates the leader to further transparency.

Enthusiasm
Understanding and speaking the purpose of your leadership gives you, the leader, meaning and direction. This is empowering and energizing. It is the source of your passion. A leader's enthusiasm is contagious. It spreads to everyone in the leader's path. In turn, those who work with the leader in supporting the purpose spread their enthusiasm to others and even back to the leader. The leader isn't walking ahead, but is willingly and joyfully joined. This gives everyone greater allegiance to the purpose. It builds hopefulness that, together, their belief and actions will fulfill the purpose that drives the school.

The New Superintendent Between a Rock and a Hard Place, continued

In the end of the matter with the basketball tournament, I was blessed to be able to resolve the complicated dispute. But the resolution went beyond the final determination (explained earlier) about that year's event. I met with the leadership of the alumni association right away after communicating the decision. We also set up additional meetings where we worked together, discussing ways to improve the processes about facility rentals. That led to additional conversations around the needs of the school—which included new windows, gym floor replacement, and a medical clinic. Eventually the district was able to partner with our alumni association to create a fully functioning clinic in the high school. This clinic is still in operation today.

DEVELOPING HEAD-CENTERED LEADERSHIP

I'm recollecting the familiar old adage, "Measure twice; cut once." It's very simple. But it reminds me that when we fail to lead effectively from the head, we end up in accidental leadership. This means we lead unwittingly—obliviously or haphazardly or both! True leadership is not accidental, but methodically approached and well measured.

You'll remember from Part 1 of this book that I believe leadership must include a way of feeling, and you'll find in Part 3 that I'm sure that a true leader is one who takes confident, decisive action—putting the hands to work. Yet in the absence of a thoughtful head with a clear sense of purpose (the why!) for all actions, and without the practice of thinking before acting, leadership can escort even the best of people, programs, and systems to a chaotic mess, where actions are disjointed and the needs of students and schools are not met.

My descriptions of leadership from the head assume some things that may not be true at all times of every leader's head. Just as I said in Chapter 1 that a truly heart-centered leader must have an open, welcoming heart—so it is that an effective head-centered leader needs an open, welcoming head. If your thinking is rigid, self-sufficient, overly perfectionistic, biased, fearful, sloppy, self-superior, hierarchical, closed to outside input, or self-protective, you won't have the capacity for the curiosity, creativity, and risk-taking needed to make the best decisions or inspire others to follow your leadership. So, part of developing head leadership is attending to your own head! Notice your thinking style and patterns. Be aware of the connections between your beliefs and your thoughts. Notice the factors that affect (nourish, impede, control, manipulate, challenge, enhance, etc.) your ability and freedom to lead mindfully.

You'll need other parts of the anatomy to do this too. All of these are connected to the brain, of course; but often we forget to use them as well as we could. I'm talking about your eyes and ears, mouth, and even that "Spidey-sense" I referred to in Chapter 2. Stay sharply tuned to your senses. You learn about your thinking and your purposes from listening to what you say, from reading what you write (be sure to do this before you click "send"!), and from watching your actions. You probably learn best about your thinking, though, from listening to and watching the responses of others to the effects of your thinking!

There are deliberate steps you can take to develop the habits of thoughtful head-centered leadership. Chapter 5 describes some leadership traits that flow from the head. Chapter 6 offers some strategies that help leaders develop these traits and put head-centered leadership into practice.

What Does It Mean to Lead from the Head?

Once you understand what head-centered leadership means and get a picture of how you can further develop it, you can attend to your purposes and actions and how they translate into practice. You can enjoy the effects of head-centered leadership as you watch such fruits as those described earlier in this chapter blossom in you and in those you lead.

Chapter 5

Traits of Head-Centered Leadership

How does head-centered leadership evidence itself? How can the leader tell when a thoughtful head is a major source of their own leadership purpose and action? How do others recognize and experience capable leadership from the head?

Here are some of the key **observable** characteristics or behaviors flowing from the source of a head that knows its purpose and thinks before, during, and after acting. Read about them to help answer the questions in the paragraph above. As leaders develop such traits, they grow further in their abilities to lead from the head.

The Successful Middle School Leader
Head-Centered Leadership Traits
The Head-Centered Leader...

Head Trait 1	Knows who they are and what they believe.
Head Trait 2	Knows the people and school they serve.
Head Trait 3	Holds and expands deep knowledge about young adolescents and successful middle schools.
Head Trait 4	Remembers that they work for and with others.
Head Trait 5	Consistently thinks before acting.
Head Trait 6	Crafts a clear Theory of Action for their leadership.
Head Trait 7	Effectively communicates their Theory of Action.
Head Trait 8	Guides the development of an all-school shared vision.

Head Trait 9	Holds to the vision.
Head Trait 10	Plans ahead for new and recurring processes.
Head Trait 11	Designs a process for reflection on events and situations.
Head Trait 12	Regularly gives affirmative, constructive feedback.
Head Trait 13	Invites and uses insights from others about their leadership.
Head Trait 14	Delegates to share responsibility.
Head Trait 15	Designs head-centered leadership development as a team.
Head Trait 16	Takes responsibility for mistakes.
Head Trait 17	Has courage.

Head Leadership Trait 1: The Head-Centered Leader Knows who they are and what they believe.

The head-centered leader works to explore and understand their personal characteristics, values, abilities, and habits that affect who they are as a person and a thinking leader. They have a deeply pondered consciousness about:

1. **Their own personal purposes and beliefs.**

They consider such components as these, and take time to describe or explain each. As you read, you might do the same. Ask yourself: "How would I describe or explain each of these?" Be sure to think about what's important to you, and why—rather than about programs, plans, or actions. The leader:

- Has a clear sense of their own fundamental assumptions, values, and motives.
- Explores their deepest beliefs about education and leadership.
- Ponders their purpose in being a leader—in particular, being a leader in the place and role in which they are now.

- Considers their beliefs that affect their attitudes in relation to the school or situation in which they find themselves or problem they currently confront.
- Asks themselves: "Why does what I do matter?"

2. **Their own personal qualities and abilities.**

The leader knows what they bring to the job, what they do well, and where they need work. They are honest in accepting their own gifts and needs and they acknowledge them to others. They think about (and describe) such personal qualities as these. As you read them, you might do the same. Ask yourself: "How would I describe my patterns or abilities for each?"

- Style and effectiveness of communication
- Ability to give clear explanations
- Work ethic and work patterns
- How and when and where I work well
- Thinking patterns (reflecting? thinking ahead? critical thinking?)
- Decision-making style (pre-planned approach or deciding on the fly?)
- Speaking abilities and comfort with speaking
- Confidence level (and where I am most and least confident)
- Level and style of organization (or disorganization)
- Level of and comfort with risk-taking
- Level of perseverance and commitment (to the school initiatives)
- Level of commitment (to my job, vision, people)
- Listening skills
- Project-planning skills
- Attention span
- Sense of humor
- Willingness to change
- Problem-solving skills
- Ability to delegate
- Comfort with feedback
- Time management
- Mediation abilities
- Sharing authority and control
- Attention to detail
- Efficiency
- Habits of showing gratitude

3. Their ways of doing things.

The head-centered leader thoughtfully examines the ways that they operate in the leader role. They consider what kinds of actions they will take or generally do take in various situations. They can describe how they go about things (actions, systems) in relation to such factors as these. As you read, you might do the same. For each one, ask yourself, "How do I do this?"

- Articulate a vision and clear sense of direction for the school
- Work with all stakeholders to build a school vision of shared values and beliefs
- Learn about the school and the people in it
- Learn about the history of the school, district, and community
- Learn about the history of specific programs and initiatives
- View and connect with co-workers
- Build an inclusive learning environment
- Exhibit cultural sensitivity and value of diversity
- Build a culture of strong, cohesive connections
- Emphasize and build trusting relationships
- Increase belonging for students and adults
- Keep the needs and characteristics of young adolescents at the forefront of all actions
- Assure that all policies and practices are student-centered
- Assure that all policies and practices are unbiased and fairly implemented
- Work to make every teacher better
- Hold to high expectations for student success and for staff performance
- Build an environment of true collaboration
- Form and work with teams
- Share leadership and authority
- Cultivate leadership skills in others
- Take, value, and make use of others' perspectives
- Initiate change and follow through
- Introduce ideas for new initiatives to staff (and other stakeholders)
- Plan, monitor, evaluate, and follow through on initiatives
- Create systems for communication (with staff, students, other leaders, families, community beyond the school)
- Promote hard work and tenacity for students and staff alike

Traits of Head-Centered Leadership

- Respond to successes and learn from failures
- Encourage and teach risk-taking
- Lead by example (show rather than tell)
- Demonstrate commitment to my job
- Model habits of lifelong learning
- Collaborate with the outside community
- Set and achieve goals and evaluate outcomes
- Remain accessible and visible in the school
- Reflect on programs, policies, procedures, and events
- Engage and connect with supervisors and other leaders
- Draw and use evidence from data
- Solicit, take, and give feedback
- Empower teachers
- Engage students' families
- Exhibit professionalism
- Display honesty
- Engender trust
- Allocate resources wisely
- Teach (well) those I lead
- Affirm and develop others
- Demonstrate transparency
- Consider succession planning
- Follow as well as lead
- Make decisions
- Solve problems
- Handle obstacles and setbacks
- Celebrate the school and the people

HEAD LEADERSHIP TRAIT 2: THE HEAD-CENTERED LEADER KNOWS THE PEOPLE AND SCHOOL THEY SERVE.

The thoughtful leader learns and appreciates the wealth of information available to teach them about the school, district, students and staff, and the community they serve. Doing this helps the leader understand the beliefs and values of people in the school community, what has gone on, and how things have been done. And learning this well gives the leader background and insights that will be foundational to any purposes and plans the leader envisions.

They delve into the values, thoughts, and actions that existed before they arrived in the job or before they initiated a change. They learn as much as possible about such factors as these, and thoughtfully integrate them into any of their own purposes or actions:

- The school setting, neighborhood, and town (or city)
- The culture of the wider environment beyond the school
- The school's flavor—how it "feels" and why
- The existing school culture and how it was built
- The deep stories of the school's (or district's) history—past challenges, successes, setbacks, inequities, lessons learned
- The school's physical and financial resources and needs
- The human resources—the people's strengths and gifts
- Current policies and procedures
- The purposes of the school and its programs—as seen by the teachers and other staff, the students, the families, the leaders, the board, the district administration, the community outside of school (their purposes as well as what they perceive to be the purposes of the school's leaders)
- All stakeholders' perspectives on school matters
- All stakeholders' needs, desires, and hopes for the school
- All stakeholders' disappointments, confusions, or disconnections
- The demographics and all the data the school keeps and how it has been used
- Past and ongoing initiatives, programs, and ventures
- Ongoing traditions
- What the people in the school community hope for in a leader

When proposing a change or new program or policy of any kind, the thoughtful leader learns about such factors as:

- The history of the problem—how and where it began
- What the current program is
- What has already been tried
- What has been successful and what has not (and why)

- What's still in place that is working
- What is not working
- Visions or reasons others explain related to the problem, the need, past solutions, or past failures
- Precedents regarding this or similar ventures
- People involved in programs or processes that this may replace
- What stakeholders hope for
- Resources needed and available

Learning well the people and school you serve enables you to be sensitive to what people have already given to existing structures and programs. Your appreciation for the history inspires you to respect the hard work, beliefs and hopes, traditions, risks, and richness of successes and lessons learned that have gone into past endeavors.

Then, even if you propose to stop, change, or replace an initiative, you can acknowledge the value of what has gone into a program or policy. You can affirm the accomplishments. You can honor and praise the progress and learning. When others realize that you are not disregarding all that has happened in the past—and especially when they understand the **why** of your proposed change—they'll trust you more. And they'll be more likely to choose to support the new approach.

HEAD LEADERSHIP TRAIT 3: THE HEAD-CENTERED LEADER HOLDS AND EXPANDS DEEP KNOWLEDGE ABOUT YOUNG ADOLESCENTS AND SUCCESSFUL MIDDLE SCHOOLS.

Don't start (or continue) middle level leadership without working on this trait! The head-centered leader is well-informed and passionate about these students and their education. The leader is cognizant of the students' needs, characteristics, experiences, interests, and individual differences and gifts. The leader is incessantly curious—always observing, listening, and questioning to find out about what the students think, feel, read, watch, like, dislike, believe, wonder about. They want to know what delights, discourages, encourages, impedes, challenges, worries, and influences these young adolescents. They ask students to help them understand what works best for their own (the students') academic success and overall well-being at school. The leader knows that their world—and the students' world—is changing fast. And this leader, along with the school community, wants to learn fast enough to keep up.

Head-centered leaders voraciously learn about best middle school practices. They are insatiable lifelong learners—eagerly reading, watching, listening, and brain-stretching with podcasts, articles, discussions with other educators, and a host of professional development activities. They take every opportunity to discuss programs, practices, successes, and failures with other middle level leaders.

The leader seeks insights and experiences from students, students' families, all staff members and volunteers, mental health advisors, and community members—particularly those who have connections with young adolescents. The thoughtful leader learns through such practices and platforms as podcasts, focus groups, parent-based site committees, Q&A sessions, small-group discussions with the leader (lunch, coffee, or a stroll with the leader), interactive websites, social media platforms, or student, staff, and family surveys. **Remember that the point of these is not for the leader to inform others.** You have other mechanisms for that. The point of the dialogue with others is to learn about the students from the students first and then, also, from others who interact and live with them.

For your own up-to-date and deep understanding of young adolescent students and the purposes and practices of the middle schools these students deserve, become a frequent reader of AMLE's book, *The Successful Middle School: This We Believe*. In particular, study the 18 Characteristics of Successful Middle Schools to reflect on how your school is implementing them (see page 9 in that book). As well, closely review the Characteristics of Young Adolescent Development and Implications for Educators to reflect on how your school is addressing these (pages 55–64). Visit AMLE.com/sms for access to these tools. You'll also find a self-assessment for the 18 Characteristics of Successful Middle Schools in Hand Leadership Strategy 11, later in this book.

> **Gray Matter**
>
> *Remember the old adage, frequently repeated by Harry S. Truman and Coach John Wooden: "It's what you learn after you know it all that counts."*

HEAD LEADERSHIP TRAIT 4: THE HEAD-CENTERED LEADER REMEMBERS THAT THEY WORK FOR AND WITH OTHERS.

An Early Lesson in Leadership

Many years ago, I worked as a waiter in a restaurant. It was a wonderful job to have as a college student. I had a flexible schedule and worked primarily for tips. The greatest benefit, however, was working for the superstar manager, Willie. Every shift that we worked together, he would start at the front door of the restaurant, greet the patrons, walk them to their seats, and bring water to get them comfortable.

*One day, I asked him why he did it. I wondered why he didn't spend his time in the office counting money and completing paperwork. Willie told me, "Our guests want to see me in the restaurant and our employees **need** to see me in the restaurant." The message I received was that the employees were important to him and* *he wanted to demonstrate the servant leadership by working* **with** *them—a trait that all great leaders exhibit. This was one of my most important experiences of what it means to be a leader.*

People don't want to follow someone who works for themselves. They want to join in with someone who works **with them**. The head-centered leader carefully considers the dynamic of the network in which they work. They know that they are not a "lone wolf" working to succeed at their own job. They truly value others and the jobs the others do for the school; they put others on an equal footing with themselves.

The thoughtful head-centered leader examines their own beliefs and attitudes about themselves in relation to **all** the others in the school community. This leader is people focused; they set aside their personal ambitions and any personal interests that are not in sync with the best interests of the entire school community. The leader is humble—modest about their skills and eager to welcome contributions and wisdom of others. They are authentic—sensitive to their own biases and honest about their missteps. They do not seek to set themselves apart as a superhero or a superior member of the school or district staff.

In their article "To Be a Good Leader, Start by Being a Good Follower," social science researchers Kim Peters and Alex Haslam advise that "without fellowship, leadership is nothing."[19] They contend that "leadership lies in the collective 'we,' not the individual 'I,'"[20] and found little evidence that it takes an exceptional person to be a leader. As well, when a leader works to show their exceptionalism, this will not only "undermine the leader's capacity to lead but, more importantly, it will also stifle followers' willingness to follow."[21] As they further explain:

> Leadership is a process that emerges from a relationship between leaders and followers who are bound together by their understanding that they are members of the same social group. People will be more effective leaders when their behaviors indicate that they are *one of us*, because they share our values, concerns and experiences, and are *doing it for us*, by looking to advance the interests of the group rather than their own personal interests.[22]

Effective head-centered leaders intentionally consider themselves part of the group. They know that what is effective for "us" is effective for the leader who is part of that "us"! This does not mean that, as a leader, you won't have some different responsibilities than others or that you won't make decisions and take actions that leaders must bear. But when you carry out your leader role, the others will know that you do it seeing yourself as part of the group—**with and not distanced from**—those you lead. When you make this distinction well, and still fulfill your leadership responsibilities courageously, don't worry that others will cease to see you as a leader. The people who work with you will clearly know who the leader is!

HEAD LEADERSHIP TRAIT 5: THE HEAD-CENTERED LEADER CONSISTENTLY THINKS BEFORE ACTING.

Head leadership is a way of describing the leader who is perpetually thoughtful—in particular, who thinks before acting. The action includes such things as coming to a decision and putting it in place, speaking in any circumstance including discussions, putting anything into writing and distributing it to others, or taking steps of any kind. A leader encounters a slew of situations and conversations a day in which they need to act; this means that the head-centered leader develops the habit of thinking first, even if they only have a short time to do so. And that thinking always includes considering the well-being of the students.

Take time to think. The thoughtful school leader ponders a situation with all the input, data, and knowledge available to make an informed decision about action. This includes input gained in such ways:

- Talking to people involved in a situation to find out what happened
- Corroborating versions of an incident
- Gathering whatever visible evidence is available
- Seeking others' perspectives, opinions, and suggestions
- Considering precedents in similar situations

- Digging to understand causes, history, and underlying emotions that might affect a decision or action
- Knowing and following state, school, and district policies, procedures, and safety guidelines relevant to an issue
- Keeping options for decisions and actions true to the school's vision
- Considering consequences, benefits, costs, and resources for any action
- Using well-planned and practiced decision-making and problem-solving processes
- Considering how different decisions or outcomes will affect all people and programs involved
- Pondering who should be involved in the resulting action
- Imagining how various actions will affect students
- Considering actions that are realistic, caring, and affordable
- Looking beyond the obvious to be open to creative solutions

Think even when you believe you don't have the time. "But!" I hear you saying. "So often, I have to act fast! I don't aways have time for this kind of fact-gathering and thinking." Dozens of times a day, a leader has to deal with dilemmas and decisions or jump into some kind of action. Here's some head-centered leadership advice for occasions when time is very short:

1. Sometimes, it might seem that there is no time to think. But in many of those instances, the world won't end if you pause for a moment. Sit or stand quietly to breathe and focus your mind and think calmly. This is especially useful in conversations and discussions. It doesn't cause any problems if you take 30 seconds or so to think before you respond. (You can even say to the group or other person, "Let's take a minute.") It can make all the difference between a useful response and something you'll regret.

2. Many decisions or actions can be delayed a bit longer than seconds or minutes. You can take care of something or make a decision at the end of the day or during lunchtime. There are occasions when the best thing to do is sleep on a problem or decision. Getting some distance enables clearer, deeper thinking.

3. When there truly is little time—if you've built up experience with thinking before acting, the thinking comes naturally and you can process things quickly.

4. When you've prepared for emergency situations, your brain quickly tells you what to do because you have thought through and even practiced this before.

5. Even when you need a significant amount of time to investigate before acting, the process of gathering information and input moves faster if you have:
   - Established, practiced processes for the information-gathering approaches in the bulleted list above.
   - The guidance of a well-formed and familiar (to all) school vision and mission.
   - Strong relationships and trust within the school that supply you with knowledge about people, needs, and situations.
   - Well-considered and well-practiced approaches for asking and listening to get at the details and help people feel safe when you are seeking observations and explanations.
   - Anticipated certain problems and difficulties and have already thought about actions to address the issue.

6. Keep this in mind: If you **don't** take time to think, you'll have more missteps in your actions and decisions. Repairing these will take a lot more time than you would have spent in thoughtfulness before the action.

Speaking is an action. Think before you speak. It's probably your most frequent action, yet it's one that often comes along with little thinking time. Effective head leadership is knowing when to speak, to whom to speak, what to say, and how to say it—in ways appropriate to a given situation, audience, and purpose. Many eyes are watching, many ears are listening, and many minds are dissecting everything we leaders say. Even in conversations, apply the above guidelines.

Pause before responding. Be prepared ahead of time so you'll have practiced what to say and not say.

Also, beware of how you speak with your fingers! The most criticized form of communication is that which comes from your written social media posts or email or text blasts. It is amazing that we can get a message out to millions of followers with the click of a mouse! It's also very intimidating (and sobering) to know that if that click is too quick, or not thoughtful enough, it can lead to great harm for students, others in the school community, your reputation, or the school and its good work.

> **Gray Matter**
>
> Head-Centered Leadership Equations:
> Crisis - Leadership = Chaos
> Crisis + Leadership = Challenge Met
> Crisis + Leadership + Resources = Challenge Overcome
> Crisis + Leadership + Resources + Action Plan = Challenge Avoided

In Chapter 6, see **Head Leadership Strategy 1: Leader's Smart Talk** on page 152 for a checklist to guide leaders in thinking about the ways they speak.

HEAD LEADERSHIP TRAIT 6: THE HEAD-CENTERED LEADER CRAFTS A CLEAR THEORY OF ACTION FOR THEIR LEADERSHIP.

Thinking before acting is part of the moment-by-moment life of an effective head-centered leader. But there are certain occasions in which the leader needs a focused and long-considered plan for why and how they will act. As I described in Chapter 4, a Theory of Action for leadership is the leader's well-contemplated purpose and how that affects the way they will lead. This is the leader saying, in essence, "Here's my vision for why I'm here, and because of that purpose, here is how I'll operate and what I'll do and what I'll lead us in doing together."

People are more likely to join in on any cause when they find it meaningful and when they see themselves as participants in making the meaning. They don't buy into an idea because of what you **say** you will do. They buy into your reasons for **why** you do something. And when they believe in your purpose, they'll **want** to get on board with energy and loyalty. Nothing gets done well when it's only the leader who's enthusiastic about it!

That's why I see a leader's Theory of Action as critical for effective head-centered leadership. It is especially useful when the leader does not have a solid relationship with the school community and thereby has to explain their beliefs, intentions, and actions in great detail. It is also useful when a change is proposed—no matter how long the leader has held the current job or how well the general scope of their leadership is already understood. Hence, the need for a Theory of Action is:

- At the beginning of a person's time as leader in a particular setting.
- And, also, at the beginning of a long-term, long-range, deep-rooted set of changes like an overhaul of the curriculum department, the installation of a new accountability system, or a revamp of the teacher evaluation process. In coaching leaders, I recommend a well-thought-out Theory of Action in these situations because leaders struggle with providing context around complex decisions, especially when those decisions are scaffolded around culture change and large-scale systems change. It is useful for any leader, be it a teacher, team leader, curriculum leader, or superintendent, who wants to enact major change that will require major action and yield (hopefully) major results.

> **Gray Matter**
>
> *Rev. Dr. Martin Luther King, Jr. said, "If you want to move people, it has to be toward a vision that's positive for them, that taps important values, that gets them something they desire, and it has to be presented in a compelling way so they feel inspired to follow."*

My Journey to a Theory of Action

As a new district superintendent, I wanted to shape a vision and plan for what I saw was needed in the district. I set out to design a framework for school improvement. I knew that I needed to take time to connect with and learn about those I led and served. I began asking questions of teachers, principals, and community members to learn their thoughts and feelings about the district. I convened groups, popped in on meetings, and even visited homeowner association gatherings. In each setting, I asked three simple questions: What are we doing that we should stop? What aren't we doing that we should begin? What are we doing that really works for you?

After several months of informal surveying, I synthesized the information I'd gathered, thus creating a Framework for School Improvement that delineated responsibility at every level from school board member to teacher.

I began to explain the framework to school staff and community members, sharing my plans and wishes for our schools. I spoke to various groups of teachers, leaders, parents and caregivers, board members, and community homeowners. I was clear and concise with my vision, even inspiring others with messages of hope and achievement. I answered questions and listened to their thoughts and ideas. At the conclusion of each event, I'd shake the hands of our new supporters and be whisked off to the next occasion.

By the fourth or fifth event, I was mentally exhausted and unable to clearly recall some of the great feedback given throughout the day. Becoming increasingly frustrated at my lack of ability to communicate the vision consistently, I knew that I needed help. I contacted a colleague of mine, Dr. James Pughsley, a former superintendent and seasoned mentor. I have often discussed the challenges of leadership with him, and he was eager to lend his support again. From his own experience, he knew well what it was like to be a new superintendent.

Upon hearing my story, he responded, "You need a Theory of Action for Change!" Then he walked me through the process of developing such a document. I focused on the need for the change and the vision of what could be different after the change (the why), the kind of leadership and process that could bring about the change (the how), and what the new procedures, components, and actions would look like (the what).

After hours of conversation, we emerged with a three-page document that I later trimmed to a one-pager with bulleted highlights for ease of speaking. Crafted with a community audience in mind, I included vision and mission statements, the process by which I would learn more about the district and community, the kinds of approaches I'd employ, and benchmark activities with a timeline for their completion. Although I had to go through several iterations before arriving at the final product, I felt myself growing at leading from my head. I had contained my message to a manageable form. I had balanced the content with understanding of the school culture. I stopped feeling so scattered.

This Theory of Action solved a huge communication problem for me as I began my second year as superintendent. It enabled me to better focus and explain the vision in a compelling, understandable way. It became the North Star for our district to follow.

> **Gray Matter**
>
> *There is nothing like getting assistance from a person who has been where you want to go and is willing to hold your hand until you get there!*

Here is a brief outline of what a Theory of Action could include. The work could be about an overview of your leadership or a plan for envisioning and instituting a particular program or change.

A Theory of Action incudes:

1. **Why?**

    Ask and answer: *Why am I here? Why do I lead in this situation? (Or for a particular plan: Why is this initiative or change needed?)* Identify the beliefs, values, and ideals connected to the purpose: *Why does this matter? What difference does it make or will it make? What has motivated me to this purpose?* This is your vision—your values plus your hopes for what can be in place of or in addition to what is now. **It sets your direction as a school leader.**

2. **How?**

    Ask and answer: *How will I do this?* Identify the organization, systems, and processes by which you will learn about the issue, the history, the school or district, and the community. Outline how you will proceed toward your purpose; identify how others will be involved.

3. **What?**

    Ask and answer: *What steps need to be taken?* Identify specific benchmark activities, practices for making the change, and a timeline for their completion.

Keep the document direct, concise, and compelling. You want it to be something with which the entire school community can connect! Vision for a school or district may come from you but it is not just about you.

In Chapter 6, see **Head Leadership Strategy 2: Creating a Theory of Action for Change** on page 155 for more details and ideas for the content of your Theory of Action.

HEAD LEADERSHIP TRAIT 7: THE HEAD-CENTERED LEADER EFFECTIVELY COMMUNICATES THEIR THEORY OF ACTION.

The head-centered leader does not expect others to follow their vision and plans blindly. They respect the fact that they work with professionals who come with their own view of the way schools should be led. The leader clearly paints the picture for others to see the vision and how they (other professionals) play a part in it.

A leader's Theory of Action is of little use until it is shared. Yes, the leader gains direction and clarity in the process of thinking about and creating the document. And the leader has an amazing blueprint for moving forward on an initiative. But others only know why or what to follow and support when the leader explains it.

Vision is direction for the school leader. Communicating it is like inputting coordinates into the GPS. Once the driver puts in the coordinates, everyone on board, including the passengers, knows the route and destination. Take the time to put your thoughts and plans into a succinct, compelling presentation. Begin with a convincing delivery of the **reasons** for your leadership in general or for the specific change you propose.

- You'll likely be sharing this through speaking. But also share it visually and in a hands-on, printed, projectable, digitally transferrable version.
- Put it on the school, district, team, or classroom webpage and social media platforms.
- Present it in a video that can be attached to any of the above formats.
- Invite feedback. Arrange a way for students, families, staff, and community members to ask questions, comment, and offer ideas about how they can support the cause.

The purpose and plans will flounder if your Theory of Action is not communicated **through behavior as well as words**. All members of the school community need to witness the promised actions taking place and see that the actions are true to the purpose (the why)—as it was explained. It is in communicating and demonstrating the Theory of Action that people understand what the leader does and why. Sharing clearly provides transparency, holds the leader responsible, and motivates the readers (and listeners) to join in on the cause.

In Chapter 6, see **Leadership Strategy 4: Beyond the Vision** on page 164 for more ideas about what to do with a vision once it's created.

HEAD LEADERSHIP TRAIT 8: THE HEAD-CENTERED LEADER GUIDES THE DEVELOPMENT OF AN ALL-SCHOOL SHARED VISION.

The visionary leader is clear in their own mind and clear to everyone else about what they believe for the education of students and about their own sense of moral purpose for their leadership. With that foundation, the effective head-centered middle school leader oversees an inclusive, collaborative process to develop an all-school vision for every school. This is separate from the leader's vision, but the two documents work hand in hand with one another.

What?

A school vision is a concise statement of what a school community believes and wants the school to become. It looks ahead, including hopes and intentions for the future. Its focus is always on experiences of students and objectives for students. Your school vision stands as a constant reminder of what's important. All sectors contribute to its formation, so it is a **collective** expression of aspirations. Its content comes from answering such questions as these:

What is really important at this school?
What does our school stand for?
Why do we exist?
What is our ultimate purpose for our students?
What really matters—and why?
What are we striving to create here?
What are the values behind what we do and how we do it?
What do we want our students to believe about themselves?
What is our deepest belief about what makes a difference for students?
What values should we all model?
What is our dream for this school?
What is it that all our young adolescent students should have?
What will things look like when we reach this vision?

The all-school vision statement is intended to be publicized to all stakeholders. It is clear and specific enough to truly show the school's purpose and guide the school's direction. The majority of school vision statements focus heavily on academic themes, but many of the dreams are broader, including social and mental health themes. Sometimes a vision is set for a particular length of time; when the vision is fulfilled, a new one is created. Sometimes the statement is a shared vision for a particular program. Whatever the vision's focus and for whatever time period, the leader makes sure it is revisited and revised (or replaced) regularly.

> **Gray Matter**
>
> *Our values + our hopes for the future = Our school vision*

Why?

In a successful middle school, "a shared vision developed by all stakeholders guides every decision."[23] There are many positive outcomes and uses for having a shared school vision, collectively prepared and agreed upon. The completed public statement:

- Articulates and advertises the purpose of your school and all its programs.
- Reflects the collective core educational values.
- Motivates with a strong reason for what everyone is doing.
- Sets a tone for everyone in the school community.
- Unifies all stakeholders around a cause; welcomes input from all.
- Serves as a guiding light, giving everyone focus on what really matters.

- Spreads inspiration—giving energy and meaning to everyone's work and learning.
- Feeds a spirit of togetherness.
- Provides a base for accountability.
- Guides all kinds of decisions, policies, procedures, priorities, and resource allocations.
- Gives all stakeholders a security in knowing where they are going.
- Sparks celebration when people see movement toward fulfilling the dream.
- Engenders greater participation, ownership, innovation, energy, trust, collaboration, and school connectedness.

And also, importantly—the school's shared vision is the foundation for the school's shared mission. The vision is what you want to become and why. The mission is what you will do to get there and how. Many schools create both a vision and a mission. The vision must come first.

Who?

By its very name and nature, a shared vision includes all those who are connected to the school. It's unlikely that everyone can take part in drafting the statement. But the thoughtful leader ensures that all groups and roles are represented. Gather input from a diverse group—students, teachers, support staff, coaches, parents and caregivers, leaders, administrators, and community members—for as wide a perspective as possible to make the document a truly collective endeavor.

How?

There are many ways to gather ideas and beliefs from the school community. The "design group" may be formed by representatives from various groups (mentioned above). In general, most processes begin with an invitation to identify the school's purpose or a series of questions to start the thinking. This is followed by individual or small-group brainstorming, after which folks bring their impressions to a larger group. Eventually, a specified "drafting group" of reasonable size works to collate and synthesize key beliefs, hopes, and ideas into a draft of a few sentences (some vision statements are just one sentence). At some point in the process, all stakeholders could be invited to a forum or given some kind of opportunity to hear or read a draft and give input. The "drafting group" then revises this to a final statement.

The thoughtful leader will find a process that works for their school, or delegate others to set up a process. The process of working together on a vision statement is invigorating and inspiring. But getting to a finished product is just the beginning. Next, the statement is published and put to use! Hopefully!

I say "hopefully" because, sadly, many schools create vision statements, then disregard them. Too often, most members of a school's staff—even administrators—don't know what's in the school vision. Even fewer parents or caregivers, students, and community members know. So many vision statements lie dormant (out of anyone's line of vision!) in a notebook, on a shelf, or on a few hard drives. Oh, the missed opportunities—because a superbly shared vision is a powerful center for the school! (Just out of curiosity, you might do a quick survey to find out how many people in your school community can repeat or summarize the school vision.)

In a school guided by someone leading from the head, this won't happen. Instead:

- First, the vision statement itself will be so clear, compelling, and inspirational that it will be easily remembered.
- Second, the vision will be well-marketed and widely championed.
- Third, the school leader will be a living model and chief promoter of the vision, connecting actions and decisions to it.
- Fourth, the vision will set the tone for the school culture. Anyone who walks into the school will know it's there and will feel its power.
- Last, the vision will be repeated and used again and again. It will be the guiding light it was intended to be. People will know it by heart.

In Chapter 6, see **Head Leadership Strategy 3: We Are Family (Building a Shared Vision)** on page 160 for more suggestions and details about creating an all-school vision. Also see **Head Leadership Strategy 4: Beyond the Vision** on page 164 for ideas about what to do with the vision once it's created.

HEAD LEADERSHIP TRAIT 9: THE HEAD-CENTERED LEADER HOLDS TO THE VISION.

Taking the Vision Seriously

I am rarely frustrated, but on this occasion, to say I was frustrated was a grand understatement.

"He said you just don't get it." One of our schoolboard members was always concise in her judgment and criticism. And direct. She never held back, and this time was no exception. My heart sank as the words reverberated through the air: ". . . you just don't get it." She was sharing the conclusion of her conversation with the president of the organization that had recently offered a chance to host a popular summer math camp in one of our schools.

I recalled the conversation with the organization's representatives. It seemed like a good program, but it didn't match our vision for academic growth in student performance at that time, so I declined the offer. The board had been in support of the vision. We had already allocated resources to chosen endeavors. This was all part of working together (the board and I) to establish priorities for the district—focusing clearly on what was most needed.

But those priorities didn't seem to resonate with the school board member in that moment. So it wasn't surprising that she was more worried about denying a potential partner than holding to the vision. Many in the district were eager for support and partnerships that appealed to our families in a more relatable way than a vision for instruction. I knew that this math camp was more instantly appealing.

My focus, however, was on long-term, sustainable change that we had agreed on, and not necessarily on one initiative or program that would engage our scholars during the summer. We did conduct the math camp at one of our middle schools the following summer. But we only held this after we determined that the program connected with our solid instructional vision and goals of the district. The board member was initially disappointed in my decision to pass on the camp the first *year. However, later she recognized the need for alignment to our wider program. The camp was more effective for our students in the context and coherence of their other math instruction.*

The "You just don't get it!" encounter did propel me to reflect and ponder: How could we prioritize our instructional vision? What guidelines do we need to decide what program or initiative will work for our school? How can our vision be our buffer between a "no" and a "yes" to a decision proposed by a superior or even by students and teachers? How can we say "no" to things that don't line up with our set priorities without alienating well-meaning partners? All these are considerations when we are serious about adhering to the vision.

Once a vision has been set and embraced—whether it be the all-school shared vision or a leader's vision for leadership in general or for a specific program—it needs to be honored. The vision is what it became for good reasons. It is based on your joint examination of values and hopes, and your knowledge of the needs of your students. The tasks you do and programs you implement are clear and have meaning because they flow from the agreed-upon vision.

The thoughtful leader reminds stakeholders of that often and uses the vision as the foundation it was intended to be. This means making hard choices (although they are less hard **because** the vision has been created). So while saying "no" to something is uncomfortable, the decision can be clear. Everyone already knows the priorities. The more you champion, publicize, use, and fulfill the vision—the more likely it will be for others to see what fits and what doesn't.

HEAD LEADERSHIP TRAIT 10: THE HEAD-CENTERED LEADER PLANS AHEAD FOR NEW AND RECURRING PROCESSES.

Are We There Yet?

A family packed up for a trip. "Where are we going?" the kids asked.

"Somewhere," replied the parents. "We're just not sure where."

The family took the dog to the neighbor's house. "So why is it that we are going somewhere?" asked the daughter, Sophia.

"We didn't think about that yet," Dad responded.

The kids looked around, but saw no vehicle. "How are we going to get there?" asked Kevin, the son.

"Hmmm," said Grandpa, "now there's something to consider."

The parents carried the suitcases out onto the porch. "Well, how will we know when we get there?" the kids asked.

"Maybe there will be some signs that tell us where we are," said Mom. She locked the house door as the family gathered on the porch.

"Are we there yet?" the kids asked in unison.

Sounds ludicrous (and unlikely), right? Yet it's surprising how often leaders or organizations embark on programs or ventures without clear answers to all those questions. Head-centered leaders oversee thoughtful planning for any new or revised procedures, initiatives, or programs. They know where they're headed, why and how this will happen, and how to tell when they've arrived. The close consideration ahead of time assures that important steps and common components won't be forgotten.

The leader assures that up-front thinking has chosen ways to be ready. They have overseen development of rubrics, steps, checklists, templates, protocols, or other tools that teach and guide everyone in the process. This includes pre-planning ways to:

- Specifically define the end objective or destination.
- Understand and articulate the purpose for the venture.
- Break large tasks into steps, setting benchmark activities.
- Set timelines for tasks and sub-tasks.
- Identify and gather resources—people, places, and materials.
- Create a system for monitoring each step of the process.

- Identify who is responsible for tasks—that is: Who plans? Who implements? For each step or task, who will see that it gets done? Who monitors? Who evaluates?
- Set a schedule for the process, including timelines for individual components.
- Define roles for teachers, other staff, leaders, students, and parents or caregivers.
- Keep records.
- Communicate progress.
- Make needed adjustments mid-course.
- Anticipate possible obstacles and ways to handle them.
- Solicit and use feedback.
- Evaluate the process and the outcomes.
- Look ahead to next steps.

Planning ahead on such components for new journeys saves a great deal of time. It avoids confusion, inconsistencies, and disorganization. It's good head leadership! It lends assurance and security to the people involved.

Thoughtful leaders also work with others to plan for recurring processes and actions—things they know will come up again and again—whether as part of creating a new initiative or just in everyday life of school leaders. They develop advance foundational strategies for how these matters will be approached and managed. Once designed, the strategies can be taught to and used by all members of the staff. They can be taught to students too.

> **Gray Matter**
>
> *If you don't have a plan, you'll operate by someone else's plan or worse, you'll operate in the chaos of a dozen plans or no direction at all.*

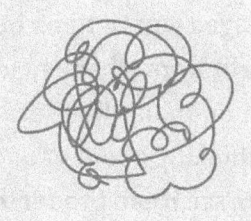

For sample guides or plans for these recurring processes—goal setting, decision making, and problem solving—see strategies in Chapter 6:

Head Leadership Strategy 5: A Goal-Setting Plan (page 166)
Head Leadership Strategy 6: A Decision-Making Plan (page 169)
Head Leadership Strategy 7: A Problem-Solving Plan (page 172)

HEAD LEADERSHIP TRAIT 11: THE HEAD-CENTERED LEADER DESIGNS A PROCESS FOR REFLECTION ON EVENTS AND SITUATIONS.

Reflection is a necessity for all aspects of leadership—when one is leading from the heart, head, or hand. This trait is about the leader's thinking to prepare for reflection. The head-centered leader designs a specific process for shining a light back on a situation and thinking about how it informs future behavior. They create this tool to provide a consistent approach to rethinking. With a regular pattern in place, the leader can coach others in the wisdom and art of reflecting upon a particular event or situation. Once others learn and practice a reflection protocol, they can use this tool on their own.

Reflection can be defined as serious thought or consideration of something in the past to inform you for future actions. Or, as my grandmother would often say, "Use your head now so that you don't lose it later." The mindful leader embraces those quiet post-action moments to pause and look back at what happened, learning from it before pushing forward. You benefit even if you reflect on something as brief as a confusing, difficult, friendly, or extraordinarily enlightening conversation!

I've encouraged you to think **before** you act. And when you do that, you'll automatically benefit from what you learned from past actions—that is, **if** you took the time to reflect on them. This sets up a cycle of thinking, acting, and reflecting. It's a lot of good thinking about your thinking.

In Chapter 6, see **Head Leadership Strategy 8: A Reflection Protocol** on page 176 for a simple guide that I use and teach for this process. Offer this to those you lead. Or use it to inspire you and others to develop something that serves the same purpose. Note: Actually, it is a great tool for life in general—in and out of school! Also in Chapter 6, see **Head Leadership Strategy 12: Journaling: Leading from the Head** on page 187 for a guide to journaling your personal reflections on your head leadership.

The Reflection Protocol in Action

A superintendent colleague of mine found himself in a crisis when local media carried a story on the ability of strangers to access school grounds and buildings without being questioned. The reporter said that they were able to enter a school from the front door and exit out the back door without being approached by an adult. My colleague was shocked and discouraged about the gaps in following well-planned protocols and angry that the media had conducted a "sneak attack" by airing the story without balancing it with some statement from the district. He was also anxious about the likely community reaction to the lapse in safety protocols. In his compounded frustration, he took to the media to vent. It was not the best approach, and he suffered ridicule for his inability to effectively communicate during a crisis.

He contacted me for coaching support. I walked him through the Reflection Protocol to help him identify what had happened so that he would not make the same mistakes again. This also enabled him to envision how to rebound from the mistake. In reflecting, he identified several actions that would improve the safety of his schools, and at the same time, would work to restore his reputation as an effective communicator. He noted to me, "If I had done this thinking before I reacted, we would have had a more successful outcome. And perhaps we would not have had any security issues in the first place."

This experience did result in improved processes. But the immediate impact for him was growth in his thought process and improvement in communication among the principals, media, and community.

As it turns out, my grandmother's advice still rings true: "Use your head now so that you don't lose it later!"

HEAD LEADERSHIP TRAIT 12: THE HEAD-CENTERED LEADER REGULARLY GIVES AFFIRMATIVE, CONSTRUCTIVE FEEDBACK.

The thoughtful leader continuously learns and practices the art of giving feedback. Now, lots of folks find this to be a difficult thing to do. Some avoid it altogether because it can be uncomfortable or they are not sure how to do it. Many staff members or students (leaders, too!) quake at the thought of receiving feedback—which makes it harder to know how to give it. Most of us humans have likely had unpleasant experiences with feedback.

It is truly a gift to give feedback that is kind and caring yet direct and growth-enhancing. Thankfully, it is a gift that can be developed. The head-centered leader does not shy away from giving feedback to fellow leaders, administrators, teachers, support staff members, students, parents and caregivers, board members, and community members.

People need feedback from each other, their leaders included. Why? They need responses to their work, actions, or attitudes to:

- Encourage them to reflect on their own work or their actions.
- Help them identify (and be proud of) what they have done well—and why and how that has worked.
- Practice thinking critically about how they can improve.
- Receive suggestions for improvement.
- Deepen trust and collaboration with their co-workers or partners in education.

But it isn't just any kind of feedback that people need. They need feedback that is:

Thoughtful—with forethought about what you will say, ask, and suggest.

Positive and well-intentioned—not harshly critical.

Specific—not trite or vague, but a response that points out explicit details and examples.

Honest—not just what you think someone wants to hear.

Timely—not days or weeks later.

Instructive—always containing suggestions for what they might try that is different.

Conversational—given in a situation where you dialogue with the other person.

Careful—given after considering who the person is, what they need, and how they might respond.

Private—in most cases, offered just to the person or group affected.

Inspiring—words that boost confidence and inspire them to do more and do better.

In Chapter 6, see **Head Leadership Strategy 9: Feedback FROM the Leader** on page 179 for a guide that can serve as a reference for thinking about and giving feedback.

HEAD LEADERSHIP TRAIT 13: THE HEAD-CENTERED LEADER INVITES AND USES INSIGHTS FROM OTHERS ABOUT THEIR LEADERSHIP.

The thoughtful superintendent, principal, teacher, support staff member, coach, or any other leader knows the value of receiving feedback on their leadership. They truly want the benefits of what can be learned from many other brains and perspectives.

The leader sets up structures for feedback—**asking** colleagues, students, and others to give them feedback **about them:** about their (the leader's) ideas, actions, performance, and behavior. There are a variety of ways to solicit such feedback. It can be through online surveys, digital communications, group get-togethers, notes under your door, single-question texts or emails, or individual conversations.

The most important part of the leader's example is using, not ignoring, the feedback—and following up to find out how others view the leader's responses. The leader's relationship with feedback is critical for modeling to the rest of the school community, as well as for the leader's own development.

The leader is eager to hear and incorporate the thinking from all stakeholders:

- Viewpoints, opinions, advice, interpretations, insights, discoveries, and unique ideas
- How they respond to the leader's words and actions
- How they view any event, program, policy, or procedure at the school
- How they believe they are welcomed or viewed by the leader
- How they believe they are listened to and valued by the leader
- How they view the leader's job effectiveness
- What they agree or disagree with
- What they question or don't understand
- What they'd like to see done differently or not at all
- What they'd like the leader to know

Definitions of *feedback* include the idea of *evaluative reactions* **along with** the idea of *using those reactions as a basis for improvement.* So using feedback to improve is intrinsic to the process. The leader who pays serious attention to it and puts it to use:

- Honors the diversity of their school community and the value of every person in it.
- Promotes transparency and honesty in school and leader actions.
- Strengthens relationships and trust with members of the school community.
- Strengthens the feeling of "us" and the view of the leader as "one of us."
- Keeps themselves on their toes.
- Expands their own self-awareness, self-examination, and reflection.
- Takes insights from the feedback to spark innovation and creative thinking.
- Finds more meaning in all their actions.
- Shows willingness to risk hearing what may be uncomfortable.
- Learns and grows as a leader.

An open-door policy, as well as an attitude of fearlessness and humility in embracing feedback, sets the tone for everyone. "Open door" means frequent presence in places where people can converse with you, ask questions, and give comments. It also means setting aside regular times in your schedule when students, staff, and family members can visit with you and tell you how you're doing.

How the leader reacts to harsh or negative feedback is a highly visible indicator of their ability to receive all feedback gladly. As tough as it may be, some of the best lessons come from your antagonists. This is where you learn and practice humility, grace, and patience. This is where you practice what you preach about welcoming all perspectives—about keeping an open mind. If you put up walls when you sense opposition or hostility, you miss precious opportunities to stretch yourself to innovative solutions. You miss wonderful chances to repair relationships.

Traits of Head-Centered Leadership

The Superintendent's Dilemma, Redux

You may remember the story in Chapter 2 about my meeting (as a superintendent) with a large group of bus drivers who were angry at hearing they would not get a deserved raise in wages. I prepared for an onslaught of complaints. Although most of the drivers wanted information and some resolutions, there definitely were antagonists in the huge crowd. During the conversation, someone commented that I was never seen in the district. I did not feel that this was true. But someone perceived it to be true, and therefore it was feedback to welcome. It prompted me to take immediate steps to communicate more often with the drivers and to show up regularly at the bus depot to check in with drivers and supervisors. I began to ride bus routes periodically to show my support. This was a major area for personal development, and I grew as a leader because of it.

Human inclination is to run away from perceived enemies, yet I encourage you to use their negative energy to sharpen your focus. Embrace what they say but not how they say it. From many accusations and criticisms, there's opportunity to glean information that improves your outcome and teaches you useful lessons in communication and head-leadership.

In Chapter 6, see **Head Leadership Strategy 10: Feedback FOR the Leader** on page 182 for a plan a leader can use to gather and use feedback on their leadership.

> **Gray Matter**
>
> *Friends keep you in the seat (of leadership), but enemies keep you on your toes. Welcome feedback from those who may seem like adversaries.*

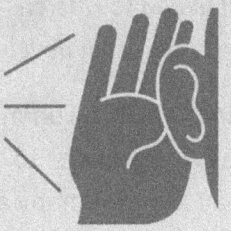

HEAD LEADERSHIP TRAIT 14: THE HEAD-CENTERED LEADER DELEGATES TO SHARE RESPONSIBILITY.

A Story from the Ages for the Ages

A story from the book of Exodus in The Bible[24] serves as possibly the first documented evidence of strategic delegation of leadership. Moses, the Hebrew prophet who led the people out of slavery from Egypt, is visited by his father-in-law, Jethro. From morning until evening, Jethro watches Moses answer questions from the crowd ("judging," as the text describes). Telling Moses that keeping up this pace "wilt surely wear [him] away," Jethro recommends delegating the work among other leaders—suggesting that only the most difficult cases should be brought to Moses.[25] Good advice from thousands of years ago. Some truths just stand the test of time, don't they!

I have always been a do-it-yourselfer. This comes from my mom who is famous for saying (over and over), "If you want something done right, do it yourself." So, from small projects around the house to preparing speeches for crowds of thousands, I have always done it myself. Well, not always—not anymore. I've learned that doing everything myself is not a thoughtful, effective, or healthy way to operate as a leader or family member. I am aware that in any school or district, even a small one, no leader can shoulder all the responsibilities. This is true for all kinds and levels of leadership.

What?

Delegation is assignment of responsibility. It is a foundational component of head-centered leadership. That's because delegation begins as a thinking skill. It is about contemplating the most efficient way to accomplish the vision and goals of the school. It is spreading the work among many shoulders. It is the leader understanding that there are others who have skills to do jobs well, even better than the leader. It's about considering priorities for the leader's time and energy, acknowledging their own capabilities and limitations, and thinking about the best use of the human resources in the school.

Why?

Some leaders fear that delegation makes them look weak or ineffective—unwilling or unable to their job well. The head-centered leader thinks differently. They see that delegation is not abdicating authority; it is authorizing creativity. They understand that when leaders delegate, they do not give away their powers; they empower others, helping others become better leaders. Head-centered leaders welcome gifts and energy of others to share leadership tasks, so that they can dedicate their time to doing fewer tasks well instead of many tasks less well.

The thoughtful leader knows that when leadership is shared, we see such benefits as these:

- More good thinking, energy, and abilities pooled to accomplish missions
- Increased chances for the best outcomes in reaching school vision and goals
- A rise in the leader's focus, productivity, and efficiency
- Leaders who can lead with a clear head

- Better use of the leader's time and energy for thinking and planning
- Leaders getting a chance to learn from others
- Expansion of others' leadership skills and confidence
- More innovation and creativity from all who have leadership roles
- Many people feeling a role in making the school a success
- Leaders able to take on some tasks they might not have been able to include before
- More people inspired and motivated about the school's purposes
- More people who understand the processes and challenges of leading the school
- Greater connection and investment for those who play a part in the management
- Strengthened relationships when people are trusted with responsibilities
- More balanced workload for leaders
- Less isolation, exhaustion, and burnout for leaders
- An electric spirit of everyone working meaningfully for the same goals

Gray Matter

You are on the right track; slow the train long enough for others to board it with you.

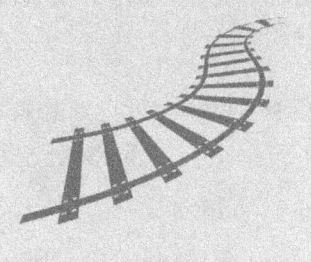

Who?

Leaders at various levels can delegate to others on their leadership team, principal supervisors*, teachers, other staff members, team leaders or department heads, whole teams or departments. Within a school structure, there are also tasks that can be delegated to students, students' parents and caregivers, or volunteers. Make use of opportunities to use the leadership capabilities of these folks.

*Principal supervisors take on significant delegated roles and tasks as leaders who lead other leaders. Someone in this role supervises one or more school principals and provides oversight for each school. Standard 1 of the Model Principal Supervisor Standards states that "Principal Supervisors dedicate their time to helping principals grow as instructional leaders."[26]

They assume many duties of school management so that principals are able to focus on instructional excellence. This position has become an important part of district management structures, particularly in larger districts.

How?

Thoughtful delegation is not about making a list of leadership tasks and doling them out. The delegation must be meaningful. This means not giving out tasks that are easy to do and require little thinking or true leadership. The tasks must be important undertakings that have purpose—tasks that flow from and further the school's vision and priorities. Given chances to share leadership, your people will soar. But they need real responsibilities to do so.

When leading from the head, the leader does not just delegate tasks, but **delegates authority** to make decisions and take other actions necessary to accomplish the task. I keep in mind this quote from experienced leadership coach Craig Groeschel: "When you delegate tasks, you create followers. When you delegate authority, you create leaders."[27]

And that's not all: The leader explains the task, the goals, and most importantly, the reasons for the task. The leader sets up a protocol for delegation so everyone knows and follows a process for understanding the tasks, moving forward, keeping records, reporting, and evaluating. And though the leader trusts the person to accomplish the task and puts the authority to do so in their hands, the leader does not just walk away. The leader coaches the "designated" leader—not hovering or overprotecting, but teaching what is needed for doing the task and then being available for support. This coaching is a way of gradually building even more leadership skills in others.

See **Head Leadership Strategy 11: Planning to Delegate** on page 184 for a model of a delegation process.

> **Gray Matter**
>
> *At some point, you must know when you're in above your head and need to call in reinforcements. Be wise enough to know when you need help and sensible enough to accept it.*

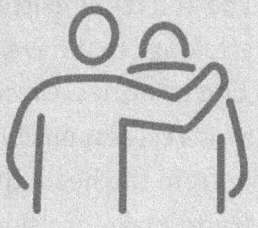

HEAD LEADERSHIP TRAIT 15: THE HEAD-CENTERED LEADER DESIGNS HEAD-CENTERED LEADERSHIP DEVELOPMENT AS A TEAM.

The leader in any school, team or other PLC, or department oversees plans for professional growth. They see that for the best and most lasting effects, professional

Traits of Head-Centered Leadership

development on any topic is relevant, long term, and job embedded. The head-centered leader clearly identifies what is meant by *leading from the head* and collaborates with others to find ways to learn more and practice it. The group intentionally includes some PD activities for learning about leading from a deep foundation of thoughtfulness—thinking about purposes and reasons before, during, and after action.

They examine the concepts or current status of head-centered leadership at their school, then search for and practice activities to develop or strengthen such areas and skills as these:

- Experiences of thinking before acting
- Practice asking "Why?"—thinking from the inside out (see Chapter 4)
- Writing visions with teams or classrooms
- Thinking about what it means to be student-centered in strategic planning
- How to gain others' perspectives (perspective-taking practices)
- Planning for how to plan
- Problem-solving skills and practice
- Decision-making skills and practice
- Goal-setting skills and practice
- The "yes" brain and the "no" brain[28]
- Growth mindsets and fixed mindsets
- Giving, inviting, receiving, and using feedback
- How each personally handles receiving feedback
- Kinds of feedback we need and how to get it
- Debriefing and other reflective thinking practices
- Expanding and using curiosity and creative thinking skills
- Expanding and using critical thinking skills
- Asking strategic questions
- Thinking about failure and setbacks

They consider and discuss how to apply head-centered leadership to:
- Planning policies and procedures
- Planning instruction
- Data and resource management
- Assessment and grading processes

Challenge your colleagues to find and share ways to apply head-centered leadership to their particular work situations, content areas, and types of interactions with students and with each other. Be sure to include support staff in the development of thoughtful leadership. Help them learn how to apply it to their jobs and responsibilities. You can teach the principles to parents and caregivers as well. Definitely teach the ideas to student leaders too and expose all middle school students (whether or not they are officially in leadership classes or positions) to the concepts of leading from the head. Developmentally, your young adolescent students are ideally situated to think about and develop their own leadership capacity. All in all, everyone can learn and grow together. That way, the effects of good leadership from the head spread widely.

Head Leadership Trait 16: The Head-Centered Leader Takes Responsibility for Mistakes.

A Mistake to Remember

As superintendent, I was faced with a decision to support the high school principal's selection of the school valedictorian or override that selection based on information presented to me. The parents of a student dropped by my office to complain that their high school daughter, who was expected to be selected as valedictorian, was recently told by the principal that another student was chosen over her. They presented a very compelling case, showing past report cards and even a recommendation from a former teacher. Needless to say, I was very surprised about the decision of the principal, noting that the parents' information and documents seemed to prove the case quite well. I assured them that I would personally see to it that their daughter be named valedictorian. They left my office very satisfied.

After they left, I called the principal and asked him to come by my office. I prepared him for the discussion; I let him know that I had made a decision but wanted to be sure he understood my reasons. He agreed to come by. But he informed me that he felt I had made a grave mistake and that he would show me proof of this when he arrived. I hung up and immediately had a bad feeling in my stomach. Had I jumped the gun and made a decision without having all the facts? I grabbed my keys and headed to the high school. This meeting could not wait until after school. If I got this one wrong, I needed to rectify it as soon as possible. Although I had asked him to come to my office, I decided to visit him at his.

When I arrived at the principal's office, he was visibly upset. "Doc." He affectionately referred to me that way. "I'm sorry sir, but that parent had no right to come to you about this. I met with her and their family attorney yesterday. She left my office satisfied with my research about the matter and agreed with the decision I had to make."

He continued, my stomach now boiling. "The parent was correct in that her daughter has the highest GPA for her senior year. What we discovered, however, was that, as a freshman, the daughter took Algebra while her nearest competitor, the actual valedictorian, took Honors Algebra. Honors Algebra was scored on a 5-point scale as opposed to the 4-point scale for Algebra. The true valedictorian has a 0.5 higher grade point average than her daughter."

My jaw hit the floor and my stomach hit the ceiling. I realized that I had failed to investigate thoroughly before acting; I acted too quickly. I reflected on my conversation with the parent and my commitment to her daughter. I would need to make this right, and it would not be easy. There was only one week before graduation, so there was no time to wait. I called the student's home and left a message for her mother to contact me as soon as possible. It was school board meeting night, so I had to prepare for the meeting. I decided that I would contact the mother again after the board meeting and clear the air. Several hours later, however, I discovered I would not have to wait.

The ringing in my ears matched the ringing of the microphone feedback as the parent approached the podium for public comments. The parent decided not to call me back to talk, but to instead share her dissatisfaction with my decision to the entire listening community. Her comments seemed to take an eternity. As she concluded, our board chair gave me a look of surprise and bewilderment. I nodded at him as I mouthed a request to respond.

As I choked the words from my throat, I was tempted to verbally dance around the matter or even blame the principal. Instead, I heard the words of my grandmother in my ear, "If you make it wrong, make it right." I proceeded to tell the whole world my error. I acted without having all the information and jeopardized the integrity of the school board policy for valedictorian selection. I caused pain for two students and their families.

Sweat dripped down my back as I admitted my mistake, apologized to the offended family and to the principal, and promised to put a system in place that validates the selection of the valedictorian without the involvement of the superintendent. As painful as it was, I took responsibility for my actions, regardless of the consequences.

You can probably imagine the humiliation I felt and the lessons I learned. There were plenty of head lessons as well as heart lessons. That's why I titled the story "A Mistake to Remember." I need never to forget the pain of that—the pain to me and to others. Many of the leadership traits I've described in this book I have learned about from difficult situations.

We must look our failings and errors straight in the eye. We must not shy away from them, put off admitting them or making things right, or pass blame on to anyone else. We take them head-on! By head-on, I mean *squarely and truthfully facing them*. But I also use this term to mean *with a thoughtful head on our shoulders*! This applies to our personal mistakes and mistakes in programs, events, and situations we have guided. Yes, others may be specifically at fault for errors or bad behavior. Those people must take responsibility for their mistakes. But head-centered leadership implores us, the leaders, to take on whatever part of the responsibility is ours.

Traits of Head-Centered Leadership

Here's one other thing: You asked for the job. Every school leader, no matter the situation, has asked to assume the role. It's a heavy mantle to carry and shouldn't be taken lightly. When it gets too heavy, and you want to drop it, remember that you chose to do it. Reflect often on this reality. Such reflection will help you recall **why** you asked for it. The **why** will help you carry on after mistakes.

> **Gray Matter**
>
> My dad told me, "It's a smart man that learns from other's mistakes but a wise man that learns from his own."

HEAD LEADERSHIP TRAIT 17: THE HEAD-CENTERED LEADER HAS COURAGE.

Courage is the "mental or moral strength to venture, persevere, and withstand danger, fear, or difficulty."[29] The thoughtful head-centered school leader acts in the face of adversity or fear—to do what they believe is right and what supports the purposes and vision of the school. Ultimately, they act to do what is best for the students, even when it is hard or scary to do so.

The strength of courage for a school leader is rooted in deep values and commitment to their purpose. It's not just being brave to look or feel brave. It's that drive to fight for what the school, the students, and everyone else in the school community need and deserve. It's the school leader fully embracing the responsibility they have for the minds and lives of students. Not only do they know with their whole being what **must** be done, they have the discipline, willpower, and faith to **do** it.

The head-centered leader knows that courageous actions are risky—and will take them to unexplored places or produce uncertain reactions. Though the results of the actions may be unpredictable at the least and outright terrifying in some cases, the leader **knows why** they take the risk. Yes, courage is usually defined by bold actions. But it is based in thinking skills—thinking about why. The thoughtful leader clearly knows why it's worth it to leap into the unknown and take the risk of a courageous stance or act.

> **Gray Matter**
>
> The good news is that when the well-pondered values and commitment are clear and strong (and deeply incorporated into the leader's soul), courage comes more easily.

And by the way, if a choice does not involve some possibility of failure, danger, discomfort, disapproval, intimidation, or hardship, courage isn't needed. Some leaders are great organizers and managers when things go smoothly, but they lack patience and fortitude in the face of adversity—even adversity as mild as disagreement or disapproval.

It takes courage to be a school leader to begin with, be it a principal or other administrator, teacher, staff member, parent or caregiver, district superintendent, or student leader. Some might say it takes an extra dose of courage or a special kind of it to lead in a middle school! For any grade-level school, there are possibilities for physical dangers and violence in and around schools—as we hear of and experience all too frequently. There are complex relationships, disagreements, rivalries, fights, harassment, unhappy parents or caregivers, disgruntled employees, city politics, strenuous state requirements, aging facilities, multiple safety concerns, community factions, nosey and non-objective news reporters—many physical, social, and psychological issues that everyone in the school community has to face. You could make your own list of matters that need courageous leadership. I'm sure it would be much longer!

In addition to the courage it takes to just **be in the role**, courage is also required to:

- Push hard and try whatever is necessary to develop each student's potential.
- Genuinely accept, care about, and advocate for every human being in the school community—even those who seem prickly, adversarial, or unlikable.
- Speak hard truths firmly.
- Stand up for others.
- Stand up for your own beliefs.
- Face and learn from failure.
- Ask for, receive, accept, and act on feedback.
- Give honest feedback.
- Be authentic and transparent.

- Articulate and act on commitment to diversity and cultural responsibleness.
- Make inclusion a priority and a reality.
- Delegate and empower others.
- Fight for policies, protocols, programs that further the school's vision.
- Challenge the status quo with new, creative, or unexpected ideas.
- Take responsibility for one's own failings, lack of knowledge, mistakes.
- Arbitrate disputes.
- Hold others accountable.
- Say "no." Or say "yes."
- Take risks.
- Step between a gun and your students and staff.

When a leader is the first to stick out their neck or take the heat, however:

- People sense stability and safety. The leader's courage inspires confidence in members of the school community that there *is* a leader who will hold to the purposes, get things done, run interference, weather storms, and solve problems.
- There is more trust in the leadership.
- People see a leader who does not give up.
- People see a leader who is **for** and **with** them, the school, the students— even if they have to take on dragons.
- Others are inspired to be brave in their work and school life.

Chapter 6

Head-Centered Leadership Strategies

Follow up your understanding of the kinds of traits that characterize those who lead from the head (Chapter 5) by putting them to work. Strategies such as those in this chapter are designed to motivate leaders and challenge them to continue growth in head-centered leadership with practical processes they can put into action right away. I'm confident these strategies will also ignite ideas that lead you and your staff to create other practical approaches to head leadership.

Overview of Head-Centered Leadership Strategies

Strategy #	Strategy	Referenced in Head Leadership Trait #
Head Strategy 1	Leader's Smart Talk	5
Head Strategy 2	Creating a Theory of Action for Change	6
Head Strategy 3	We Are Family (Building a Shared Vision)	8
Head Strategy 4	Beyond the Vision	7, 8
Head Strategy 5	A Goal-Setting Plan	10
Head Strategy 6	A Decision-Making Plan	10
Head Strategy 7	A Problem-Solving Plan	10
Head Strategy 8	A Reflection Protocol	11
Head Strategy 9	Feedback FROM the Leader	12
Head Strategy 10	Feedback FOR the Leader	13
Head Strategy 11	Planning to Delegate	14
Head Strategy 12	Journaling: Leading from the Head	11

Head Leadership Strategy 1: Leader's Smart Talk

Purpose: Leaders examine how they speak and set intentional plans for improving what they say and how, when, and where they say it.

The following **Leader's Smart-Talk Checklist** contains practices that lead to overall mindfulness and wisdom in a leader's communication. These practices can nudge you toward more appreciation of the power of language, even down to the tone of voice, manner of delivery, or a single word choice. Most apply to messages or interchanges that are either spoken or written. Here's how to use the checklist:

STEP 1	Answer each question thoughtfully with a rating on the line before the item: **1** Usually **2** Sometimes **3** Rarely For each one, think of actual situations to verify that you do this regularly.
STEP 2	Choose five of the items marked 1. Identify some ways and situations in which you do this. Then commit to continuing those smart speaking habits!
STEP 3	Choose five of the items you marked with 2 or 3. For each one, set a goal or two for specific ways to be smarter about this aspect of talking.
STEP 4	Share your outcomes and thoughts with a trusted colleague. Enlist them to notice and affirm when you show mindful speaking and to help hold you accountable where you need to rethink or do better.

Head-Centered Leadership Strategies

Leader's Smart-Talk Checklist

Use this to gauge your speaking habits and think about what you do well and where may need improvement. Answer each question, writing 1 for Usually; 2 for Sometimes; or 3 for Rarely.

Ask, "When I speak, do I..."

	Do so after thinking and planning ahead?
	Choose words cautiously with the listener or reader in mind?
	Remain conscious of my tone and body language at all times?
	Stay fully present and positive when talking?
	Discuss, converse, or present in a relaxed and agreeable manner?
	Exhibit care and compassion?
	Speak more about us than about you or them or I?
	Use language inclusively and respectfully?
	Consider ahead of time what the audience needs?
	Use timing, a tone, or word choice that is appropriate for the audience?
	Communicate messages and responses clearly and to the point?
	Position myself in a place that shows openness and connection with the listeners?
	Read my audience—carefully listen and observe as I speak?
	Pause in conversations before giving a response?
	Only hit "send" after careful rereading of digital messages?
	Reread anything I write, allowing time between readings?
	Listen as much as I speak?
	Ask questions to invite, affirm, and listen to other's opinions and perspectives?

The Successful Middle School Leader

Leader's Smart-Talk Checklist (continued)

	Invite questions and answer them honestly?
	Tell why when explaining a program, decision, policy, or idea?
	Tell how whenever I explain what will happen?
	Exercise strong self-control in personal use of social media?
	Use caution around microphones?
	Take great care about what I say in private, too?
	Frame messages in a positive light?
	Bring solutions?
	Project hope?

Ask, "Do I avoid..."

	Sounding insistent, superior, arrogant, abrasive, or annoyed?
	Using the word "but"? (Use "and" instead!)
	Speaking when someone else knows more about the topic or situation than I do?
	Overwhelming listeners with "you" messages?
	Talking too much, or using a lot of extra words or educational jargon?
	Saying or writing anything that can be offensive or demeaning?
	Talking over others?
	Blaming other people or groups?
	Assuming that everyone who shares a certain role or similar characteristics thinks, feels, or believes alike?
	Boring the listeners or readers?
	Making promises I can't keep?

Choose five of the items you marked with 2 or 3.

For each one, set a goal or two for specific ways to be smarter about this aspect of talking!

	Item	Goals
1		
2		
3		
4		
5		

HEAD LEADERSHIP STRATEGY 2: CREATING A THEORY OF ACTION FOR CHANGE

Purpose: Leaders use a guide to outline a Theory of Action for Change.

Those who lead from the head, with that spirit of perpetual thoughtfulness, are willing to change and guide change. The need for change is inevitable in schools. Things around you change—demographics, technology, educational needs. When a change of considerable magnitude is needed, it's helpful to design a leader's Theory of Action for Change for that initiative. This strategy gives instructions and a template for doing your thinking. (See the template, **Planning a Theory of Action**, found later in this strategy.) If you wish, you can adapt the elements on the template to use it for creating a Theory of Action for your leadership in general instead of making a plan for change.

The ideas you gather with this strategy will not comprise the entire finished product. However, do try to write a polished version of your opening vision statement. But for the rest (the how and what parts), you'll only outline an at-a-glance version.

PREPARATION

- Make sure you have worked at developing the attributes described in Head Leadership Traits 1, 2, 3, and 4 in Chapter 5. That work challenges you to deep thinking about yourself, your purposes and vision, your abilities—and about the others you serve. The thinking you do there sets a foundation for any Theory of Action you produce. Have those pages handy.

- Review Head Leadership Trait 6 in Chapter 5 with its background and information on Theories of Action.

- Begin the outline on the following template by giving a title or topic for the proposed change as well as the current date and the projected completion date or duration of the initiative.

- Armed with your contemplations from Head Leadership Traits 1–4, and 6 in Chapter 5, begin creating your vision (purpose).

STEP 1: THIS PART TELLS WHY

- Ask yourself such questions as these to help state your purpose. (You could also think of this as your vision or dream. I'll use these terms interchangeably).

    What's the reason or purpose behind proposing this change?
    What's happening now that begs for change? What's the need?
    What evidence shows that a change is needed?
    Why does this matter?
    What unwavering beliefs and values of mine are behind my reasons for doing this?
    How will things be different when this vision becomes real?

- Brainstorm terms or phrases that answer some of these questions. Use them to write a draft of the purpose. Remember that this is informed by your beliefs and values. Make it clear, concise, and inspiring. Some visions can be stated in one sentence. Try to stay with no more than two or three. Rework this until you feel that it is just right. Getting feedback (Step 5) will give you input that may lead to revision. Write your finished draft of the statement on the planning template.

STEP 2: THIS PART TELLS HOW

- Ask yourself:
  How will this be done?
  How will I go about this?

- How the change will take place is about the kinds of approaches, systems, relationships, resources, collaborations, delegations, organization, groupings, communication (meetings, interviews, emails, group discussions, etc.), monitoring techniques, and people that will form the process. Answering the question of how outlines your ways for getting the information and data, history, input, schedule for working, and combinations of people—things that will help set a plan for designing and carrying out the actions to take everyone to the fulfillment of the vision.

- On your planning template, note thoughts and ideas for showing **how** you'll go about guiding the process.

- Go back and cross out those you don't need, leaving the best elements.

STEP 3: THIS PART TELLS WHAT

- This is the **action** part of the plan. Ask yourself:
  What steps, practices, or activities will I undertake?
  What steps, practices, or activities will I recommend be undertaken by others?
  What all needs to be done and who will do each part and when?
  What actions will monitor, follow-up, evaluate, reflect on the process?

- On your planning template, note thoughts and ideas for showing **what** you will do.

- Choose actions (strategies) carefully. Think about the sequence and timing. For each action, be ready to explain why that was chosen and how it will further the cause.
- Go back and cross out those you don't need, leaving the best elements.

For the ones you keep:
- Identify benchmark goals or activities.
- Note a projected time for getting to each benchmark.

STEP 4: LOOK AHEAD TO THE DREAM
- Add a statement to tell how you will know when the vision is fulfilled.

STEP 5: GET FEEDBACK AND THEN POLISH
- Again, when you're instituting a plan that will affect many people and many aspects of the school, classroom, team, or district, there will be plenty of occasions for input and feedback. And there will be revisions to the plan before a working draft is in place. But your overview version will kick things off.
- Enlist some trusted others to read and respond to the overview. They can let you know if it is understandable and compelling. They may have some suggestions for additions, deletions, or other improvements.
- Prepare your final draft in an attractive manner for sharing.
- Then **do** communicate it to the rest of your stakeholders. It does little good if it is kept in your own heart, head, and computer.

See **Head Leadership Strategy 4: Beyond the Vision** in this chapter for suggestions about how to communicate and share a vision with others. Also, review Head Leadership Trait 7 (in Chapter 5) for ways thoughtful leaders communicate their personal visions.

Head-Centered Leadership Strategies

Planning a Theory of Action

Topic or Proposed Change

Why? Ideas:

Why? (Best draft of your purpose.)

How? Ideas:

What? Ideas:

Benchmarks: **Time:**

HEAD LEADERSHIP STRATEGY 3: WE ARE FAMILY (BUILDING A SHARED VISION)

Purpose: Leaders oversee a plan for the formation and use of a school-wide shared vision.

Here is one option for a process that may help you as you design your shared vision. Perhaps form a task force of diverse representation (a "design team") to conceive the best process for your school.

The core concepts for the head-centered leader to remember are:

- If it is to be truly a shared vision, all segments of the school community will be represented in its creation.
- Experiences and needs of students, and outcomes for students, must be at the center of this vision.

PREPARATION

Re-visit Head Leadership Trait 8 in Chapter 5. This defines the all-school shared vision, explains its reasons, and gives ideas for how it is formed and who is involved. Keep these pages handy as you all work together on a shared vision. Plan for a few sessions for this process—it won't happen all at once.

STEP 1

Form a group with representatives from all parts of the school community. Include students as well as staff and parents. Be sure to get a diverse group—a good cross section of the whole school community. Choose people, or let people volunteer. It's helpful to get people who are able to invest the time and energy in the process and who are interested in the topic of the change. You won't be able to open the group to everybody, but representatives can solicit ideas from others in their segment or with similar roles.

The group needs to be large enough to be representative and to gain a wide diversity of perspectives, but not so big as to be unmanageable. Some recommend 10–30 for the size. In some of the process, the group will be broken into smaller groups.

STEP 2

Begin with the whole group so they can all feel welcomed. Let them all know how important each one of them is to the process, and how important it is for them to gain contributions from others they represent. Tell them that you'll ask them to think about the purpose of the school and what their dreams are for the students and the school. Don't define vision formally yet or outline the process.

STEP 3

Many recommend that you begin by letting individuals think first because it gets at raw insights free of influences from others. Provide paper and pencils for everyone. Tell participants that you will ask (or show on a screen) a few questions. Encourage them to brainstorm words or phrases that show their personal answers to the questions or thoughts about the subject. Assure them that there are no right or wrong answers.

> Start with questions that get at core values. For example:
> *What is really important to this school?*
> *What are core purposes for the school?*
> *What does (or should) the school stand for?*
> *What are the values behind what we do and how we do it?*
> *What really matters at this school—and why?*
> *What does the school value most?*
>
> Move on to questions about visions for the future.
> *What should we strive to create here?*
> *What is your deepest belief about what makes a difference for students?*
> *What is your dream for this school?*
> *What is it that all our young adolescent students should have?*
> *What will things look like when we fulfill our dream?*

Ask or show the questions slowly, first about values, second about the future. Give time for participants to think and jot down words or phrases.

STEP 4

Split the group into pairs or groups of three. Guide the groups to share their thoughts with one another and first discuss core beliefs and purposes about school and students and education. They can share anecdotes, experiences, and observations that help identify values and purposes. They can share perspectives both of current values at the school and what they think the values should be.

Next, guide them to share and discuss their thoughts, aspirations, wishes, and hopes for the future for the students and the school.

STEP 5

Come back together as a whole group. Define what a shared vision is. You can use this definition I wrote in Chapter 5, Trait 8, or use your own.

*A school vision is a concise statement of what a school community believes and wants the school to become. It looks ahead, including hopes and intentions for the future. All sectors contribute to its formation, so it is a **collective** expression of aspirations.*

- Emphasize the collective nature of the vision.
- Explain some reasons for creating a shared vision. (See Chapter 5, Trait 8.)
- Describe the process that will be followed.

If you wish to look at vision statements from other schools, you could share some at this point. (Some leaders or vision design teams want to focus only on their own school and community and not draw attention away from it by looking at other visions.) Or you could do that at a later stage in the work of the committee.

If the school has a current vision statement, review that. Take some time for people to point out what they see in that vision—identify underlying values and the future hopes.

STEP 6

Break into slightly larger groups, about four people. Each group works to identify key ideas, terms, and phrases from the lists of the group members—common themes and ideas that they feel have the greatest importance.

STEP 7

Rejoin the whole group, where each small group shares its key ideas. A scribe records these and the whole group brainstorms to pull ideas together into sentences. Sentences might begin with such phrases as *We believe our school . . .* or *All of our students deserve . . .* or *We wish for a school that . . .*

STEP 8

Next, designate a small "drafting committee" to craft the ideas into a vision statement of one to three sentences. When the larger group reconvenes, they all read and listen to the draft and discuss until they reach consensus.

STEP 9

This can be a time where everyone in the school community is invited to respond. You might host a meeting where people can come voluntarily to give feedback and suggestions. Or choose some other way for everyone to have a chance to examine and respond.

STEP 10

The "drafting committee" makes necessary adjustments.

OTHER ADVICE

- Encourage the committee to write a vision that is inspiring, compelling, and forward thinking. It must be appealing to the whole community.
- The vision should be specific about what we believe and hope will happen or become true.
- Encourage the committee to make sure the vision statement is not vague, outdated, too complex, shallow, or unrealistic. (Make sure it doesn't promise something the school cannot deliver.)
- Consider a duration for this vision—what do you see as the time frame for fulfilling it?
- You'll know, and your readers will know, that the final product is right if you feel motivated and energized to get to work helping the dream come true!

Head Leadership Strategy 4: Beyond the Vision

Purpose: Leaders guide the creation of plans for publicizing, using, and fulfilling the shared vision.

Many people have worked hard to form a statement that represents the collective hopes and dreams—the shared purpose for the school. Now the work continues; because if the vision is ignored after its creation, it will be lost.

- Create an overall plan for spreading the good word, helping all stakeholders understand the vision and become inspired to help realize it, and for putting it to work.
- Decide how to "mobilize the troops" to carry the vision beyond the paper.
- The vision is a great unifier, and people are more likely to persevere when they have a common goal and know how they can help.

Here are some components to consider as you form your plan. Make sure this planning, too, is a collaborative venture—students included.

- **Show it off! Help others learn about and understand the plan.**
    - Communicate the plan to everyone.
    - Hold Q&A sessions to be sure everyone understands it.
    - Market it.
    - Feature it everywhere around the school community.
    - Interpret it and show it through art (students can do this).
    - Set it to music, rap, or poetry. Share it on TikTok or Instagram (students can do this).
    - Post it in classrooms, offices, hallways, cafeterias, gymnasiums.
    - Project it on the screen or read it at every meeting—board meetings, faculty meetings, assemblies, school gatherings.
    - Include it on all newsletters. Post it on the school website, class websites, team websites, and other school social media sites.

- Publish it in the town newspaper.
- Enlist students to share their understanding of it and help publicize it.
- Ask for, listen to, and incorporate feedback about it.
- Enlist everyone in quoting it and keeping it alive.

- **Get busy implementing and using it.**
  - Follow up with creating a mission that sets steps for fulfilling the purpose stated in the vision. Involve others in this process.
  - The vision is a strategic document. Consult it. Operate by it. Let it guide you to identify priorities.
  - Appy it to how you use time, resources, and energy.
  - Align decisions, plans, programs, and actions to it.
  - Remind teams, departments, and clubs to use it (and align with it) if they form their own visions.
  - Memorize it.
  - Involve students in finding ways to use it.
  - Re-check understanding of it periodically.
  - Let the school community know about ways you are fulfilling the vision. Share milestones in notes, newsletters, text or email blasts, public announcements, newspapers. Make it into a headline or logo for school, team, or class websites.
  - Ask stakeholders to notice and point out examples of the vision being reached.
  - Periodically, invite stakeholders to give reflections on how they view the progress of the vision's fulfillment.

HEAD LEADERSHIP STRATEGY 5: A GOAL-SETTING PLAN

Purpose: Leaders guide collaborative development of a consistent approach for goal setting.

Whether you are setting a goal for a short project or for a long-term or all-school venture, it's wise to have a general process and protocol already in hand. Work collaboratively to design yours, making sure it is adaptable to many uses—by students as well as adults.

This example of a process for setting and accomplishing goals uses the SMART goal concept[30]—adapted to be SMARTER goals (as many recommend). See the following two templates at the end of this strategy: The **SMARTER Goal Guide** details expectations for what a SMARTER goal looks like. The **Setting My Goal** form provides a template for setting a goal.

Setting a goal is just the beginning. Goals are meant to be achieved. Here are other expectations to consider when designing a protocol for setting and reaching goals; be sure to also think these things through ahead of time.

- Teach the process and expectations (protocol) to everyone before they use it.
- Always check to see if goals are SMARTER. Don't proceed until they are.
- Be sure that the person can articulate the reason for the goal.
- Teach others to break goals into mini-goals to make the process manageable and give places to pause and assess progress. Benchmarks must also be specific and measurable.
- Coach people through the processes of goal setting **and** achieving until they master it.
- Be sure that resources—people, materials, space—are readily available for working toward goals.
- Before goals and mini-goals are set, communicate expectations for a reasonable time frame.
- Arrange for time, personnel, and guidelines to evaluate progress along the way.

Head-Centered Leadership Strategies

- Include in your protocol a standard method of monitoring and reporting.
- Prepare for adapting or replacing a goal when necessary.
- Encourage folks to celebrate each accomplished step.
- Be sure that time is allotted for review and reflection throughout the process. Supply a few questions for focusing the reflection.

SMARTER Goal Guide

As you design goals, check them against these requirements for SMARTER goals.

Specific	The goal clearly states what I want to accomplish. It tells precisely what I want to happen, and why. Details are well-defined and can include who will be involved.
Measurable	The goal is something that can be measured. These are the exact criteria (numbers, amounts) I will use to measure progress toward the goal and accomplishment of the goal. The work will be broken into manageable mini-goals so I can track progress.
Achievable	The goal is attainable and realistic. It is limited enough to reach within the available resources and time frame. There are reasonable skills that I can use or develop to reach the goal. I have access to the space, resources, and help needed to accomplish it.
Relevant Rigorous	The goal matters to me. I can explain why and how reaching it will make a difference. I can relate it to my interests. It fits my personal purpose (or supports the school's vision) or both. The goal is something that inspires me. The goal is challenging enough to push me a bit beyond where I am now, but it is not so hard that it will be impossible for me to accomplish.
Time-Rleated	The goal can be reached in the time available. I have target dates for starting and finishing. I have a timeline that includes target dates for each benchmark. The timeline also includes time for periodic reflection and changes that may result.
Evaluated	I have questions ready for evaluating my progress throughout the process of working toward the goal. I know who will join or coach me in those evaluations.
Reviewed	I have questions or prompts for reflection on the outcomes—looking back at what I did, what changes I might make, how I overcame obstacles, and looking forward to what my next goal might be or what I might do differently next time.

Setting My Goal

Write your goal. Then plan steps to follow toward goal accomplishment.

Goal *Write your clear, specific goal. Include a statement of how you will know when you reach it.*	

	Mini-Goals (Steps to reach the goal)	Target Date
1		
2		
3		
4		
5		
6		

Resources Needed	
Help Needed *Name and what you need from each person*	
Reviewers *Name two persons to give feedback as you work and finish*	

HEAD LEADERSHIP STRATEGY 6: A DECISION-MAKING PLAN

Purpose: Leaders guide collaborative development of a consistent approach for decision making.

A *decision* is a conclusion that you reach after consideration. When you make a decision, you make a choice between ideas that might work in a situation. Investigate good decision-making models and work collaboratively with colleagues to set a process that can be used by all leaders in the school. It's a good process to teach to students too. Our young adolescent students have capabilities to participate in many decisions connected to their school life and personal learning. Here is one example of a decision-making protocol.

STEP 1: REVIEW YOUR PROCESS

- Review: *Who will be involved in gathering information? In identifying alternative choices? In making the decision? In communicating the decision? In putting it into effect? In evaluating outcomes?*
- Reconfirm how this kind of decision will be made. Ask: *Will the final decision be made by one leader? By group vote—majority rules? By consensus? By choosing the alternative with more pros than cons? With some other method?*

STEP 2: DEFINE THE SITUATION THAT NEEDS A DECISION

- Ask: *What, when, and where is the situation? Why is a decision needed? Who is involved? What outcome do you desire from the process of deciding? How will you be able to tell if the decision was a good one?*

STEP 3: BECOME INFORMED ABOUT THE SITUATION

- Think about what you need to know before deciding.
- Gather as much relevant information as possible.
- Get a variety of perspectives.
- Seek information and insight from people who are mostly likely to have

experience and knowledge about the topic.
- Focus on facts rather than opinions.
- Look for precedents of decisions on similar questions or situations.

STEP 4: IDENTIFY VIABLE OPTIONS FOR DECISION

- Find a few possible decisions that might work.
- Sometimes it may seem that there are only two choices—either this or that. Ponder to determine if there might be others.
- Don't overload on the number of options.

STEP 5: ANALYZE ALTERNATIVE CHOICES

- Weigh the alternatives. Ask what might happen with each alternative.
- Identify benefits and consequences of each.
- Pay attention to evidence as you weigh the options.
- Consider possible impacts on people, systems, budgets, programs, and time.
- Ask what message each alternative choice would send.

STEP 6: MAKE THE DECISION AND SET AN ACTION PLAN.

- Choose the best alternative. Use your pre-decided method for reaching the decision.
- Decide how to put it into effect. Make a plan that identifies who will do what, and set a timeline.
- Make the decision in a timely manner. Don't let it get separated (time-wise) too far from the situation that called for a decision.

STEP 7: COMMUNICATE THE DECISION

- Communicate decisions and reasoning behind it to the people who need to hear your conclusion.

- Be direct, honest, and kind.
- Be confident in your decision.
- Take full accountability for the choice, even if it is not popular.
- Don't procrastinate communicating.

STEP 8: ACT – IMPLEMENT THE DECISION
- Act on the decision. Follow through on your plan.
- Stick to the plan, but be flexible where needed.

STEP 9: MONITOR AND EVALUATE OUTCOMES
- Monitor the progress of putting the decision into effect.
- Ask for feedback about the decision and the resulting actions.
- Examine the impacts on people, plans, programs, resources, etc.
- Evaluate the decision by watching the outcomes.
- Ask: *Did we meet the objective? Did it work out the way we hoped? Who benefitted? Were there any negative effects? Was this the right decision?*

OTHER ADVICE:
- People may be included in discussing options even though they don't have a vote.
- Stay objective and unbiased. Pay attention to the facts and data. Try hard not to be swayed by people's personal attachment to their suggested option.
- Pay attention to past errors in making decisions.
- Don't include too many people in the decision.
- Take time to reflect on the decision and its outcome. What did you learn in the process?

HEAD LEADERSHIP STRATEGY 7: A PROBLEM-SOLVING PLAN

Purpose: Leaders guide collaborative development of a consistent approach for problem solving.

A *problem* is a situation in which something is wrong. There is some standard from which this situation or behavior varies. Part of solving any problem is identifying how far from that standard is or is not okay. The thoughtful leader works collaboratively with colleagues to set a consistent process that can be used in many situations throughout the school. Your young adolescent students can learn and apply such a protocol to many learning and living problems.

This process outlines for everyone how problems will be solved and put into effect, and who will be involved. Here is one example of a problem-solving protocol:

STEP 1: Review your process.

- Review: *Who will gather information? Identify and discuss alternative choices? Describe and communicate the solution? Put it into effect? Evaluate outcomes?*
- Reconfirm how the final solution will be chosen. Ask: *Will the solution be chosen by one leader? By group vote—majority rules? By consensus? By choosing the alternative with more pros than cons? With some other method?*

STEP 2: Examine your attitude about the people and situation.

- Don't see problems as needless distractions.
- Believe that each problem is an opportunity to learn and stretch.
- Keep an open mind; welcome possibilities that you have not seen or tried before.
- Realize that a problem may point to a deeper need for a strategy or policy change.
- Avoid blaming.
- Avoid letting bias against persons or actions involved cloud your judgment or impede finding the best solution. Be ready to apply solutions equitably.
- Empathize with those involved in the problem.

STEP 3: Describe the problem.

- Ask: *What happened or what is happening? Why is this a problem? What went wrong? What would be the ideal from which this varies?*
- State the problem in one sentence.

STEP 4: Clarify the problem.

- Dig deeper to get a clearer and more holistic understanding of the problem.
- Gather as much information as possible with research and feedback.
- Clarify: *Where and when did this happen? How long has this been going on? Has this happened before? What is unique about this problem? How urgent is it to reach a solution? Who is involved? Who else is impacted?*
- Talk to the people involved.
- Get input from others who may not be directly involved but have relevant insights to offer.
- Ask: *What are the root causes? What other problems are beneath the surface, contributing to or triggering this problem? What else must be addressed in solving this problem?*
- Ask: *Is this a people problem or a process problem?*

STEP 5: Generate ideas.

- Having gathered information and insights, brainstorm many possible solutions that might work. Don't stop to examine or discuss each one. Just get them out there on paper or screen.
- Generate many—the more, the better—within a reasonable amount of time, of course.
- Be creative. Take risks. Think outside the box.
- Keep the particular people or situation in mind. Think about what might work for them.
- Look for precedents. Think of what has been tried before and worked well.

- Consult others who have connections to the matter or skills that could lend good ideas.
- Ask the people involved in the problem to make suggestions for solutions.

STEP 6: Analyze and cull the alternative solutions.

- When you have several, weigh the pros and cons of each one.
- For each one, ask: *What is most likely to happen with this option? What is the best that could happen? What's the worst that could happen?*
- For each one, ask: *Can this really be done? Do we have the resources to do this, including the people to make it happen?*
- For each one, ask: *Does this align with our school vision and mission? How?*
- Narrow the possibilities to a short list of feasible options.

STEP 7: Examine each option more closely.

- When you've culled the list to a few good possibilities, weigh the viability of each one.
- Examine more closely what might happen with each alternative.
- Identify benefits and consequences of each.
- Consider possible impacts on people, systems, budgets, programs, and time.
- Pay attention to evidence as you weigh the options.
- For each one, ask: *How will this affect each of the people involved? Who else will be affected, and how?*
- For each one, ask: *Will others agree with this? Will it really get used?*
- For each one, ask: *What message will this send?*

STEP 8: Choose and develop the best solution.

- Choose the strongest alternative. Use your pre-decided method for reaching the decision. (Some recommend choosing the option for which you'll be best able to deal with the worst possible outcome.)

- Be sure you can explain the solution.
- Decide how to put it into effect. Create an action plan that identifies who will do what, when, and where. Set a timeline for your plan.

STEP 9: Communicate the solution.
- Explain the solution and the reasoning behind it to the people most affected by the problem and the solution. Get them on board with the plan.
- Communicate the solution promptly, clearly, and succinctly, without blame or judgment.
- Be confident in your choice.
- Take full accountability for the solution.

STEP 10: Put the plan into action and follow through.
- Follow through on your plan.
- Stick to the plan, but make adjustments as needed.

STEP 11: Monitor and evaluate outcomes.
- Monitor the progress of putting the solution to work.
- Ask for feedback about the solution and the resulting actions.
- Evaluate the solution by watching the impacts and outcomes.
- Ask: *Did we fix the problem? Did we address underlying causes? Did it work out the way we hoped? Who benefitted? What were the greatest benefits? Were there any negative effects? Was this the right solution? How can we tell?*
- Be prepared to try a different solution if this does not fix the problem.
- Take time to reflect on your problem-solving process. Ask: *What did we learn? What systems or behaviors should we put into place to avoid this problem in the future?*

HEAD LEADERSHIP STRATEGY 8: A REFLECTION PROTOCOL

Purpose: Leaders design, use, and teach a standard process for reflecting on a specific event or incident.

Reflection is revelatory work. It's an opportunity to step out of a situation or moment and look at something as if through a window from the outside. Reflection on past action offers space and calm to make sound judgments; it informs and refines future actions. It is definitely a head-centered habit to have ready when something needs rethinking. Here's one example that I've seen work for others. Adapt the steps slightly for use by students.

STEP 1: DISCUSS REASONS AND GUIDELINES WITH YOUR STAFF.

Your colleagues need to understand the importance of reflection and why you see the need for a standard protocol. Show the following example or develop your own. Discuss some guidelines. Help others think about situations in which this process should be used (since it's not realistic to do this in every circumstance). Think about when and where to do the reflecting, and how to decide who should be involved.

STEP 2: APPRECIATE THE BENEFITS OF THE PROCESS.

Besides helping the user(s) to remember, rethink, learn, and improve, capturing reflections leaves a record of what happened—when, where, and with whom. When people join together for reflection, the protocol offers powerful opportunities to collaborate and connect. The stronger sense of shared purpose that results will lead to better solutions and better performance in future situations.

STEP 3: PRACTICE USING THE PROTOCOL.

Apply it to a recent situation or any incident your group suggests. The following template, **Post-Event Reflection Questions**, will serve as a guide. You can adapt the template to your own ideas, changing or adding questions. If you don't use such a written record and guide, be sure to find another way to capture your thoughts. Don't count on remembering all those when the quiet is over!

STEP 4: PUT IT TO USE IN REAL-LIFE SITUATIONS.

Apply it to a recent situation or any other meeting or incident your group suggests. Keep the process fairly short so that the practice does not become burdensome. Don't overlook instances where the reflecting is best if it includes students, teachers, support staff members, student family members, or others. Be sure to reflect, not only on difficult situations, but on events that were uplifting, successful, fun, or informative!

Post-Event Reflection Questions

Use this guide to review and record your impressions about an event or situation.

WHAT? Objective question— get a clear description *What happened? What did I observe or hear? What did I do? Who else was there? What did others do? What was the situation or event? Was there a problem or issue? What was the outcome?*	
So WHAT? Reflective question—engage personal and emotional responses *Why reflect on this? Why does this matter? What emotions did tis trigger? What concerns, surprises, frustrates, pleases, excites, confuses me? What emotional responses did I see from others?*	
Now WHAT? Instructive question—guide toward improved future action *What did I learn? What did we learn about each other? What was successful? What was missing? What could have been done better? What should we change?*	
Then WHAT? Directive question—identify next steps *What's next? What needs to be addressed right away? What will we do differently next time? What strategies might work? What other ways can we use to learn from the situation?*	

Head Leadership Strategy 9: Feedback FROM the Leader

Purpose: Leaders plan specific ways to strengthen people and their performances with frequent constructive, affirmative feedback.

This strategy offers guidelines for a leader to use as they set processes for giving feedback. See the **Leader's Guide to Giving Feedback** (found later in this strategy). You can consult this before giving feedback or use it as a checklist to reflect on your feedback habits. Share it with others, including students.

Before you begin offering feedback,

- Make sure others in the school understand that giving and receiving feedback is a normal part of a learning community.

- Remember why you do it:
    - To reflect and affirm (with clear examples) what is strong, useful, helpful, or effective
    - To point out what could be improved
    - To offer concrete suggestions for ways to improve
    - To coach others to review and reflect with self-feedback

- Examine your own attitude and intentions. Approach feedback-giving from a place of care and connection. Drop any of your own agendas. Go forward thoughtfully, with empathy and attention to a trusting relationship.

- Don't limit feedback comments or sessions to occasions of problems or need for improvements. Those are important. But often give feedback solely to point out strengths. This, too, helps others do their jobs well. But be specific. Tell how the action or behavior makes a difference.

- Prepare. Be clear about what you will say and what suggestions you will give. Distinguish feedback from advice. Feedback leaves the person with a clear picture of what they should keep doing and what else they should do (or what they should do differently).

- Choose an appropriate time, place, and context.

- Give it promptly—soon after an event, performance, project, etc.
- Ask permission to give feedback; make an advance arrangement. Let the person know the topic and the timing. In most cases, feedback should be private.
- Address one issue or matter at a time.

After offering feedback,

- Always ask for feedback on your feedback. Give others a chance to tell what they learned, what was most helpful, what they suggest to you about your feedback practices.
- Revisit the person later to follow up on how the feedback suggestions are working.

LEADER'S GUIDE TO GIVING FEEDBACK

Use this to inform and double-check your feedback-giving habits.

Good feedback is:	
Purposeful	Feedback should affirm and inspire improvement. Look for what is done well; suggest what could be done to improve.
Clear	State observations and ideas simply and straightforwardly. Don't complicate comments with wordy explanations that are not helpful.
Fair	Clarify for yourself the criteria for the work. Give feedback only on matters that are requirements for the work. Be equitable with responses and evaluation. Don't go easy on some people and hard on others.

Specific	State clearly what you observed, heard, or read. Give examples. Describe the parts, steps, or words that worked well; explain the impact—what happened because of this. Ask questions or make specific suggestions for what might be changed or added; explain how this would impact the situation or product.
Instructive	Include only comments that teach something. Avoid overused comments that offer no specifics or ideas for growth—including praise: *Good job! You can do better. This is much improved. Great! Lacks clarity. Spectacular! Doesn't follow the code of conduct. I like where this is going. The task is unfinished. This caused problems. That was not a good idea. Incomplete. Inspiring! Too long! Too short! Too noisy! Too ordinary! Too bothersome!*
Actionable	Give comments that can be put to work. Continuing something that went well; offering concrete, measurable ideas for what else to try. Focus on realistic, doable solutions. Help them set goals that they can attain—and know when they reach them.
Collaborative	Treat the feedback session as a conversation. Let the other person explain and show why they did what they did. Give them a chance to point out the strengths and needs for improvements. Ask questions. Dialogue. Listen.
Objective	Avoid moralizing or judging. Give statements about the behavior, the action, the situation, the writing or performing—not the person.
Affirming and Uplifting	Avoid any comments that diminish or degrade. Be kind and sensitive to the individual. Affirm the work. Demonstrate your belief in the person's ability to make their work or behavior or efforts the best possible. When suggesting changes, be sure the person hears your confidence in them. Leave them energized and inspired.

Head Leadership Strategy 10: Feedback FOR the Leader

Purpose: Leaders design processes to solicit feedback about their own leadership styles and actions.

Most schools know the value of gaining feedback from stakeholders in order to design and improve programs, policies, procedures, and events. But often one kind of feedback is forgotten: feedback **for** the leader. This is feedback from others in the school community, including students, that provides honest, constructive insights to help a leader be the best at their job. The thoughtful leader develops specific structures and processes for getting this kind of feedback.

Components of a process for feedback to the leader about the leader:

1. **First, ask for it.** Don't count on a "policy" that says it should be done. Go after it yourself. Don't count on people spontaneously telling you their responses to your way of running the faculty meeting yesterday, or your communication style, or the messages you give with your body language, or the way you conducted their latest staff-evaluation interview.

   Be thoughtful and creative about how to gain feedback. There are unlimited possibilities. Here are some:

   - Consult a trusted colleague, personal leadership coach, or mentor. Ask the kinds of questions that the person in the role can answer.
   - Plan periodic (but regular) face-to-face chats with individuals or small groups.
   - Set up post-event debriefing sessions with staff. This could be after a meeting, assembly, parent gathering, student encounter, or any other event for which you took a leadership role. Ask others to reflect to you how it went, what you handled well, what positive things resulted, what you missed, what you got wrong, what you could have done differently, what reactions they felt or saw from others.

- Use a variety of approaches. Solicit feedback with one-question emails to several people, online surveys on specific topics or events, focus groups, or short conversations.
- Use some structures where you invite feedback on a specific characteristic, action, or event.

2. **Welcome it.** Let go of reluctance and fear. Go after feedback with an open heart, open mind, and humility. Let all your language (and body language) show that you are eager to listen and intend to put the feedback to work. Receive it with respect and gratitude. Relax. Get in the spirit of mutual trust and human connection. Keep and show your sense of humor.

3. **Seek feedback that helps you reach stated goals.** Ask for feedback that weighs your actions against what you said you were going to do, against values you have espoused, against attitudes and behaviors you have promoted. Ask people to think about the school vision as they assess your performance. Ask for feedback on how you are holding to the school vision (or the leader's stated vision).

4. **Look for concrete examples.** Always ask for concrete examples. Ask others to tell you specifically what you did well (so you can continue that) and what you actually did or said that needs to be different.

5. **Solicit solutions.** Ask questions that invite concrete examples and specific ideas for solutions you can realistically and affordably put into action. Really dig into it! Eagerly look for input. Ask clarifying questions. Don't walk away without satisfaction that you know what to do next.

6. **Be consistent.** See that feedback practices are ongoing and strong. Don't let them fizzle away.

7. **Use it.** Along with asking for feedback, this is the top feedback priority. You don't get any feedback if you don't ask for it (except maybe behind your back). But it means nothing if you don't listen, accept, and implement it. Repeat the feedback you found helpful. Tell how and when and why you are going to use it. Point it out when you do. Let folks know its good effects.

Questions such as these inspire feedback. Ask for specific examples as part of each answer.

- *What is the most helpful thing I did or said?*
- *How have I been supportive of you in your job?*
- *What could I do differently about _____?*
- *What did I do well?*
- *Was my communication on _____ clear and helpful?*
- *In what ways could I be more effective at _____?*
- *What is the least helpful thing I do to support you in your job?*
- *How have I helped your child succeed?*
- *What else do you and your child need from me?*
- *What was helpful about my feedback to you?*
- *What do you notice that you and other students need from me that they are not getting?*

HEAD LEADERSHIP STRATEGY 11: PLANNING TO DELEGATE

Purpose: Leaders set a consistent protocol for delegation and teach it to others.

Get ready to delegate thoughtfully. Use the following template, **Delegation Framework**, to outline components of your preparations for giving responsibility to another person or group. You can fill this form out ahead of time, or complete it when you meet with the designee. Let it serve as a record for the plans you've made and the expectations for the task.

STEP 1: PLAN AHEAD.

A. **What?** Identify the task or responsibility. Write it in a clear sentence or two.
B. **Why?** Explain the reason for the task. Why should it be done? Why does it matter?

C. **Who?** Choose the person or team with skills and time suited to the responsibility.

D. **Expectations?** Define exact expectations for success. What should the final outcome be or the final "product" look like? You could write this in the form of a SMART goal—state a clear goal that is specific, measurable, achievable, relevant, and time-related.

E. **Measure progress?** Set benchmark goals so all can gauge and reflect on progress.

F. **How long?** Set a timeline with deadlines for benchmarks and for completion.

G. **Reporting and checking in?** Decide what process will be used for the person to keep records and to report to the leader.

H. **Coaching?** Decide who will be available for help and support along the way.

I. **Evaluation criteria?** Let the person know how the task and responsibility will be evaluated, by what criteria, by whom, and when.

J. **Preparation? Resources?** Think ahead about what training, information, or resources you will need to supply to the person as you hand over responsibility.

STEP 2: MEET WITH THE DESIGNEE.

Plan a session for passing the responsibility on to another person or group. Communicate the tasks, responsibilities, and reasons clearly. Collaborate with the person on the expectations and details of the task(s). Allow time for discussion and questions. Agree on the timelines and the processes for accountability and evaluation. Confirm their understanding of all the components. Be sure that both parties are clear on the extent of the responsibility and authority given to their charge.

STEP 3: KEEP IN TOUCH.

Though the leader trusts the person to accomplish the task and puts the authority to do so in their hands, the leader does not just walk away. The leader coaches the "designated" leader—not hovering or overprotecting, but teaching what is needed for doing the task and then being available for support. This coaching is a way of gradually building even more leadership skills in others.

Delegation Framework

Outline the details and expectations for a responsibility you are delegating.

The task or responsibility	
The reason for the task	
Expectation for finished product	
Benchmark goals	
Time frame for benchmarks and completion	
Reporting and recording expectations	
Evaluation criteria	
Who will coach and check in?	
Who will evaluate? When?	

HEAD LEADERSHIP STRATEGY 12: JOURNALING: LEADING FROM THE HEAD

Purpose: Leaders follow a practice of journaling to reflect on their experiences with head-centered leadership for purposes of understanding and enhancing their abilities and practices.

Reflection is slowing down to think about yourself, your actions, and your experiences. It is critical to growth as a leader and to your self-care.

1. Intentionally set aside a regular time, maybe 15 to 30 minutes. Protect this time.
2. Select a quiet place. Turn off devices and avoid distractions.
3. Put down your thoughts in paragraphs, sentences, phrases, outlines, poetry, or a narrative format. There is no one right or best way.
4. Choose a theme to ponder, or a topic or prompt, and get started.
5. Be honest. Notice your feelings as you write. Note those as well.

Some ideas for a journal entry:

- Where and when you were effective in thinking before acting; where you might have missed opportunities for more thinking or fact-gathering
- An overview of the week, pondering what you learned about leading from the head
- Head-centered leadership strategies you consciously used and how they worked
- Revisit examples and situations in which head-centered leadership was needed and analyze how you used (or did not use) such leadership effectively
- One thought or lesson learned from a short encounter
- Examples of head-centered leadership you have witnessed
- Personal experience of any of the "fruits" of head-centered leadership (see Chapter 4)

- Thoughts on a Chapter 5 trait related to the status of your head-centered leadership
- A look at an important value and how it connects to your leadership from the head
- Thoughts about goals you want to set for yourself
- Thoughts on your whole head-leadership style or direction (or any facet of it)
- Or any other ideas about head-leadership matters

The journal guide template on the next page, **Journaling Head-Centered Leadership**, is an example of a tool you might create to record your thoughts. This particular sample could be used for a general overview of your week.

Journaling Head-Centered Leadership

Use this to guide in your reflection. Add other ideas if needed.

Theme, event, or topic for reflection today	
My best head-leadership moment	
Another example of head-centered leadership that I observed in myself	
A head-centered leadership trait that I needed but didn't use	
Something someone taught me this week about my thinking	
An important value and how it connected to my head leadership this week	

PART 3

LEADING FROM THE HAND

Chapter 7   **What Does It Mean to Lead from the Hand?**
Chapter 8   **Traits of Hand-Centered Leadership**
Chapter 9   **Hand-Centered Leadership Strategies**

The Successful Middle School: This We Believe
Characteristics Crossover

- Educators are specifically prepared to teach young adolescents and possess a depth of understanding in the content areas they teach.
- Curriculum is challenging, exploratory, integrative, and diverse.
- Health, wellness, and social-emotional competence are supported in curricula, school-wide programs, and related policies.
- Instruction fosters learning that is active, purposeful, and democratic.
- Varied and ongoing assessments advance learning as well as measure it.
- Policies and practices are student-centered, unbiased, and fairly implemented.
- Leaders are committed to and knowledgeable about young adolescents, equitable practices, and educational research.
- Leaders demonstrate courage and collaboration.
- Professional learning for staff is relevant, long term, and job embedded.
- Organizational structures foster purposeful learning and meaningful relationships.

Chapter 7

What Does It Mean to Lead from the Hand?

Leadership in the Lunchroom

Nana used to say, "Boy, say what you're gonna do, but do what you're gonna say." I've remembered those words hundreds of times, especially in my various school leadership roles. This occasion, in particular, stands out.

As the assistant principal of a middle school, one of my many duties was to monitor the cafeteria. At the time, we split our student body of 800 students into four lunch groups, serving each group for a 30-minute session. Every day in the busy lunchroom with groups coming and going was an adventure.

One day near the end of "third lunch," a group of students got up to leave their assigned table. I reminded all the students, via the megaphone I had wrapped around my wrist, that they should clean up behind themselves. For some school leaders who have not had the privilege to monitor lunch in a middle school, this might be a scenario that you can only imagine. But for others, it's a vivid reality. Right after I reminded students to clean up their tables, this group of students turned away from their littered table and walked toward the exit without so much as a napkin or straw in their hands.

I was livid! I wanted to grab that bullhorn and run to the nearest seventh grader and yell until I passed out. But the good habit I'd honed of paying attention to emotional triggers took hold. I paused a moment to think. I asked myself, "Is there a better way?" Yes, there was!

I got the attention of everyone in the cafeteria (I did end up yelling a little) and asked the students who had been sitting at that particular table to come back into the room and stand by their table. I took a bus tub (a plastic rectangular box-like container often used in restaurants to clear dishes from tables) and a towel, and I silently cleared and cleaned the table.

After I finished, an astonishing thing occurred. Students began to applaud and cheer. I was shocked but couldn't show my surprise at their reaction. I just took a bow and asked that every student follow my example. I had spoken the words of reminding before but, as Nana taught me, "though words have power, actions have more."

Hand-centered leadership is the leadership of action. It's the part of leading where an educator makes clear **what needs to be done** and gets busy **doing** it—visibly, consistently, and eagerly. The earlier parts of this book, with their spotlights on leadership from the heart and head, have shown a leader who knows the school community members and connects with them heart-to-heart and who approaches all planning of the school's work with deep, strategic thought before action. I've given much attention to the importance of creating action plans that are deeply rooted in the purposes and dreams of the school community (**why** we do what we do) and are founded on serious consideration of **how** to operate and **what** outcomes we hope for.

To be fully effective, the school leader does not stop there. The goals cannot be met without strategic systems and protocols that are easy for everyone to follow. And even the smartest systems or plans will falter if the leader hands out the details of necessary actions, passes out jobs for others to do, then closes the office door and waits to receive reports about what happens.

When you lead from the hand, you literally use your hands and feet to carry out the plans that have been so carefully designed to accomplish the school's vision and mission. This is the **action part** of any initiative or policy. You not only do what you say you'll do, but you also inspire, lead, and join everyone else in getting the action items done. Such leadership:

- Sets the tone for engagement, organization, and transparency within implementation of all action plans.
- Focuses all actions on the priorities that have been set.
- Keeps plans on track, seeing that all the moving parts work together.

- Supports the processes for accountability, monitoring, and evaluation of actions.
- Sees that accomplishments and the people who take part in them are celebrated.

Successful hand-centered middle level leadership is solidly based on a commitment to the needs of your young adolescent students—giving preeminence to actions that build and support a culture of excellent instruction and overall well-being for them. To do this, the leader knows that it takes open hands and many joined hands for successful action. Leadership from the hand is a venture of shared leadership and collaboration—with thoughtful delegation and coaching from the leader. As a leader, you become the chief model of cooperative action.

THE FRUITS OF HAND-CENTERED LEADERSHIP

When the hand is the source of leadership, acting in union with other hands to follow well-articulated goals and plans, such results as these naturally follow:

Togetherness and Trust
All the people involved in any plan gain the sense of "we." They see that planned actions are for the purpose of doing something important for "us," with the leader being "one of us." It is not only that they have a shared purpose, as stated in the school vision or in the reasons for key projects—they also experience joined hands and shared energy to get the action done. As staff members, students, and other stakeholders leap into action together, they know they are not alone. Smart plans under strong hand leadership induce greater connection, deeper relationships, and increased interdependence. With true interdependence, trust increases. In doing tasks together, people grow in trust for each other, trust for the leaders, and trust in the system.

Certainty and Security
When action is planned carefully with sensible systems and clear protocols,

the processes run smoothly. People know what to do and why. They know when, where, how, and for how long. The goals and expectations are specific; they have no doubts about where they are headed. They know the steps to follow. They have checkpoints along the way so they know how they're progressing toward goals. They know who is supporting them and how. They know the criteria for doing their jobs well. All of this is part of a good system for action, and together these factors provide certainty and security for everyone involved. When leaders join hands with the other participants to reach objectives, the certainty and the security doubles.

Productivity
With smart leadership from the hand and the strategic plans and actions that result from it, **things get done**. Time and resources (including human energy resources) are not wasted. Confusion and disorganization are avoided. People involved feel the sense of joint accomplishment. They see movement toward the goals and the final outcomes. With guidance from the leader, people stick with the plans, and the plans work.

Visibility
Hand leadership is the easiest aspect of leadership to see. Because it is about the whole process of reaching goals, this leadership is right out there for all to observe. Thus, it offers the leader an extraordinary opportunity to serve as a model for the entire school community of how to start and follow through on accomplishing the school's missions.

Growth
One of the rewards and great joys of a smoothly operating action plan is the growth for all the folks who are part of making it work. Skills of communication, social interaction, problem solving, cooperation, creativity, and leadership blossom. People get better at taking on responsibility, gain comfort with increased authority, and learn countless other lessons along the way. Leaders get better at leading.

What Does It Mean to Lead from the Hand?

Confidence
As integral parts of successful action, people see themselves making a difference. They gain importance and self-reliance. When people are trusted to take on a role of action, and when they do it successfully, they become more independent. They are energized to work harder. They gain the confidence to take on more action. This is true for the leaders too. As effective action results in goals accomplished, the leader is emboldened to take on new challenges and calculated risks. The leader gains self-confidence as well as confidence in their co-workers (be they students, parents and caregivers, staff members, or community members).

Loyalty
People form unique bonds when they are part of a process that leads to visible results and improvements. Earlier I mentioned the togetherness that results from good hand-centered leadership. This bond of completing actions together for shared values transforms to commitment and loyalty to the school, to each other, and to the successful systems. The participants following hand-centered leadership get fully behind the action. They believe in the process and the leadership. And they're ready to dive into the next set of tasks—with enthusiasm.

Satisfaction
It's fulfilling to be part of a team of people working together for a valued cause. The leader and those with whom the leader joins find personal and group satisfaction. This sense of gratification is not only an end-of-project reward. With well-planned protocols, the entire process is inspiring and satisfying. The experience boosts morale and joy for each person involved.

Leadership in the Lunchroom, continued

Later in the week of the "silent lunchroom cleanup demonstration," some students began to ask for buckets and mops. The lunchroom was never left with messy tables like that again. I can say that I did plenty of reflecting on the best reactions to such a situation. Realizing much later that no student jumped right in to help me that day, I considered that there might have been some other ways to respond. Though the situation did improve, appointing an official group of student cafeteria-cleanliness supervisors (or recruiting a volunteer group) might have been an even better option. Or, I could have turned the problem over to the student group to come up with their own solution. The situation was as much a lesson for the leader as for the students.

DEVELOPING HAND-CENTERED LEADERSHIP

Leadership from the hand is the logical companion to leadership from the heart and leadership from the head. The hand, too, is an integral part of the successful leader's anatomy. And thank goodness for it! Those hands (with plenty of help from feet, eyes, ears, mouth—and yes, head and heart as well) are busy during all the waking hours—moving, demonstrating, teaching—to get done what needs to be done.

In Part 1 of the book, I said that to be an effective heart-centered leader, your heart must be open and welcoming. In Part 2, I said that to be an effective head-centered leader, your head needs to be open and welcoming. So it is with the hand. Leadership from the hand is successful only if your hands and arms are wide open and welcoming. But that description may not be true for all leaders. If your hands are withdrawn, tightened into fists, selective about whom they welcome, or hiding behind an office door, you can't effectively lead, model, or coach necessary actions. If your hands won't get down into the dirt, get scraped up or even bloody, do heavy lifting, or hold hands with others, you won't be able to go places you need to go, do work you need to do, or join with the people you need to join to make the brilliant action plans work.

There are deliberate steps you can take to develop the habits of hand-centered leadership. Chapter 8 describes some leadership traits that flow from the hand and Chapter 9 offers some practical strategies that leaders can use to put hand-centered leadership into practice.

What Does It Mean to Lead from the Hand?

Once you understand what hand-centered leadership means and get a picture of how to develop it further, you can attend to the hand in your views and practices. You can enjoy the outcomes of hand-centered leadership as you watch such fruits as those described earlier in this chapter blossom in you and in those you lead.

Chapter 8

Traits of Hand-Centered Leadership

How does hand-centered leadership evidence itself? How can the leader tell when their hands are a major source of leadership purpose and action? How do others recognize and experience leadership from the hand?

Here are some of the key **observable** leadership characteristics or behaviors flowing from the source of hands-on action that directly leads to getting the work of the school done. Read about them to help answer the questions in the paragraph above. As leaders develop such traits, they grow further in their abilities to lead from the hand.

The Successful Middle School Leader
Hand-Centered Leadership Traits
The Hand-Centered Leader...

Hand Trait 1	Shows up, sleeves rolled up.
Hand Trait 2	Understands and communicates the need for systems.
Hand Trait 3	Creates a clear and compelling vision of instruction based on deep knowledge of young adolescents.
Hand Trait 4	Ensures that the big-picture plan is successfully executed.
Hand Trait 5	Establishes and follows a system for managing projects.
Hand Trait 6	Sets clear expectations, deadlines, and responsible parties for action items
Hand Trait 7	Nourishes a collaborative, inclusive environment for learning and working.
Hand Trait 8	Operates from a "touch it but don't hold it" mindset.
Hand Trait 9	Anticipates problems and meets them head-on and hands-on.

Hand Trait 10	Uses data to inform instruction and decisions.
Hand Trait 11	Keeps students at the center of all policies and plans.
Hand Trait 12	Chooses curricula and academic supports purposefully, strategically, and collaboratively.
Hand Trait 13	Prioritizes and cultivates excellent instruction.
Hand Trait 14	Develops and nurtures professional learning communities.
Hand Trait 15	Commits to relevant, long-term, and job-embedded professional development.
Hand Trait 16	Acts to properly resource the school or district.
Hand Trait 17	Follows through with courage and commitment.

HAND LEADERSHIP TRAIT 1: THE HAND-CENTERED LEADER SHOWS UP, SLEEVES ROLLED UP.

When effectively leading from the hand, the leader shows up in the halls; on the playground; outside the front door; in the classrooms; in meetings of faculty, teams, or departments; at pep rallies and field days; at school events on-campus and off-campus; and in the community. They show up with their whole self—alert, present, and tuned in. Their hands and feet and all their senses are "in the game." And others around them can tell. How?

The actions are visible. Others can observe the leader:

- Listening, watching, asking, affirming, nudging, teaching, welcoming.
- Hauling and carrying and digging and sweating—setting up tables, putting up banners, joining playground games, cleaning up after storms, helping parents or caregivers carry heavy musical instruments into the school, or patching holes in the courtyard.

Traits of Hand-Centered Leadership

- Paying attention to the jobs people do—showing that they know what kinds of tasks are done by everyone who works or volunteers at the school.
- Stepping into other roles in the school—teaching lessons in partnership with teachers or to give a teacher a break, supervising the lunchroom or playground, serving up lunches, or mopping floors.
- Taking risks—being the first one to step forward and stand up for a staff member or student, boldly model culturally responsive behaviors and policies, jump into the fire to manage a crisis, or fight for adequate funding for the school programs.
- Joining hands with others in a game of tug-of-war or in the metaphorical tug-of-war of keeping the school moving toward fulfilling its vision.

On full display are the leader's energy, passion, and unshakable beliefs that every student can achieve and that every person in the school makes a difference in meeting the school's goals.

> **Gray Matter**
>
> *You have two hands and 10 fingers for a reason. To be an effective middle school leader, you'll need them all to join hands in cooperation and to literally build the fulfillment of your vision.*

In 2004, researchers from the University of Minnesota and the University of Toronto, supported by the Wallace Foundation, set out to identify school leadership practices that directly or indirectly foster improvement of educational practices and learning—and to discover how this influence happens. The largest study of its kind, researchers collected data over two years from 180 schools in 43 districts across the nations—schools of varying size, level, type, and student demographics. The study's key conclusion is this: "Leadership is second only to classroom instruction among all school-related factors that contribute to what students learn at school."[31]

Researchers in this study also noted that **they were unable to find any cases of a school with overall improved student achievement in the absence of talented leadership**.[32] Though most of the effects of leadership on student achievement were indirect, they were powerful because the school leader's actions **directly** influence the relationships across the school community, every teacher and all the instruction, the entire climate throughout the school, and all the attitudes, policies, plans, and procedures that affect student achievement.[33]

As other researchers, revisiting this topic a decade later, explain: Research since 2000 shows that the impact of an effective principal has been underrated. The impact of a principal's action on student achievement, they say, "is greater and broader than previously believed."[34]

In Chapter 9, see **Hand Leadership Strategy 1: Wild and Wacky Actions** on page 244 for some ways to help leaders spur stakeholders to action in following the school vision and executing major plans.

Also in Chapter 9, see **Hand Leadership Strategy 2: Job Check-In** on page 246 for a process to help leaders tune into all the hands at work in the school.

Hand Leadership Trait 2: The Hand-Centered Leader Understands and communicates the need for systems.

Gratitude for the System

I wanted to keep the grass on my lawn healthy and green. I hauled out the hose and sprinkler, tried to find the best spot for it, then trudged across the lawn to turn on the faucet. I repeated this every day, sometimes more than once in the hottest weather. But then the brown spots started to show up. So my new daily routine involved troubleshooting—dragging the hose and sprinkler around to try different placements—hoping to get all the spots watered.

Eventually I gave in and bought a second hose and a second sprinkler—and one of those gizmos that allows you to hook two hoses to one faucet. Now I had double troubleshooting, slogging around on the lawn pulling two hoses to get the right spots. Inevitably, there were always some places that didn't get enough water. And I often ended up out there holding the hose to hand-water those spots. About this time, my neighbor had a sprinkler system installed. So now, I did my tedious watering while he smirked at me from across the fence.

I finally relented and reached for my cell phone to dial the number I saw on the installation truck in front of my neighbor's house. Yes, it cost more money (I wish I hadn't blown the $200 on the hoses and sprinklers!). Thank goodness for the professionals; how I appreciated their skills. And how wonderful it is to be able to flip the switch and watch the system at work!

The successful middle school leader harnesses the resources and invests the time up front to install systems for execution of action plans. This includes processes that are part of a successful plan—such things as coaching, collaboration, scheduling, accountability, feedback, and evaluation. Yes, it takes work. With smart leadership, hands get busy and dig the trenches. The leader is right there in the forefront with their hands in the dirt.

With a well-designed and well-communicated system in place, the leader is not always having to pull out the hose in despair to water struggling patches or put out fires. The hard work saves time and resources in the long run. It also diminishes uncertainty. Good systems set a foundation for organization, stability, and clarity. All participants in the action know the reason for the action, and they have guidelines for what to do and how to do it.

The hand-centered leader knows that building systems builds trust. A great example of this is the organizational structure of teaming, which fosters deep, long-term colleague relationships and student-teacher relationships and offers a strong experience of connectedness and trust among students, students' families, teachers, and the school.

Also, once built-in structures and protocols are in place, processes work smoothly to accomplish the system's purpose—without being specifically dependent on particular persons. That is, instead of choosing a particular type of person to do the work, or depending on the leader to be there, staff members can trust the system to work. They don't need to worry if the leader is having a bad day or running late. They don't have to wonder if a process will proceed correctly or fairly. They work the system. An example of such a system is a pre-designed and pre-approved formal teacher evaluation process that determines mastery of instruction through the use of rubrics for assessment. A teacher who wants to become a master teacher or attain the highest marks on the evaluation does not need to "schmooze" up to the evaluator. They do not need to worry about the evaluator's objectivity. Instead, the teacher needs to study and practice the evaluation instrument. Growth and performance of the teacher move forward, without variation due to the person in the role of administering the appraisal.

The strong hand-centered leader also knows that systems don't work well when siloed. When a leader changes one part or process in a particular system, they realize that this will affect other systems or parts of a system. They identify the ramifications of that change and plan for additional adjustments. For example, if the superintendent or leadership team wants to adjust the start times for middle schools in the district, they consult with the directors of transportation, nutrition, and human resources. Changing the start times for middle school students from

8:45 am to 8:00 am requires the buses to run earlier, the cafeteria to serve breakfast earlier, and the teachers and support personnel to arrive at school earlier.

Other examples of interdependent systems that are critical to middle schools are:

- The transition programs for students coming into middle school and moving from middle school to high school.
- The instructional systems for middle school students taking high school courses.

In these examples, elementary, middle, and high school officials must plan jointly and seamlessly interconnect their systems. When any programs develop, or changes occur that affect other schools, programs, or departments, the hands-on leaders collaborate with one another to minimize disruptions and maximize benefits for students and teachers.

HAND LEADERSHIP TRAIT 3: THE HAND-CENTERED LEADER CREATES A CLEAR AND COMPELLING VISION OF INSTRUCTION BASED ON DEEP KNOWLEDGE OF YOUNG ADOLESCENTS.

I have learned that if you do not give your team or learning community a vision for the work, they will make it up as they go along. Effective hand-centered leaders work with others to build a joint vision for what they hope will come about for their middle school students as a result of their master instructional plan. Vision, by definition, is a picture of where schools and districts desire to reach. It is the reason behind the instructional plans and actions you design.

In Part 2 of this book, I gave plenty of attention to vision-setting. I wrote about a leader's vision for their leadership and about vision-setting for the entire school or for a particular project or initiative. Here, I note that effective middle school leadership from the hand also includes a clear vision for instruction, since successful student achievement is at the center of what you strive for in your school. So, before identifying specific objectives, actions, strategies for curriculum, teaching, and learning, the leader makes sure that everyone:

- Has strong understanding of instructional and curriculum needs for young adolescents and
- Knows where they hope instruction will lead.

(Of course, any vision you set for instruction will align with or flow from your overall school vision, or may even be at the heart of your school vision.)

Here are two of the instructional visions that I have seen or used:

Every child, every day, college bound.

Every scholar, every day, ready for life.

In Chapters 4 and 5, I described vision as a dream. Successful middle school leaders foster and act out of an instructional vision by gauging the capacity of the school, determining the appropriate baseline data, and setting goals that seem just beyond reach. I know that setting goals beyond the reach of the school may sound illogical; but that's why the vision is a dream. Yes, it is just out of reach, but still within the school's power to reach. That's what keeps everyone continuously striving for the next level. It is what your students deserve.

From that instructional vision, the hand-centered leader takes action, hand in hand with teams or other PLCs, to create plans and protocols focused on student data, student work, student outcomes, and student academic, social, and emotional needs. Think of the instructional vision as your North Star, and your school improvement plan or other master instructional plan as the map.

See **Hand Leadership Strategy 1: Wild and Wacky Actions** in Chapter 9, page 244, for some ways to help leaders ignite stakeholders to action and enthusiasm around visions.

HAND LEADERSHIP TRAIT 4: THE HAND-CENTERED LEADER ENSURES THAT THE BIG-PICTURE PLAN IS SUCCESSFULLY EXECUTED.

It is likely that your school has a strategic plan. This might be a Theory of Action extended with a specific action plan for the school or district. Or it might be framed as a school improvement plan or an instructional plan. As discussed in Chapters 4 and 5, the effective leader guides the development of such a plan, with input from all stakeholders in the school or district community, and with involvement and affirmation from the school board. The creation of the plan involves much good thinking and draws input from a diverse pool of perspectives, including insights and ideas from students. The plan is also developed with firm commitment to equity, with safeguards to assure that it impacts and benefits everyone equally. Creating such a plan is a dynamic and meaningful collaborative process.

The successful hand-centered leader takes the plan beyond its vision and design to ensure that the strategies (actions) of the plan, in fact, lead to goal accomplishment. Now, this may seem obvious: Of course, plans were written with strategies to get things done. Isn't that why they are strategic plans? And isn't it a given that the leader would see the plan through to completion?

In reality, **it is easier to form a strategic plan than to successfully implement it**. Statistically, many strategic plans hardly ever come off the shelf; large percentages of goals go unmet; and in many schools, only a small percentage of employees even see the plan. Data on the success of strategic plans across many organizations also show that, on average, leadership teams spend very little time actually executing strategies, and few organizations have a fully implemented monitoring and tracking system.[35,36]

The successful hand-centered leader knows this reality and boldly leads processes that beat these odds. One such process is the **balanced scorecard**.[37] This is a "performance measurement framework" that places "strategy as the centerpiece of a dynamic leadership and management system."[38] It has had worldwide success in enabling organizations to actually achieve the targets of their strategic plans.

The balanced scorecard is based on using measurable indicators of success for goals your school has set. The focus is on strategies that produce short-term results as part of accomplishing the long-term plan. Basic tenets of a balanced scorecard are:

- "If you can't measure it, you can't manage and improve it."
- "Measurement motivates."
- "The simple act of measuring and monitoring causes people to pay attention to what is measured."[39]

The goals of a master plan are often broad. It's tempting to have many goals—since we leaders always want to do more. I recommend following the idea of "wildly important goals,"[40] where you name and hone in on the most critical of the ideals you want to reach. Even with a refined set of goals, a school can only move forward toward execution when the goals are defined by objectives and strategies that can actually be measured and accomplished.

Successful strategies are the linchpin of a balanced scorecard. They derive from identified needs revealed by careful review of the school environment and data. Research-based strategies, matched with measurable strategies, form the heart of the action items. The "hand" of leadership spearheads the professional development and resources necessary for doing these tasks well. Then the action is formally launched.

The balanced scorecard approach balances your attention among:

- Your baseline plan with its clear goals and strategies with measurable indicators;
- The collective effective actions implementing the strategies;
- Consistent gathering of data as you measure and monitor progress on each strategy; and
- Achievement of stated outcomes.

This serves as an ongoing report card for your school—not one that only gives grades at the end of the quarter, semester, or year—but one with which you can see various aspects of school environment and performance all the time. At any point, you can compare current performance against baseline measures and against the target performance you desire in the future.

Sometimes parts of a strategic plan are managed separately, leading to ineffective execution. The beauty of the balanced scorecard is that it is a collective management system. It links all components of the strategic plan into one management system. Like a marching band—though there are different instruments and band sections, everyone moves to the same music and for the same purpose.

When I was the superintendent of Jackson Mississippi Public Schools, the decision to use the balanced scorecard as a centerpiece of our accountability system helped lead to significant gains in the student achievement ratings of our middle schools. It was the laser focus on measuring and monitoring progress on well-chosen strategies that made the difference. Since then, I have worked with other schools and districts that have found success when they added the balanced scorecard to the implementation of instructional plans.

> **Gray Matter**
>
> *Use your hands to pass along effective strategies and help scaffold existing ones.*

See **Hand Leadership Strategy 3: Focus on WIGs** in Chapter 9, page 248, to guide your group in writing and pursuing wildly important goals.

Also in Chapter 9, see **Hand Leadership Strategy 4: A Balanced Scorecard Plan** on page 251 for a general guide to the contents of a balanced scorecard process.

Hand Leadership Trait 5: The Hand-Centered Leader Establishes and Follows a System for Managing Projects.

In order to fully execute an instructional plan or any other strategic plan, break it down into manageable parts. The hand-centered leader sets a management and oversight process with a format and tools for designating projects—each of which is the operation or fulfilling of a segment of the overall plan. All people who work on a project are aware of its connection to the overall plan.

The combined processes of a balanced scorecard and great project management turns a school or district's goals into real work that is carefully organized and delegated. Together, these two approaches produce a practical, effective process for putting strategies into action.

Once an instructional plan is launched, with its specific measurable strategies identified, its success is dependent upon good monitoring. Anyone who leads from the hand knows that every system needs a check. Thus, they develop a standard protocol for all projects. Each step in the management process is a check on the system and must be completed chronologically before moving on to the next.

The number of projects that work together to satisfy the goals of the overall plan will depend on the plan's complexity. But whether there are few or many projects, each one is critical to the meeting of your important goals. Let's look at an example of a project: If your instructional vision is that *every scholar will have the adequate preparation to be college and career ready*, one of the objectives (tasks to help you get to the goal) may be to build students' language skills. Within that, you may form a project aimed specifically at reading proficiency.

The general steps to manage a project are:

1. **Establish a goal (or goals) for the project.** For the above-named project, the goal could be to improve reading proficiency by a certain percentage.
2. **Determine objectives (sub-goals).** Objectives may be to provide professional development training for teachers and instructional aides; to increase classroom time for students to engage in reading instruction

targeted at both word skills and understanding of complex texts; and to provide regular tutoring for struggling readers for at least a full semester.

3. **Determine what is needed to accomplish the objectives.** Identify personnel, time, space, and materials needed to accomplish objectives.

4. **Identify strategies, with measurement indicators, to accomplish each objective.** List actions that will be done for each of the objectives above. Ask: *What will be done to provide the necessary PD? What topics? How will schedules be arranged to give more time for reading instruction? What word skills will be taught, by whom, and how? How will progress be measured? What comprehension and deep-reading skills will be taught, and how? How will progress be measured? What will be the content of the tutoring? How often and how long will the tutoring last? How will progress be measured?*

5. **Review assignments and timelines that have been set.** Create an organizational chart identifying people, defining roles and responsibilities, and showing deadlines.

6. **Put strategies into action.**

7. **Monitor and evaluate the process and progress according to previously set guidelines.**

The school leader or "head" leader of the overall plan regularly schedules meetings with key partners to receive status updates on project components. This creates a rhythm of results and accountability. Participants review action items that were assigned as well as address any hindrances to progress. It is important to have decision makers at the meeting and not a department designee. If there is a part of the project that is dependent upon a decision being made, the group should not need to wait on an answer.

Given that there will be several concurrent projects as part of meeting goals, a good strategic plan allows for many leaders to manage different projects concurrently.

In Chapter 9, see **Hand Leadership Strategy 5: Planning for Project Management** on page 252 for a checklist to use in creating a map for managing a project.

Hand Leadership Trait 6: The Hand-Centered Leader Sets Clear Expectations, Deadlines, and Responsible Parties for Action Items.

One common barrier to clean operations of a plan is unclear explanation or instruction. When one leads from the hand, they make sure that expectations, responsibilities, persons in charge, and time frames are clear. These things are not just defined in writing as part of your project map or other plan; they are clearly communicated by the leader. They are discussed, defined, and refined collaboratively.

At times the clarification requires teaching and demonstration. The hand-centered leader may need to walk the action team through each phase of a particular project. This leader knows that the best action plans work only when each person involved has both an understanding of the overall scope of action plus an unequivocal view of their precise role, including:

- The exact actions they will take
- The expectations for how they will do their tasks
- Criteria for successful accomplishment of their tasks
- How actions and outcomes will be recorded and reported
- A timeline for meeting each benchmark goal, as well as for the final goal for their action

Traits of Hand-Centered Leadership

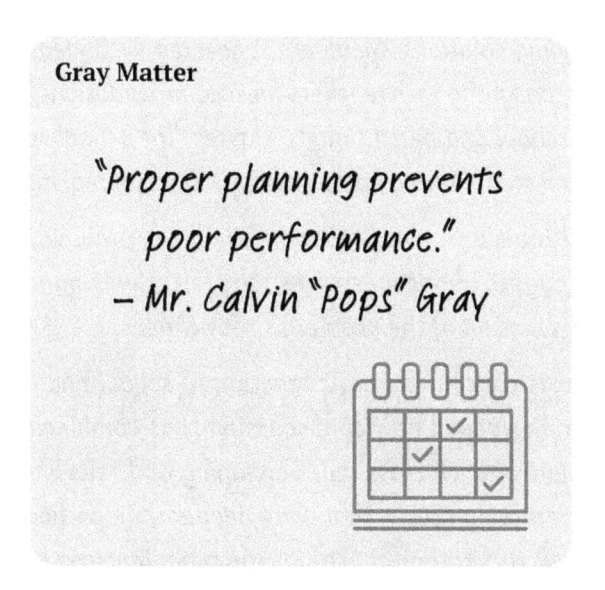

> **Gray Matter**
>
> *"Proper planning prevents poor performance."*
> *— Mr. Calvin "Pops" Gray*

This leadership from the hand was on full display as I observed a superstar middle school principal lead her administrative team in a very difficult conversation about attendance—or in this case, the lack thereof. Attendance had been part of school goals, but the work was clearly in need of a reset.

Tackling Tardies and Attendance

The pandemic had lingering effects on Dexter Valley Middle School, just as it has had on many schools. None were more devastating than the attendance of the students both to class and to school.

Principal Maxwell opened the meeting of her administrative team: "Please take a look at this and tell me what you see." She motioned toward the printout she had just distributed. As I looked at the report and at the team members, I noticed broadening eyes and looks of disbelief. The report showed that nearly all the 625 students enrolled at the school had 10 or more tardies to class and five or more absences from school.

I sat back in my chair, imagining what would happen next. I fully expected the team to point fingers and find excuses or perhaps blame one another or the teachers. What happened was a true testament to effective leadership. Everyone, including the principal, began to acknowledge the problem and their own part in the situation. They started recommending solutions. Members suggested such ideas as beefing up the PBIS program and consulting with teachers for recommendations about incentivizing students to be at school and be on time to classes. The school counselor offered to speak with individual students and host Saturday school for making up time and work.

Principal Maxwell looked in my direction, "Well, Dr. Gray, what do you think?" I offered other thoughts about incentives, but felt it was important to shift the conversation to discussion of the problem's root causes.

"What do we think is causing lethargic reaction to school and class attendance?" I asked. The question opened up rich discussion that combined ideas for making the opening moment of each class more engaging and relevant to students with thoughts about addressing causes that were deeper than perhaps just the draw to hang out with friends rather than get to class on time. Teachers brainstormed about next steps, including strategies, timelines, persons responsible, and follow-ups.

After the team gathered and synthesized the ideas that would form components of a plan, Principal Maxwell stepped in to help pull everything together. The team responded eagerly in the final steps to polish a solid plan to address the attendance issue. The principal delegated specific tasks, clarifying expectations for each and answering questions along the way:

- Ms. G., the assistant principal overseeing instruction, would ensure that teachers had an engaging plan for the first three minutes of class that included "do now" work and a clear process in place for students to follow as they arrived in the classroom.

- In her support of teachers, Ms. G. would see that each teacher post both learning intentions and success criteria on the classroom whiteboard or screen so that students could clearly see what was expected of them upon arrival to class.

- In addition, Ms. G. would monitor and support teachers as they stood at their doors during class change.

- Mr. R., the assistant principal overseeing student support, would begin the new initiative with a student assembly to explain the new processes.

Traits of Hand-Centered Leadership

- *Students who were chronically tardy or absent (or both) would meet Mr. R. for one-on-one meetings to discuss underlying causes of their tardies or absences.*
- *Mr. R. would then request a home visit from the student-support specialist to determine the amount of support needed from both home and school.*
- *In addition, Mr. R. would leverage his already established relationships with the students to encourage timely arrival to school and class by discussing serious consequences for continued late arrival in a way that allowed students to maintain their dignity. In other words, he laid down the law, remained firm but fair, and applied some tough love where necessary.*
- *The group would meet again in three weeks to share insights gained from talking to students, teachers, and the student-support specialist.*

As a result of the new measures, attendance began to slowly improve. The end of the school year was approaching, so Principal Maxwell built in some field trip incentives along with an end-of-the-year dance as a way to let all the students know she cared about them as well as about their timely arrival to school and class.

HAND LEADERSHIP TRAIT 7: THE HAND-CENTERED LEADER NOURISHES A COLLABORATIVE, INCLUSIVE ENVIRONMENT FOR LEARNING AND WORKING.

When leading from the hand, the effective middle school leader fosters and depends on people **acting** harmoniously together. The leader cultivates an environment where all members of the school community know that they are needed. This is not just about warm welcome speeches that the leader gives now and then. Such an environment is rooted in the leader's absolute belief that everyone has something to contribute and that all those contributions are critical to meeting the vision and goals for a successful middle school. The leader embraces a diverse and rich pool of ideas, perspectives, and talents. They actively lead the staff and others in the school community to take collective responsibility for student success, for performance on projects and initiatives, and for holding to high expectations for inclusion and respect.

The leader is aware of the many rewards of inclusive collaboration. They see and develop the following:

- Better ideas! More ideas! More creative ideas! Stronger outcomes! More desire to support outcomes that one has helped to produce!
- Expanded exposure to the experience, abilities, and perspectives of others
- A stronger, more cohesive force for action; higher productivity
- Joint commitment to putting strategies to work
- Getting things accomplished more agreeably and efficiently
- More frequently heard voice for all members, including students
- Space for everyone to contribute safely
- A closer community with buy-in and connection from students, staff, and families
- Increased ownership of the school and its beliefs, goals, and action plans
- A deeper sense of security and optimism about the school, vision, and action plan
- Joint accomplishments that lead to authentic connections
- Increased staff retention and job satisfaction; higher morale
- Heightened trust and participation of families
- Stronger communication and trust among staff members
- Increased meaningful learning; collaboration is a wonderful pedological strategy—for students and adults!
- A visible demonstration of who the leader is—as *one of us*—**acting along with** the students, family members, colleagues, other leaders, and members of the outer community
- Outcomes, decisions, and actions that are more effective, inclusive, fresh, and engaging
- An overall higher-spirited, more optimistic, and more comfortable culture

Traits of Hand-Centered Leadership

Under hand-centered leadership, collaboration is used as a powerful way to build up (affirm, teach, strengthen, empower) others. As a group collaborates, the leader sets a model of identifying specific contributions and abilities of others. This boosts the group's awareness of one another's skills. Others join and further the leader's example of noticing and affirming others' gifts and contributions. People become more confident and courageous. With a gain of respect and support from others, they try new things.

> **Gray Matter**
>
> *We are all empowered by the confidence and contributions of one another.*

Professional learning communities, such as instructional teams, are foundational as powerful models of collaboration at work. There are many other opportunities for small groups, departments, advisory groups, task forces, site councils, or other configurations of members to collaborate. Students, parents and caregivers, administrators, staff members, community leaders, and school board members can all lend ideas and hands in settings with one another to accomplish meaningful tasks. The hand-centered leader oversees design of a consistent protocol for collaboration that can be used across various groups and situations.

In Chapter 9, see **Hand Leadership Strategy 6: A Protocol for Collaboration** on page 255 for guide to planning for collaboration.

Hand Leadership Trait 8: The Hand-Centered Leader Operates from a "touch it but don't hold it" mindset.

When leading from the hand, the leader resists the urge to micromanage every project. Like the head coach of a football team, the leader gives team members the playbook, teaches them the rules and expectations, designs maneuvers and strategies, warns them about hazards, and enthusiastically sends them off to get the job done on the field. The coach is nearby to continue guiding and supporting but not to take over the job of any of the players.

Earlier in this book, I described successful delegation as a trait of one who leads from the head. I included it in that section because delegation begins with thinking—thinking about the best use of a leader's time and talents and about the most productive ways to get things done using the talents of many. Yes, delegation is a thinking skill. But it is also a skill of action.

When a leader has put their passion and energy into guiding a plan's development, there can be a strong pull to hold every project of the plan close to the chest. It is tempting to feel as if you, the leader, can do each action better than anyone else. However, once leadership is shared—following prepared protocols for delegation that include processes for selecting someone with the capabilities to lead a project—the effective leader should be able to confidently hand over responsibility.

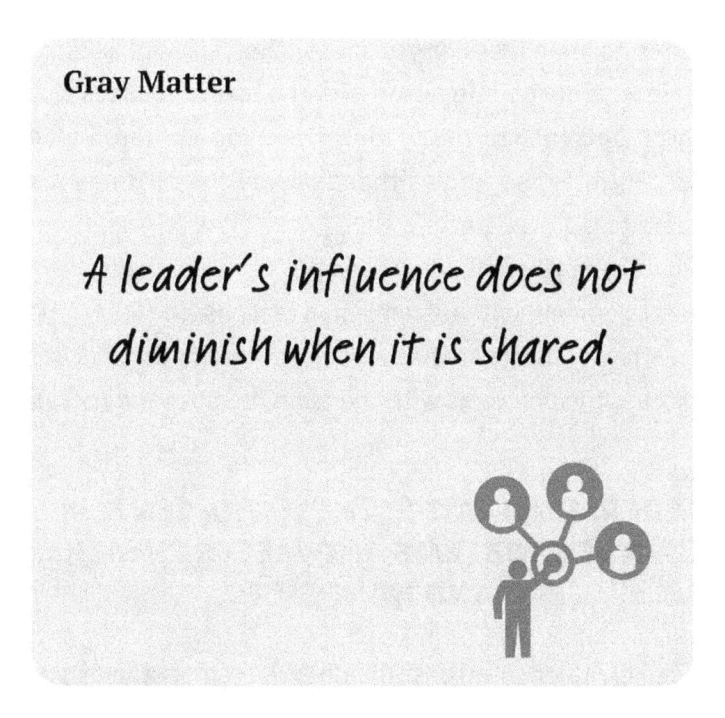

> **Gray Matter**
>
> *A leader's influence does not diminish when it is shared.*

I hold two hand-centric images when delegating to accomplish goals and fulfill visions. They have become my mantras for shared leadership.

1. **"Touch it but don't hold it."** The leader creates touchpoints for checking on and supporting the person to whom responsibility has been designated. The hand is extended when it is needed. But the leader does not operate as if it were their own responsibility.

2. **"Operate with hand over fist."** The gesture of hand over fist is a salute that opens some martial arts events. The right hand held in a fist represents the weapon, a symbol of strength. The left hand covers the fist, softening or suppressing it. This is a symbol of civility, morality, and wisdom. The symbols together signify strength while respecting the skills of the other person by restraining the strength. Covering one's fist also represents humility—showing that the person knows they are capable of making mistakes. In the context of school leadership, "hand over fist" means that the leader controls their own power out of respect for the other person's strengths and abilities.

If a leader tries to manage every project, they show a lack of confidence in others. Part of the wisdom of delegation is that a leader realizes that there are jobs that others can do better than the leader. The hand-centered leader truly wants the best results possible, and knows that the way to get those results is to trust capable co-leaders to do their parts well.

In the case where management of part of a project is not going well, the leader does not withdraw the assignment without very good reasons. The leader examines the situation closely to learn why things are not working according to plan. Before taking back a project, they discuss the problems with the team member and try to find solutions.

Hand Leadership Trait 9: The Hand-Centered Leader Anticipates Problems and Meets Them Head-on and Hands-on.

Any good plan is likely to encounter some unexpected obstacles and missteps. The effective middle school leader guides in full awareness that things don't always go as planned. The leader embraces these truths by:

1. **Preparing for possible disruptions or even failure of the plans.** They identify and anticipate snags and delays as parts of planning for any specific initiative. They collaborate with others to design strategies to have ready for the predictable obstacles.

2. **Paying attention to the first signs of a problem.** Think of the check engine light in your car—how sometimes you hope it will go away the next time you start the car, or be corrected by a simple oil change. Life experience has probably taught you that the longer you ignore the blinking light without investigating the reason, the more damage is done to the car. And the repair is way more costly than it might have been originally. So it is in the educational world. We might be tempted to overlook warnings, perhaps because we fear it might unearth our own mistakes or mistakes of the staff. But the wise school leader knows better than to ignore those small signs; they know that when disregarded, problems just get more serious.

3. **Acknowledging the problem and meeting it head-on and hands-on.** I use *head-on* in the sense that the leader doesn't shy away from getting to the root of an issue. And I use *hands-on* to mean that once the leader clarifies and understands the reason for the problem, they get busy collaborating with others to find the best remedy and to act on it.

4. **Encountering problems with these beliefs and responses:**

    - Transformative leaders don't get mired in frenzy or disappointment.
    - They don't let even major missteps get them off track from pressing toward the vision or goal, or from following the plan.
    - They are flexible enough to make adaptations in the plan when needed.
    - They remember that they are not alone; they know they have others alongside and that they'll climb over obstacles together.
    - They learn everything possible from the interruption or failure.
    - They let the situation unleash passion, innovative thinking, better action, and optimism—in themselves and others.

Disheartened, but Not Defeated

No leader, regardless of their experience, likes to get bad news. For school leaders, that is especially true when it comes to the results of student assessments. "What am I going to do?" I said out loud as my curriculum director announced that the district would be assigned a failing grade for performance on the state assessment. The news came in the midst of a day of touring five schools with our deputy of operations and chief of schools.

We had actually just been talking about where we thought we had landed in school accountability. Over the recent years, the state had changed standards, achievement tests, and the accountability rubric. We had installed numerous systems to address learning deficiencies, but it was not enough to outpace the constant revisions in the state's accountability system.

When I got the call with more complete information from our departments of research and evaluation, I had to sit down. "Check again, please," was all I could muster in response. The second check of the scores yielded the same result. We would not be celebrating an upgrade in state accountability status as we had hoped. The news was bad, and we were disheartened.

In the moment, disheartened felt like an understatement. However, it was just the wakeup call we needed. At first, I was heavyhearted and unsure how to move forward. After some thought and prayer, I remembered to do what I always do—look at the data again, mine it for nuggets, and dig some more.

Yes, we felt that the state had done us a disservice by frequently changing the accountability goalposts, but we knew we could not let that stop us. We dove back into the details and discovered several data points that exposed our fault lines. We were disheartened but not disillusioned and not defeated.

With further reflection, we recognized that we had no Plan B. We had mistakenly put all our energy and effort into one approach without even considering that it might fail. So we went back to work—all hands on deck. Further digging into the testing results led us to discover a gap between the curriculum department's training of teachers on standards implementation and the teachers' actual comfort with and capacity to unpack standards and teach them well. We hired some experts to retrain our curriculum team, who then retrained the teachers.

Leading from the hand, we were able to act to learn from our mistakes, find answers, and make repairs for a more successful outcome. With the improved practices inspired by our honest self-examination, the district realized gains at all grade levels with the most impressive increases at the elementary level.

HAND LEADERSHIP TRAIT 10: THE HAND-CENTERED LEADER USES DATA TO INFORM INSTRUCTION AND DECISIONS.

Successful hand-centered middle school leaders understand that data alone are only part of a greater story. They know that allowing data to solely drive our decisions can negate the fact that there is a story behind each data point. Students come to school under various conditions and situations. They may perform well during instruction but arrive to school on test day with a headache, under duress from an argument with their parent or friend, or even hungry and irritable from lack of proper nutrition. A data point may tell how well the student performed on an assessment but not why.

According to Susan B. Neuman, who is part of a research team at New York University studying how data-driven instruction is enacted in a group of schools serving low-income students, "our most vulnerable students are measured, examined, rubricked, labeled—and denied the meaningful instruction they need."[41]

Neuman argues that our students today are deluged with data. Some classrooms are literally data-centered. The students' classroom time is "driven" by bar graphs, spreadsheets, and color-coded charts. For many students, data-driven instruction is based on an assumption that when students see where they fall on the data chart, they'll be motivated to achieve more (which is proven not to be true). And the time spent on raising testing scores robs students of the kind of instruction they need—which is "content rich and focused on students' interests, goals, and achievements."[42] Neuman recommends a change in the way schools use data to this:

- Look at student work to inform data.
- Don't try to "motivate" students with data.
- Don't teach to items on the test.
- Be "data-informed," not "data-driven."
- Broaden the definition of data.[43]

Data can contribute a goldmine of information that can make school life better for students, raise achievement, increase students' beliefs in themselves as learners, and improve instruction. But it can't be just data that comes from standardized tests; it must be data from a wider variety of sources and of a wider variety of types.

When you lead from the hand, you encourage teachers to regularly gather information from observations, mini-lessons, daily assignments, group learning experiences, and many other classroom activities. You remind teachers to pay attention to what they can learn from the signals students continually give about their work processes, their accomplishments, their struggles, their gaps. Teachers and leaders can notice students' eagerness of participation (or lack thereof) and their body language. Such pieces of daily information are gems that let us know how students are learning, what they know, how they see themselves as learners, and what they need.

In summary, here's the difference between data-driven and data-informed instruction and decisions: In the first, data controls the decision making. Decisions are made on written evidence only—primarily standardized test scores when it comes to instruction. Data-informed decisions take the data off the golden pedestal. It recognizes the limits of what test scores tell. It considers data as one of many factors and kinds of information that contribute to making a good decision. **Instead of data driving instruction, the students' lives, needs, and work drive instruction.**

HAND LEADERSHIP TRAIT 11: THE HAND-CENTERED LEADER KEEPS STUDENTS AT THE CENTER OF ALL POLICIES AND PLANS.

Policy in Need of Revision

We had a serious dilemma: cell phones. Students continued to ignore the requirement to keep phones in their lockers. According to teachers and staff, cell phones were everywhere, and principals felt powerless to control them. Although a new policy was in place, it seemed unable to stem the tide.

The real issue was the lack of "teeth" in the policy. We needed a policy that would be widely accepted and enforceable, student friendly as well as teacher supported. We realized that, when used properly, cell phones could be a great resource in the classroom. Teachers could use software to quickly access student knowledge about a particular concept. They could also get feedback through web-based audience response platforms, which allows students to text responses to questions and display the results immediately. We also knew that students and their families feel a greater sense of safety when students can have cell phones on them at all times.

Still, the question that all the adults were asking was, "Is there a way to let the students keep the cell phones on campus and not be distracted by them?" I had an idea that was risky but, in the end, could reap great benefits. (It's an idea that probably should have been put to use when we first worked on the policy.) I took the question to our student school board.

A few weeks earlier, I had assembled the student school board representing schools in the district. They had been selected through an application process where they wrote essays explaining what they would do to support their school and represent youth voice. In monthly meetings, they discussed challenges that their respective student bodies presented to them. As representatives of fellow students, each student board member was laser-focused on resolving the various issues that were priorities in their school. Cell phones were high on each of their lists.

At the meeting, I presented them with the problem. I asked them to create a policy to address the problem. I provided each of them with a copy of the current policy and walked them through each section. We then reviewed what state code had to say about student property rights and appropriate consequences for violation of code. We also spent some time reviewing what other school districts had in place. The last part of the meeting was spent taking notes as the students discussed the pros and cons of ideas for a revised policy. After an hour of discussion, the students emerged with a solid first draft of the new cell phone policy. Although it would take a few more meetings to get to a final draft for the school board to review and ratify, I was very proud of the work done by this outstanding group of young adolescents. They were even prouder of themselves.

Later, as I reviewed the draft of the new policy with our district counsel, some themes emerged. I noticed more satisfying outcomes of this policy-drafting than the specifics of the policy. The process itself showed true leadership qualities from our student board.

- *During conversation and drafting of the policy, student board members began to sharpen their abilities to collaborate and discuss difficult issues.*
- *They deftly exercised the skills of balancing advocating for what they personally believed and inquiring more about the opinions of others.*

- *They each truly represented their constituents.*
- *In the throes of discussion, no one voice became more dominant than others. The student board seemed to value one another's opinions and reflect a genuine sense of respect and comradery for one another.*

According to AMLE's *The Successful Middle School: This We Believe,*

Successful middle grades educators and leaders intentionally examine the policies and practices that guide teaching and learning within their schools to ensure that all students' academic and personal needs are met. This goal is upheld when policies and practices are student-centered, anti-racist, academically rigorous, and responsive to the realities of students and their families' lives.[44]

This cell phone story deals with just one example of the many policies and practices school leaders must develop and oversee. As I reflected on the students' final work, I was impressed with the strength of their voice. That was a key step in developing a student-centered policy. The outcome was certainly responsive to the realities of their lives in that it satisfied their and their families' needs for them to have phones nearby and because it acknowledged learning occurs in today's world via the cell phone. The policy valued teachers' need to have the students' attention and instructional use of phones for academic value. The specifics of the rules and consequences were fair and written clearly to provide for equitable application. The students crafted a policy that worked because it was reasonable, fair, and had student support and engagement. It worked for students, teachers, and families.

> **Gray Matter**
>
> *With a little ingenuity, we can always find a way to gain student insights, reflections, and critical thinking for every part of the policy-creating process.*

In Chapter 9, see **Hand Leadership Strategy 7: Student-Centered Policy & Practice Check-Up** on page 258 for a checklist that will help leaders examine their policies and practices for focus on students' needs.

Also in Chapter 9, see **Hand Leadership Strategy 8: Say Your ABCs** on page 262 for a tool that can engage parents in monitoring their child's school success.

HAND LEADERSHIP TRAIT 12: THE HAND-CENTERED LEADER CHOOSES CURRICULA AND ACADEMIC SUPPORTS PURPOSEFULLY, STRATEGICALLY, AND COLLABORATIVELY.

Choices of curriculum and other academic supports for students are some of the key actions guided by a middle school leader. When leading from the hand, the successful leader takes an active role in developing collaborative processes with teachers, PLCs, other leaders, and parent-caregiver representatives to make these critical choices in line with the students' needs and with the school's vision and goals.

Middle school leaders sometimes frustrate vendors by saying "no"—because they have a greater "yes" inside. Purposeful, collaborative, and strategic selections mean the leader has worked with the others to determine criteria, goals, and outcomes expected from any product or service an educational vendor or consultant can offer. These connect directly to the previously determined vision and goals of the school's instructional plans.

Schools are bombarded with all kinds of flashy, attractive programs, digital options, and other materials. For the most part, these are presented as engaging and challenging for students and easy to use. Many schools and districts mistakenly ask the book company or software developer to advise them on the right product for their student academic achievement needs.

However, to see the results that students and their families deserve, the hand-centered leader uses the school's own well-crafted plans, carefully gathered data, and broad collaboration to lead the way when deciding what instructional supports to adapt. The leader has engaged appropriate personnel in a targeted review of materials. In addition to looking for materials that support the goals of their school's instructional plan, the leader ensures that materials they consider are culturally relevant, challenging, and developmentally appropriate for middle school students. The curriculum team or committee has reviewed materials for rigor, integration, alignment with standards, and inclusion of SEL skills. The "greater yes" leaders have inside is "yes" to the decisions that have already been made about what their students need.

Under leadership from the hand, the same collaborative process applied to purchases is used to make choices about other services and resources the school might use or establish. These academic supports may be in the classroom, in the school, after school or during the summer, or off the school campus. These are such supports as tutoring, extra classes, counseling, enrichment courses, summer learning experiences, or technology learning assistance.

Whatever the material or service, school boards can support purchases with confidence and an expectation of improvement. This is because they have seen that the curriculum team has chosen with strategic focus on the needs and development of their young adolescent learners.

For a practical overview of what curriculum in the successful middle school looks like, consult AMLE's *The Successful Middle School: This We Believe* (2021), pages 27–35.

HAND LEADERSHIP TRAIT 13: THE HAND-CENTERED LEADER PRIORITIZES AND CULTIVATES EXCELLENT INSTRUCTION.

The hand-centered middle school leader knows that instructional leadership is a joint role. It is a venture for "us" rather than one for "them" or "I" or "him" or "her." Instructional teams or PLCs are powerful partners in most of the actions of instructional leadership. Middle level students are also part of the "us"; they have capabilities to take strong roles and offer valuable input into designing, planning, performing, monitoring, and evaluating their learning activities.

The effective leaders involved with instruction are committed to and knowledgeable about young adolescents, equitable practices, and educational research. They assure that these students are at the center of all decisions about instructional practices. To offer the most effective instruction possible to students, leaders prioritize such actions as these:

- Hire educators who are specifically prepared to teach young adolescents and possess a depth of understanding in the content areas they teach.
- Collaboratively establish and implement common expectations of rigor and ensure that all staff understand how they apply to specific subject areas.
- Oversee the creation of collaboratively designed, standard ways for teachers and other staff to keep regular checks on each individual student to see that no one falls behind.
- Align instructional strategies to adolescents' needs and middle level standards.
- Assist teachers in gaining access to and learning the best practices and materials.
- Encourage teachers to keep a strong focus on student performance.

- Take on the teacher role; the leader who is no longer in a full teaching role stays close to instruction by taking opportunities to teach or guide learning activities.
- Promote use of instructional practices that are:
  - Varied in content, materials, and activities.
  - Active and interactive.
  - Collaborative.
  - Novel, unexpected.
  - Engaging and relevant for young adolescents.
  - Flexible enough to address different interests and passions of different students.
  - Rich in meaningful content, apply to themes, ideas, and questions that matter.
  - Develop higher order thinking skills and metacognition.
  - Purposeful; students understand why they are doing tasks or learning about something.
  - Connected to real-life problems or topics.
  - Clear; students understand the expectations of learning activities.
  - Designed to promote student choice and develop autonomy.
  - Structured to include feedback and student self-reflection.
- Available to help teachers
  - Use multiple measures to assess student progress, including checks for understanding and performance tasks.
  - Monitor data to ensure that every student has access to supports within and beyond the school.
  - Ensure that assessments are aligned to the standards and instructional strategies.
  - Apply visible learning principles; teachers pay attention to how students "see" and understand the task, how they do it, and what they believe about what they can do and about how well they can do it.[45]
- Support teachers heartily, giving extra attention where needed. Leaders watch and listen, taking time to mentor, give helpful feedback, notice areas to affirm and encourage.

- Assure plenty of time and advocacy for teacher collaboration, vigorously supporting teams and other PLCs as structures that engender excellent instruction.
- Support and boost teacher competence and confidence. "Collective Teacher Efficacy is the collective belief of teachers in their ability to positively affect students."[46] According to John Hattie's research on influences related to student achievement, this particular influence lands at the top of the list of positive correlation with student achievement.[47]

In Chapter 9, see **Hand Leadership Strategy 9: Leaders Trading Places** on page 263 for a way to get leaders sharpening their classroom instruction skills, and **Hand Leadership Strategy 10: Learning About Learning Walks** on page 264 for a way to use a leader's informal, nonevaluative classroom observations for instructional improvement.

HAND LEADERSHIP TRAIT 14: THE HAND-CENTERED LEADER DEVELOPS AND NURTURES PROFESSIONAL LEARNING COMMUNITIES.

The inclusion of professional learning communities (PLCs) within a school is a key component of a successful middle school. A PLC, such as an interdisciplinary team, is a group of educators that meets regularly to work together for two major purposes:

1. To raise students' academic skills and achievement and foster all the factors that nourish students' well-being.
2. To learn and grow professionally, to improve their own professional knowledge and teaching skills in order to better teach the students.

One basic understanding about PLCs is that teachers working together, rather than in isolation, is the absolute best way to ensure that students learn and have all the support they need to thrive. When leading from the hand, the middle school leader knows that one of their most important actions is to guide the creation and sustaining of a network of PLCs that encompass all the students and teachers across the school. These structures are prime examples of collaborative thinking, planning, and action. The different strengths, personalities, and teaching styles of the group members combine to form a rich mixture of perspectives and abilities to bring about the best results for young adolescent students.

PLCs have different configurations in different schools. In general, a PLC is made up of teachers across different subject areas or different departments, or across one grade level or more than one grade level. Sometimes leaders and other staff members play parts as members of the group. In many middle schools, PLCs are interdisciplinary teams at one grade level.

The PLC structure and processes:

- Promote deep relationships among teachers, between teachers and students, and among peers—contributing to improved learning for students and work settings for teachers.

- Set and follow common goals and expectations across the team or community for learning, for instructional supports, and for assessing learning.

- Set and follow common protocols and expectations for classroom operations, behavior, and discipline.

PLC members meet and collaboratively work to:

- Set a vision and goals for their group.
- Discuss and improve student work, progress, and factors affecting their work.
- Stay aware of how each student is faring academically, socially, and emotionally.
- Share responsibility for students' success and struggles.
- Focus on what they see with students; intervene before problems become bigger.
- Pay attention to and gain information from in-class data.
- Discuss and correlate curriculum, instruction, lesson plans, assessments, and activities.
- Plan schedules for learning activities, assessments, homework, and group events.

- Prioritize identifying students' needs and adjusting teaching, content, or processes to meet them.
- Engage in professional development together to offer the best instructional practices, try new strategies, and hone instructional skills.
- Continuously learn—reflecting, re-evaluating, and improving.
- Give honest and important feedback to one another.
- Work together—hard, and hold each other accountable for results in student well-being and achievement.

The hand-centered leader's role is to see that such a PLC process is underway, then to vigorously act to sustain it, establishing the best conditions for it to flourish. Some critical actions of this role for you as the leader are:

1. Understand that the PLC process must begin with training in the purposes and practices of effective PLCs. Become knowledgeable about PLC processes and practices.
2. Provide ongoing time and opportunities for PLCs to grow together professionally, including ongoing training in the effective processes of PLCs (for teachers and leaders).
3. Absolutely, positively, see that adequate time is scheduled for PLCs to meet and plan together. The whole concept will fail without sufficient and well-used meeting time.
4. Fight for adequate funding to support PLCs. Don't let your guard down on this.
5. Be fully committed to the need for and benefits of PLCs. The successful middle school leaders are the head cheerleaders for PLCs.

For assistance in building and sustaining high-performing PLCs, see AMLE's comprehensive guide to the elements of effective teaming, *Successful Middle School Teaming* (Berckemeyer, 2022).

> **HAND LEADERSHIP TRAIT 15: THE HAND-CENTERED LEADER COMMITS TO RELEVANT, LONG-TERM, AND JOB-EMBEDDED PROFESSIONAL DEVELOPMENT.**

Few actions a leader takes are more critical for the sustained level of excellence in their middle school than that of creating and sustaining excellent professional development processes. Effective leadership from the hand sets a high value on quality learning opportunities and continuous growth for the staff. Effective leaders want to do all they can to enable their educators to get better at accomplishing the many actions of their jobs. They recognize the powerful impact this makes on the students' personal and academic development.

Though one-time conferences, speakers, or webinars are a helpful part of the professional development picture, hand-centered leaders prioritize long-term teaching, coaching, and support over single events. The best training and polishing of skills take long stretches of time, broad learning experiences, practice, feedback, reflection, and more practice. The best learning also takes place primarily in the professional's job setting.

Professional Development Plans and Calendar

The hand-centered leader, passionate about purposeful PD, works collaboratively with teachers, other staff members, and other leaders to:

- Identify areas of needs for adult learners' growth and develop a list of targeted initiatives or topics for development. These choices are purposeful, and should be aligned to already established school improvement goals or PLC goals.
- Design a cohesive PD plan and calendar for the year to focus on the matters of greatest importance.
- Set clear expectations for implementation of presented practices and strategies and monitor their implementation and use.
- Provide room in an overall PD plan for personalized activities to allow for individual differences and needs. Also allow room in the plan for professional

development activities that teams or other PLCs designate as critical for their group.
- Consider a variety of settings and situations through which adults can learn, and people who can help them grow, such as teams teaching one another, individual coaching, an outside consultant working in the school with repeated seminars, on-site workshops using on-staff teachers, off-campus workshops, visits to other classrooms or other schools, university courses, or coaching from leaders or other colleagues.
- Identify classrooms within the school or in other schools in the district that demonstrate strong instruction and results; encourage teachers to visit these classrooms.
- Develop a year-long calendar of professional learning for the instructional leadership team members to build consistency in their assessment of teacher practice and ability to provide immediate feedback.
- Assure that professional development focuses on implementing high-impact instructional strategies designed to create meaningful learning experiences.
- Include time for teachers to engage in processes to increase their expertise in their content areas.
- Assure that professional growth activities:
  - Are varied and engaging.
  - Allow for collaboration—sharing of good ideas as well as challenges and solving problems together.
  - Are purposeful and relevant to the staff members' needs.
  - Offer opportunities to practice strategies.
  - Include feedback.
  - Include time for reflection.

The hand-centered leader knows that leaders need sustained professional development too. They directly engage in PD sessions, sometimes as a leader or facilitator. Whether or not they lead the session, this leader is still an active participant in all facets of the learning.

Hand-centered leaders also plan for continuous PD targeted specifically on leadership skills. Be sure to include the topic of improving leadership from the hand as a topic for learning. Any of the traits in this chapter or the fruits of hand-centered leadership in Chapter 7 can be topics for growth in leading from the hand. Successful middle school leaders establish a regular (at least weekly) habit of reflecting on their own leadership as part of their continuous learning.

Professional Development through Teacher Observation, Support, and Evaluation

For teachers, and other staff, the processes that are set for observation and job evaluation also serve as professional development. That's the point of your staff evaluation protocols! Successful middle school leaders follow a system of frequent contact, communication, and feedback with staff members. Sometimes they observe classrooms to focus on learning in action—strictly observing, not evaluating, what's happening for the students. They offer coaching where needed. They plan collaborative sessions where they can join with the staff member to reflect, celebrate strengths, and discuss areas for more learning. They join teachers in co-teaching to help strengthen specific strategies. (They can do the same "job-sharing" sessions with other staff members.)

In Chapter 9, see the following strategies that enhance professional development and school improvement:

Hand Leadership Strategy 9: Leaders Trading Places on page 263 for a way leaders can learn and practice skills by stepping into different instructional roles.

Hand Leadership Strategy 10: Learning About Learning Walks on page 264 for a way to use a learning walks process as a professional development tool.

Hand Leadership Strategy 11: Self-Check on Middle School Characteristics on page 267 to collaboratively assess implementation of the characteristics of a successful middle school.

Hand Leadership Strategy 12: Journaling: Leading from the Hand on page 270 for a guide to journaling your reflections on this hand aspect of your leadership.

Hand Leadership Trait 16: The Hand-Centered Leader Acts to Properly Resource the School or District.

I've defined leadership from the hand as leadership of action. When we think of actions, we think of the visible contacts with students and staff and other members of the school community. We think of school improvement plans taking hold. We think of a leader out there working hard on what matters to the school. One critical set of actions by school leaders may not be as exciting to watch as these. But it is a critical pillar for all the others. The hand-centered school leader realizes that the school or district is a learning organization and takes actions to properly resource it. Just as there is an art and science to teaching, there is a business side and an academic side to school.

The business side of school includes such actions as hiring personnel, staffing school offices, providing supplies to teachers and students, operating buses and district vehicles, funding specific programs, stocking school pantries and refrigerators, and even retaining attorneys to help craft policy. The school principal or superintendent may not be the person in charge of the overall financial picture; most districts have financial managers for that. But school leaders strategically shape their individual school budgets to support all operations of the school. From Title I budgets to fundraisers for the library, the school leader is focused on properly resourcing the school. Superintendents strategically shape district budgets. In many cases, curriculum directors, athletic directors, music department heads, and others in such positions also act to form and promote their respective budgets.

In each case, the process consists of a series of actions. Yes, the leader brings good, thoughtful head leadership to the picture; the leader approaches the budgeting tasks with heart open to the hearts and needs of other members of the school community. But, in the end, they must **act** to make the numbers work, to make recommendations, and to advocate for adequate funding for the initiatives and plans that matter. They do this after carefully gaining information and insights from parties affected by the programs or departments.

This is not the most glamorous of actions in the leader's slate of responsibilities. But with courage, an open mind and heart, and open eyes and ears, they can comfortably join hands in collaboration with others to get this action done.

Hand Leadership Trait 17: The Hand-Centered Leader Follows through with Courage and Commitment.

As I said earlier in this part of the book, leadership from the hand is likely the most visible aspect of school leadership. I described this leader as "the chief model of cooperative action." The number and variety of actions are countless. A foundation of successful middle school leadership is unwavering commitment to their work. This, too, is visible. Others see this in action, but they also hear the leader voice their dedication. This effective leader is committed to:

- The young adolescent students.
- All the people who participate in the life of the school and district.
- Their leader role and all the responsibilities that accompany it.
- Forwarding the school's vision, beliefs, and goals.
- Giving their best, doing whatever it takes.
- Showing up, being present, being available.
- Taking risks when necessary for the good of the students, school, or district.
- Leading change and innovation while assuring stability and honoring tradition.
- Always explaining reasons and intent.
- Championing and furthering diversity.
- The school's visions and plans.
- Excellent teaching.
- Empowering others.
- Engagement.
- Continual collaboration.
- Clear communication.
- Patience and persistence.
- Keeping forward momentum on initiatives and plans.

Traits of Hand-Centered Leadership

- Enjoying the surprises, victories, and challenges of working with young adolescents and the families and staff members who love and support them.

The effective hand-centered leader sees things through—their job, their promises, the school's plans and projects. They celebrate successes with colleagues; they hold hands and courageously move forward in rough times. Despite challenges, failures, or lack of support, they stick around and keep leading with optimism and energy.

When members of your school community—in particular your staff, students, and their families—watch your courage and commitment, they feel more secure and loyal. They see you as reliable and trustworthy. They believe that things will get done without wasting time and resources, that you'll stay on the path that has been set by the vision, and that you'll keep your word.

An Unusual School-Improvement Strategy

"It's a party!" was the response to the confused expression on my face as I entered the principal's office. Moments before, when I drove into the school parking lot, I noticed a local food truck and a delivery truck dropping off one of those bounce houses often seen at kids' birthday parties. The smell and sounds of popcorn popping and whiffs of barbequing hotdogs greeted me as I entered the school's front door. I had seen some academic data from the previous year and knew that leadership would be an uphill battle for any principal, so when I arrived at the school, what I least expected to see was the makings of a festival fit for champions. I had to find out what was happening.

Dr. Vonda Beaty had just assumed the leadership of a very troubled middle school. The data was poor, the community was in decline, and the culture of the school building was toxic. As the new principal, she had every reason to believe the task at hand was unattainable. Her newly acquired school was anything but new. The building was in disrepair, the air conditioning unit constantly broke down, and the grounds were in desperate need of attention. Yet, despite all the problems, Dr. Beaty decided to throw a party.

I joined her in her office; it was just two weeks before the opening of school. Even I, the eternal optimist, had to ask her why she was throwing a party. She said, very simply and matter-of-factly, "Our scholars and teachers need a lift, not a lecture." Dr. Beaty decided that the best approach to improvement was to celebrate small successes and acknowledge the hard work of her sixth graders who, alone, showed improvement over the past year.

Her immediate supervisor encouraged a more "compliance-centered" approach to improvement, requiring teachers to submit improvement plans and students to attend mandatory tutoring. Yet Dr. Beaty was determined to approach this situation as she had at the other schools she'd led. Her approach: First, show the people she leads that she cares about the whole person and is willing to celebrate small victories. Then, allow that support to grow into overall improvement. Her bets paid off. Two years later, her school was designated as a level 5 school—the highest academic achievement distinction available based on state test scores.

Chapter 9

Hand-Centered Leadership Strategies

Follow up your understanding of the kinds of traits that characterize those who lead from the hand (Chapter 8) by putting them to work. Strategies such as those in this chapter are designed to motivate leaders and challenge them to continue growth in hand-centered leadership with practical processes they can put into action right away. I'm confident these strategies will also ignite ideas that lead you and your staff to create other practical approaches to hand leadership.

Overview of Hand-Centered Leadership Strategies

Strategy #	Strategy	Referenced in Hand Leadership Trait #
Hand Strategy 1	Wild and Wacky Actions	1
Hand Strategy 2	Job Check-In	1
Hand Strategy 3	Focus on WIGs	4
Hand Strategy 4	A Balanced Scorecard Plan	4
Hand Strategy 5	Planning for Project Management	5
Hand Strategy 6	A Protocol for Collaboration	7
Hand Strategy 7	Student-Centered Policy & Practice Check-Up	11
Hand Strategy 8	Say Your ABCs	11
Hand Strategy 9	Leaders Trading Places	13, 15
Hand Strategy 10	Learning About Learning Walks	13, 15
Hand Strategy 11	Self-Check on Middle School Characteristics	15
Hand Strategy 12	Journaling: Leading from the Hand	15

HAND LEADERSHIP STRATEGY 1: WILD AND WACKY ACTIONS

Purpose: Leaders devise unexpected actions to rally staff, students, and other stakeholders around a vision, project, plan, or initiative.

Many of a leader's actions have to do with designing and guiding plans of various sizes. Every new or repeated venture will succeed best—from the earliest brainstorming collaborations to the implementation—when all those affected by it are inspired to get on board. Sometimes, to do that, a teacher, principal, superintendent, or other leader just needs to fire up the troops with unexpected actions.

Wild About WIGs

When I first learned about WIGs (wildly important goals) and the phenomenal results organizations were realizing from the breakthrough changes in goal achievement described in The 4 Disciplines of Execution,[49] *I was sure it was right for our district. I just needed to ignite the flames in the stakeholders affected by my leadership. I knew that it might seem like a stretch to introduce this business practice into an educational setting. So I tapped into my inner middle school teacher, donned a wig, and led my colleagues into the world of wildly important goals.*

The results were far beyond what I anticipated. Other colleagues donned wigs. Passion and commitment spread like wildfire throughout the schools' staffs, students, and families. Hallway billboards featured the goals and revived our focus on raising student achievement. Morale went through the roof, and many schools in the district made great advances in their accountability ratings within the next year.

If you want to drum up excitement about important goals, the wig strategy can spread beyond one school leader. Get everyone wearing or making wigs. Pass them out when you present the idea. Or provide an assortment of recycled materials for folks to make their own. Enlist students to make wigs for their teachers and other staff members—and for themselves. Pretty soon everyone in the school will be wearing profoundly creative wigs and chanting the wildly important goals! You can take to the streets in a parade or pace the school's front yard with signs and wigs. It's a great way to advertise the goals of the school or district to the entire community.

The "wild-and-wacky-actions" strategy is certainly not limited to wigs and goals. It has dozens of applications to generate enthusiasm and participation for all sorts of plans or programs. As the leader, take the leap (or plunge). Remember: Leadership from the hand means that the leader does whatever it takes! And who is more suited to outrageous antics than middle school leaders (joined by the students and the staff)? So inspire and enlist others in important ventures with such actions as these:

- Show up in full theatrical makeup.
- Wear an outlandish costume.
- Dress up like a drum major, borrow the middle- or high-school marching band, invite the staff to the playing field, and lead the band in a rousing version of the school song. *(I have done this. It was far better than any back-to-school motivational speech!)*
- Ride down the halls on a unicycle.
- Skydive into halftime at a soccer or football game (why not?) and make an announcement about a fabulous new initiative.
- Set up one of those dunking pools. Stakeholders who commit to support the project get to toss a ball to try to "dunk the leader!"
- And . . . you devise others.
- Get into the habit of thinking outside the box to inspire! Enlist students to help brainstorm! Recruit staff members, parents or caregivers, or community members in actions to bring attention to the good cause.

Later in this chapter, see **Hand Leadership Strategy 3: Focus on WIGs** to guide your group in writing and pursuing wildly important goals.

Hand Leadership Strategy 2: Job Check-In

Purpose: Leaders purposefully learn about the work that is entailed in the various jobs of staff members and volunteers.

An effective hand-centered, collaborative leader understands the skills and responsibilities that are assigned to those who work in the school. Knowing what is required of others in their jobs is essential if the leader is to effectively collaborate and delegate. As a leader, you could go through files and read all those job descriptions that are part of the hiring process. But better yet, you can actively watch and join workers to learn about their jobs.

This strategy offers an organized way to check up on what you know about what others do, and to expand your knowledge even further. You can use the template on the next page, **Who Does What in the School?**, or design one suitable for your specific situation. Here's the way it works:

Step 1 Identify the job categories throughout the school. Don't forget all the varieties of faculty jobs, plus support staff, other leaders, and volunteers. Make more copies of the following template, if needed, to list all categories.

Step 2 Make initial notes about what you think are some key job skills or responsibilities in each category.

Step 3 Pay visits to workers in the categories. Ask questions. Watch what they do. Join them for a while. Note the persons you engage and the dates.

Step 4 Add your new knowledge to your notes. Reflect on how this connects to what you thought you knew about the jobs.

Step 5 Repeat these steps a few times each year.

Hand-Centered Leadership Strategies

Who Does What in the School?

Identify jobs in your school and note your knowledge of each one.

Job Category	Notes About the Job	Visits, Dates

HAND LEADERSHIP STRATEGY 3: FOCUS ON WIGS

Purpose: Leaders take steps to identify the most important goals of a plan along with measurable strategies to fulfill the goal.

A WIG is a wildly important goal. The concept is described in *The 4 Disciplines of Execution: Achieving Your Wildly Important Goals*. This book, the result of years of research and trial-and-error practice with hundreds of companies, offers organizations a remarkable way to move forward and complete goals. As they caution early in the book, the disciplines (rules) in this process may seem simple, but "they are not simplistic."[50] The idea is applicable to goal execution for plans and projects of all sizes.

This strategy is a starting point for thinking about WIGs, and doing some general planning for their successful execution. I have found this concept, beginning with WIGs, to be a strong foundation for accomplishing any set of goals we might choose. It can be the first component of a balanced scorecard system. This strategy is an introduction to the first two disciplines, offering a way to practice writing a WIG plus identifying some measurable strategies that can help you accomplish the goal. (For complete execution of WIGs, you'll also need two other disciplines: "keep a compelling scorecard" of ongoing progress and "create a cadence of accountability."[51] Consult the book mentioned above for the full picture.)

Discipline 1: Focus on the Wildly Important.

Identify fewer goals than you might be inclined to follow, bringing sharp focus onto those that are critical. Remember that your goals derive from the baseline data you've collected that informs where you are now and what the needs are for future work.

Discipline 2: Act on the Lead Measures.

When I described the balanced scorecard approach in Chapter 8, I emphasized the importance of identifying strategies that can be measured.

Lead measures are those that have high possibility of achieving a goal and those that can realistically be influenced by your staff. They are indicators that are more in your control on a daily basis.[52] These are such things as formative assessments, weekly or quarterly grades in specific courses, or class attendance and participation.

Lag measures are more final goals, such as graduation rates or district results on yearly state assessments. We can't measure these on an ongoing schedule. We have to wait until later in the year to get these results. But success with *lead measures* influences the *lag measures*.[53]

Use the following template, **WIG Overview**, or a similar guide to practice identifying a WIG, considering strategies for accomplishing it, and defining measures for the strategies.

WIG Overview

One Wildly Important Goal

Strategy

Strategy

Strategy

Some Lead Measures

Some Lead Measures

Some Lead Measures

Some Lag Measures

Some Lag Measures

Some Lag Measures

HAND LEADERSHIP STRATEGY 4: A BALANCED SCORECARD PLAN

Purpose: Leaders practice outlining a balanced plan for any initiative.

As I described in **Hand Leadership Trait 4** (in Chapter 8), a balanced scorecard system is a management approach for successful implementation of strategies. It balances these components:

- Goals written with measurable strategies
- Actions to implement strategies
- Measuring and monitoring of progress
- Achievement of stated outcomes

In many cases, a balanced scorecard plan encompasses the whole of strategic planning for an organization (in education—a district or school). So creating such a plan is a major undertaking. This strategy offers a snapshot of steps for outlining a balanced scorecard process. For Steps 1–3 below, review the previous strategy in this chapter (Strategy 3: Focus on WIGs).

Step 1 Set major goals. Focus on the wildly important. Remember from the previous parts of this book that your big goals are part of the vision, the dream—where you want to be in the future. Remember also that these goals are responsive to the realities of where you are now.

Step 2 Identify strategies that can lead to goal achievement. These are specific outcomes that can be measured.

Step 3 For each strategy, identify the ways these can be measured. Identify *lag* measures and *lead* measures. Your measurements will use your starting baseline data as the comparison point for benchmarks that are part of the forward plan.

Step 4 Assign specific projects to act on strategies or groups of strategies. (See Strategy 5: Planning for Project Management in this chapter.)

Step 5 Set a timeline for measuring and monitoring progress at various benchmarks and final outcomes for the WIGs.

HAND LEADERSHIP STRATEGY 5: PLANNING FOR PROJECT MANAGEMENT

Purpose: Leaders oversee creation of visual maps as part of planning to manage projects that will meet one or more chosen goals of the overall strategic plan.

The only way to accomplish everything in a major plan is to break the actions into manageable projects. Each project, then, needs its own planning and management process. A **project map** is a visual representation of the process that will be used for completing a project. It shows such components as tasks, milestones, expectations, stages or sequence, and schedules. It organizes and prioritizes tasks, and pictures the relationships between the parts of the process. There are many formats, such as a chart, diagram, or path—with other visual elements such as color coding.

The beauty of a project map is that everyone can see and understand the big picture of the plan and envision how their actions fit in. All people involved know the path, the goals, and who is responsible for what. The map also promotes good communication, transparency, and efficient monitoring of progress.

A project map may be complex. Its level of complexity depends on how broad the goal is and how many moving parts it has. Multiple companies offer software for project mapping and management, with accompanying tools for tracking and analyzing data. Some allow for tailoring a system to your school or specific project. Or you can create your own map template, customized for your needs. I've worked with districts where we designed our own. See the **Project Map Checklist** on the following page for components we regularly included on our maps. This can help you with your own map design process.

Mapping advice:

- Keep the visual clear; use concise labels.
- Place names or responsible parties and deadlines close to the tasks on the visual.

- Allow for flexibility. You can't know everything that will happen, but you can plan for the unexpected. When time, personnel, or budget restraints pop up, keep focused on the top priorities.
- Stay on top of progress. I scheduled regular meetings with key partners to receive status updates on high priority parts of the project. This helped create a rhythm of results and accountability. We reviewed action items and addressed any obstacles to progress. If there is a part of the project that is dependent upon a decision being made, the group should not need to wait on an answer. Be sure to have the right people in the room.
- When the project is complete, collaboratively evaluate your mapping structure and project management process so that you can fine-tune it for future projects.

Project Map Checklist

Include these components on your project map.

	The strategic plan goal—WIG that the project supports
	Project goal
	Project objectives—These are desired outcomes.
	Brief project description
	Leadership organization—If the project has a management leadership team, show a chart or table of those roles, role descriptions, and names.
	All tasks to be done to meet objectives. Show in a logical order. • Expectations from each task • Persons assigned to the task • Timeline, deadlines for the task • Resources needed for the task (human, physical items, space, financial)
	Milestones—Identify milestones that will be evaluated (with dates)—this might be done with color coding.
	Project dependencies—Visually link tasks and activities that depend on another task being underway or completed.
	Project risks and constraints—Risks are unexpected events, positive or negative. Constraints are things such as time, money, and other resources.
	Project assumptions—Briefly identify what you assume about the budget, other resources, staff abilities, timeline, and tasks.
	Monitoring—Include a maintained visual status update report on work
	Wrap-Up—Include notations about how work will be evaluated or reviewed.

HAND LEADERSHIP STRATEGY 6: A PROTOCOL FOR COLLABORATION

Purpose: The leader oversees design of a common set of actions that can be used to guide collaborative tasks.

In a successful middle school, collaboration is a habit. It becomes a natural way that decisions are made. Departments, leadership teams, and PLCs follow regular and ongoing patterns of collaboration. Beyond that, sometimes collaborative groups are formed for specific tasks—short term or long term. These might be such groups as a task force, advisory board, or site council. There can be a variety of purposes for collaborative groups, such as to: create or evaluate a policy, solve a particular problem, gather information to inform leaders about a topic, design and implement surveys, or advise school officials of student needs or concerns. When people are brought together for a particular purpose, a standard protocol for collaboration serves as a helpful guide.

As a leader defining and describing a collaborative task, remember to:

- Always give a task that is meaningful, that matters.
- Keep students at the center of the purpose for any collaborative venture.

Here are some necessary steps and components for such a process. You might create a template that can be used for planning any collaborative group task or experience. See the sample **Collaboration Guide** at the end of this strategy.

Task and Purpose: Write a clear statement of what is to be accomplished and why.

Expectations: Explain the outcomes that are expected. Be clear about how the group will know when they have completed the task successfully.

Details: Describe the sub-tasks of the task, as well as how and where the group will work. This helps to set milestones for the progress.

Resources: Provide information about what people, materials, and funds are available. Include such tools as decision-making or problem-solving models.

People: Identify and invite appropriate persons for the task.

Roles: Outline roles needed for accomplishing the task or set of tasks, identifying goals or responsibilities for each role.

Processes for Working: Prepare guidelines for how the group can work well together with suggestions for communication, active listening, respect, equal participation, inclusion of all viewpoints, time management, etc. Let group members know how and where (and from whom) to get help when they need it. You might create a separate pamphlet or guide sheet on this topic to provide to all group members. Model these skills yourself as you work with a group.

Timeline: Define expectations for schedules and completion of each sub-task as well as the whole task.

Accountability: Clarify how the group will keep records and report progress and accomplishments, and identify persons to whom they will report. Emphasize that part of collaboration is shared group responsibility for accomplishing goals as well as individual accountability for particular roles.

Reflection and Feedback: Specify processes and provide questions for reviewing, reflecting, and giving feedback on the group processes and success.

Getting started:

Gather the group together. Explain the task, sharing some sort of a written guide. Arrange for the group to start their work by getting to know a little bit about each other. Members can share their own goals, purposes, and aspirations for the process. Encourage them to ask questions of you and one another so that they can go away with a clear picture of the important matter they'll address and who it is that will join them in the task.

Collaboration Guide

Supervising Leader:	
Task Description	
Purpose	
Expected Outcomes	

Sub-Tasks	Due Date

Group Members	Roles

Reporting Process	Reflection and Feedback Process

HAND LEADERSHIP STRATEGY 7: STUDENT-CENTERED POLICY & PRACTICE CHECK-UP

Purpose: Leaders work collaboratively with staff to develop a checklist to guide them in determining if **policies and practices are student-centered, unbiased, and fairly implemented**.

The bolded words above form one of the 18 Characteristics of Successful Middle Schools described in AMLE's *The Successful Middle School: This We Believe*. The section of the book that explains this characteristic goes on to say that "successful middle grades educators and leaders **intentionally examine** the policies and practices" to see that this is the case.[54]

It's easy to claim that "policies and practices are student-centered, unbiased, and fairly implemented." But just what does this mean? And how do we know for sure if ours—newly created or well-established—meet these criteria? Well, successful hand-centered leaders see that the phrase is adequately defined and that the policies and practices are carefully checked against those definitions. Here's one suggestion for setting up a process for the examinations. Be sure to include students in this process.

1. Gather a collaborative group, representative of stakeholders affected by or involved with policies and practices, to form a list of criteria or questions for deciding: "Is this true of our policies and practices?" The group might draft one or both of these:
   - Some overall questions that can be applied broadly to the school's systems or kinds of activities and experiences offered to students
   - Questions or criteria that can be applied to individual policies or practices

   Group members may solicit input from a wider number of people as they do their work.

   As an outcome, the group could form a document that includes a rating system to show the level of development or compliance with the criteria (such as a numerical system or a "yes," "no," or "somewhat" scale).

2. Form other groups as needed to do the review(s). These groups use the criteria to conduct a close examination of existing policies and practices. Since schools have dozens, different groups may work with different categories of policies or practices over a period of time.

3. Be ready for some astonishing and stimulating discussions in both processes (1 and 2)!

4. Identify policies or practices that need rethinking or revision based on the results of the examination.

See the next page, **Questions for Policy & Practice Review,** for some ideas to spark your own work.

Questions for Policy & Practice Review

Use these to inspire ideas for your own examination of policies and practices.

In general, ask: Does our school do this? or Do we have this? or Does this happen?

	Systems to gather student input and build opportunities for student voice?
	A student council, student school board, or student peer review board where school policies and practices are either vetted or created, or both?
	Multiple opportunities for multiple students to be involved in decision making?
	A model of instruction in which students are collaborative co-planners in what they learn, how they learn it, how they show what they learn, and how it is evaluated?
	Students have access to and teaching about school policies?
	Social-emotional learning is a tenet of curriculum and instruction?
	Track data to examine disparities in students' school connectedness and in discipline practices, including expulsions and suspensions?
	In-school and after-school organizations and clubs with enough variety and inclusivity to engage students of all different interests, skills, cultures, identities?
	Ethnic studies integrated in the curriculum?
	Restorative justice approaches to discipline?
	Food programs adequate for food-insecure families?
	Purposeful understanding of and involvement with the wider community?
	Intentional staff recruitment (including leaders) to model diversity and appropriately represent the makeup of the community and student body?
	A wide diversity of voices among the staff?
	Policies that assure all students of all ethnicities, identities, and socioeconomic status are welcomed and safe?

Questions for Policy & Practice Review
(continued)

Examining a specific policy or practice, ask: Is this or does this . . . ?

	Clear about its purpose?
	Anti-racist?
	Academically rigorous?
	Culturally responsive?
	Identity neutral?
	Responsive to realities of students' lives?
	Responsive to realities of student's families' lives?
	Create unequal burdens for some students or families?
	Attentive to the whole person?
	Without bias toward any individuals or groups?
	Applied with equity to all students, family members, staff members?

HAND LEADERSHIP STRATEGY 8: SAY YOUR ABCS

Purpose: Leaders offer students' families a way to monitor their children's path toward school success.

Early warning systems help educators determine interventions to reduce such risks as dropping out of school. Research has identified the **"ABCs"—attendance**, **behavior**, and **course performance** as the strongest predictors of high school completion.[55,56,57] Grade 9 course performance, in particular, has been shown to correlate strongly with high school graduation.[58]

This strategy takes this information and turns it into an easy-to-use tool for parents and caregivers—and for students themselves—to know what to watch to gauge their general trajectory for success. Share this tool with families to catch students at risk and act to change their path. It's a simple habit that only takes a few moments.

Tell families: "**Say your ABCs** each time you get a report card or progress report in any class. If you watch these three data points, you will have a good indication of how well the student is doing in school."

Share the ABC information: Do this in back-to-school speeches. Put it in writing (in the Student Handbook, in newsletters, on hall posters, and on the school social media).

Accentuate the positive: Emphasize that regular attendance to school and classes, appropriate behavior in classes and throughout the school, and strong performance on class assignments and assessments are main indicators of school success.

Alert families to the early warning signs of trouble: Chronic absenteeism or truancy, repeated discipline incidents (including suspensions or expulsions), and struggles in completion of classwork or low grades and poor assessment results (for in-class assessments as well as summative assessments) signal a need for help.

Send reminders: Every four weeks, tweet, post, and robocall every family. Here's my sample message: "Parents and caregivers, when you receive your child's report card, simply say your ABCs. Check your child's attendance, behavior, and course performance, particularly in math and language. If anything is lagging, please contact your child's teacher. If all indicators are strongly positive, celebrate your child's hard work!"

HAND LEADERSHIP STRATEGY 9: LEADERS TRADING PLACES

Purpose: Leaders refresh and learn skills by stepping into different instructional roles.

Principals, superintendents, instructional leaders, and many other non-teaching leaders are often in roles that make decisions related to instruction. Yet, many spend little (or no) time as a teacher or a learner in classrooms. Any leader that has a connection to instruction in the school needs such time. The most conventional way is to take turns now and then teaching a class period, a group of lessons, or even a full day.

This strategy challenges the middle school hand-centered leader to "get their hands" into the middle of instruction in a classroom—but with a twist. The idea is for the leader to trade places with someone in an instructional or learning role in a classroom or extracurricular learning setting. This gets leaders into classrooms. It gives also gives leaders a chance to see their leadership role through the eyes of others who trade places with them. Here's how it can work:

Step 1 The leader identifies a person in an instruction-related role (or asks for volunteers).

This can be a:

- teacher in any content area
- teacher in a different content area than theirs (if the person is a teacher)
- a teacher assistant
- a student (or pair of students)
- a coach or director of any program where teaching and guiding is involved

Note: You'd also need to arrange for an adult to be present when the students are doing the job trade.

Step 2 Both parties agree on a schedule for the trade. Start with times that are relatively short, but long enough for a meaningful experience.

Step 3 Each party prepares some advice or instructions about how to do their job. This might be a pamphlet, chart, digital guide, or other format. For example, the advice might be: "How to Be a Successful Sixth Grade Math Student" or "Guidelines for the Assistant Principal's Morning." The beauty of this is that each person is responsible to decide what is important for their "substitute" to know about how to do the job well.

Step 4 Arrange a period of time for each party to review their instructions and for a short Q&A exchange, if needed. Add any other preparation you feel is necessary.

Step 5 Make the trade.

Step 6 Schedule a debriefing session to reflect on and discuss such questions as: What went well? What was challenging? What was learned about the other's responsibilities? What was surprising?

This is an awesome learning experience for everyone involved. It keeps everyone closer to the realities of instruction and learning.

HAND LEADERSHIP STRATEGY 10: LEARNING ABOUT LEARNING WALKS

Purpose: Leaders design or review their processes for using brief, nonevaluative observations of classroom learning processes.

A learning walk is a leader's brief, structured visit to a classroom (or several classrooms) to watch learning in action and gather data on what is happening with instruction. Because these are short (3-10 minutes), leaders are able to visit each classroom often. The multiple quick visits give a progressing view of instructional patterns and issues while showing consistent interest in the teacher and students. The informal visits are strictly observational—not evaluative. Each one is always followed by a prompt dialogue with the teacher to solicit reflections and share feedback.

Use these guidelines to design or review your process for short observational visits to classrooms.

Characteristics of learning walks:

The process is intended to be structured, meaning that:

- PLCs or other teacher groups work with leaders to design the structure and expectations—including expectations and questions for the post-visit discussions. Teachers have input into the system for collecting data.
- All teachers have an orientation to the process.
- The visits have a focus. Teachers know what observers are looking for and what kinds of questions and thoughts will be discussed afterward.
- Though visits are unannounced, they are frequent enough that they become routine.
- Teachers orient students to the process of learning walks so they know what to expect.
- Teachers know that there will always be a debriefing and discussion following a visit.

Leaders look for:

The focus of learning walks may vary. Some use the walks for quick three-minute check-ins with the teacher and students. Others may focus on aspects that take longer to observe. For a focus on instruction, leaders note such factors as:

- Level and evidence of student engagement
- Implementation of effective practices
- What students are learning
- How students are learning
- Student interaction with content
- How learning strategies and curriculum plans are being used

- What's going well in terms of teaching
- Learning supports available in the classroom
- Evidence of students' thinking
- Evidence of planning
- Alignment of instruction to school goals and standards
- Where students or teachers face challenges

Learning walk must-do's:
Whatever the specific reason for the learning walk:

- Hold to the focus of the visit. Look for what you said you were going to look for.
- Pay attention to first impressions.
- During a visit you might ask students to tell you about what they are learning or how, but do not talk to the student or teacher if it interrupts the instruction.
- Use a pre-planned system for collecting data. Remember that evidence is what you see or hear in the moment, not what you presume or have heard before. Keep your system simple.
- Use the post-visit discussion for specific, constructive feedback. Use this as an opportunity for teachers to reflect on and explain their practices, identify their challenges, and share their improvements.
- Remember to avoid judgmental comments.

Other outcomes:
Learning walks provide information beyond the data and discussions that are helpful to individual teachers; the leader also gains. Leaders gather a series of instructional snapshots from across the school, which:

- Allows leaders to assess overall implementation of strategies.
- Informs plans for future professional development and school improvement.
- Gives a sense of the whole cadence of the school's learning environment.

Hand-Centered Leadership Strategies

Variation:
Authors and education professors Douglas Fisher and Nancy Frey suggest that teachers do such observations of one another. They find that when teachers take nonevaluative walkthroughs of colleagues' classrooms, they can greatly enhance their own learning and improve their teaching skills.[59]

HAND LEADERSHIP STRATEGY 11: SELF-CHECK ON MIDDLE SCHOOL CHARACTERISTICS

Purpose: Leaders collaborate with others to examine their implementation of the characteristics of a successful middle school.

AMLE has identified 18 Characteristics exhibited by successful middle schools in *The Successful Middle School, This We Believe*.[60] Every school can make a habit of reflecting periodically on the status of their school in relation to these characteristics. This can help leadership teams, instructional teams, or other collaborative groups reflect on strengths, needs, and progress. The results of a self-check can inform such processes and components as goals, team planning, strategic plans, management, and professional development priorities. For a more thorough exploration than this activity can provide, school can also utilize The Successful Middle School Assessment. Using an anonymized survey instrument, the Assessment measures implementation of the 18 Characteristics through a series of evidence-based exemplars and teams can choose to also include versions for families and students. The Assessment is coach-led and provides teams with a comprehensive report that baselines implementation and outlines areas of strength and growth. You can learn more at amle.org/SMS.

Step 1 Gather a collaborative group suited to your purposes for a general review of how you are doing with the characteristics.

Step 2 Using the following table, **Where Are We on the Characteristics?**, agree on one of the three rankings for each characteristic. You can use colors for an easy way to visualize results.

Step 3 After viewing the finished picture, use the results to identify areas for celebration and to set goals and priorities for improvement.

The Successful Middle School Leader

Where Are We on the Characteristics?

	Characteristic	**Green** *We do this consistently*	**Yellow** *We do this sometimes*	**Red** *We don't do this yet*
1	Educators respect and value young adolescents.			
2	The school environment is welcoming, inclusive, and affirming for all.			
3	Every student's academic and personal development is guided by an adult advocate.			
4	School safety is addressed proactively, justly, and thoughtfully.			
5	Comprehensive counseling and support services meet the needs of young adolescents.			
6	The school engages families as valued partners.			
7	The school collaborates with community and business partners.			
8	Educators are specifically prepared to teach young adolescents and possess a depth of understanding in the content areas they teach.			
9	Curriculum is challenging, exploratory, integrative, and diverse.			

10	Health, wellness, and social-emotional competence are supported in curricula, school-wide programs, and related policies.			
11	Instruction fosters learning that is active, purposeful, and democratic.			
12	Varied and ongoing assessments advance learning as well as measure it.			
13	A shared vision developed by all stakeholders guides every decision.			
14	Policies and practices are student-centered, unbiased, and fairly implemented.			
15	Leaders are committed to and knowledgeable about young adolescents, equitable practices, and educational research.			
16	Leaders demonstrate courage and collaboration.			
17	Professional learning for staff is relevant, long term, and job embedded.			
18	Organizational structures foster purposeful learning and meaningful relationships.			

Hand Leadership Strategy 12: Journaling: Leading from the Hand

Purpose: Leaders follow a practice of journaling to examine their leadership practices and enhance abilities to lead from the hand.

Reflection is slowing down to think about yourself, your actions, and your experiences. It is critical to growth as a leader and to your self-care.

1. Intentionally set aside a regular time, maybe 15 to 30 minutes. Protect this time.
2. Select a quiet place. Turn off devices and avoid distractions.
3. Put down your thoughts in paragraphs, sentences, phrases, outlines, poetry, or a narrative format. There is no one right or best way.
4. Choose a theme to ponder, or a topic or prompt, and get started.
5. Be honest. Notice your feelings as you write. Note those as well.

Some ideas for a journal entry related to leading from the hand:

- Your best hand leadership moment or experience this week
- An opportunity for strong leadership from the hand that you missed, and why
- An overview of the week, pondering what you learned about leading from the hand
- One thought or lesson learned (about your hand leadership) from a short encounter
- Examples of effective hand-centered leadership you witnessed
- Personal experience of any of the "fruits" of hand-centered leadership (see Chapter 7)
- Reflections on any of the traits in Chapter 8 as they relate to the status of your hand-centered leadership
- Hand-centered leadership strategies (from this chapter) you consciously used and how they worked

- Gratitude observations—names of people whose actions have assisted or uplifted you this week
- A look at an important value of yours and how it connects to your leadership from the hand
- Or many other reflections. Ideas will come to you!

The template on the next page, **Journaling Hand-Centered Leadership**, is an example of a tool you might create to record your thoughts. This particular sample could be used for a general overview of your week. You might put blank template pages into a notebook, use an actual book-like journal, or capture your thoughts in a digital format as if you were preparing to write a book.

Journaling Hand-Centered Leadership

Use this to guide in your reflection. Add other ideas if needed.

Theme, event, or topic for reflection today	
My best hand-leadership moment	
Another example of hand-centered leadership that I observed in myself	
A hand-centered leadership trait that I needed but didn't use	
Something I noticed about how my leadership from the hand affected someone else	
An important value and how it connected to my hand leadership this week	

Middle School Leader, You Are Built for This!

Final Thoughts

Your anatomy has fitted you ingeniously for this job. Leadership is a way of **being**; and the human organism that you **are** has all the components—heart, head, and hands—to **be** an outstanding middle school leader. It's often said that leaders are born. But I believe that leaders are developed. Due to your anatomy, you have unlimited possibilities for development. You can develop a holistic leadership from the heart, head, and hand. I say holistic because these sources of leadership can each grow and flourish best when they develop simultaneously, weaving together with mutual interdependence.

Now, a principal, teacher, coach, curriculum director, or other leader can be spectacular at leading from one (or even two) of these sources, but any one or two alone is less effective without the others. Unless all three are functioning well and in harmony, a leader will not be the amazing and effective leader that our young adolescents deserve.

As you arrive at the end of this book, I challenge you to keep reflecting on your strengths with each part of the leadership-anatomy metaphor. I challenge you, equally, to acknowledge places where you can grow—so that you are able to develop balanced leadership that comes from your open heart, sharp mind, and effective hand.

Be grateful for your anatomy! One of the remarkable things about it is its ability to grow and change, adapt and learn. That's a good thing—it is an absolute must that middle school leaders avoid falling into stagnation or complacency. The students are changing, their needs are changing, and the world is changing ever so fast. Our students are keeping up. We leaders have got to keep up with them. Here are some suggestions to renew and energize you on your middle school heart, head, and hand leadership journey.

NEVER UNDERESTIMATE YOUR APTITUDE FOR GROWTH. AND NEVER STOP LEARNING!

Live in a constant state of growth and development. Just as the body has to be fed to grow and be strong, effective leaders consume information, connections, experiences that help them grow professionally, emotionally, and spiritually. Keep finding out what students need and what will work well for your school. Keep taking chances. Push yourself beyond your limits. Take on challenges that require you to enter new territory and grapple with new concepts. When I was a teacher in elementary school, I noticed my principal had a heavy load of responsibilities and asked, "Ms. Williams, what's one thing I could take off your plate today?" It turned out to be a life-changing question for me—launching me to new places. Don't hesitate to take gutsy risks.

KEEP YOUR EYES AND EARS ON THE STUDENTS.

Young adolescent students, as they navigate the astounding changes in their lives, are glorious gifts to middle school leaders. Hang out with students. Watch them. Let them inspire you with their energy and creativity, their passion for novelty and change, their brilliant and innovative ideas. Listen to them. Consult them. Ask them to teach you what it's like to be a middle school student. (Keep your mind open to being shocked, awed, and moved.) Tell them what it's like to be a middle school leader. Take their advice. Truly, there is nothing more refreshing and enlightening than time spent with a bunch of middle schoolers. Treat yourself to the delight, challenge, surprise, and laughter they bring you. This increases your warmth and appreciation for them. It enables all leaders to provide middle school students with what they need most from you—your grace, patience, and persistent dedication.

DRAW STRENGTH AND INSPIRATION FROM OTHERS.

We know that middle school leadership jobs can be highly taxing mentally and intensely draining emotionally. Draw refreshment and comfort from your colleagues, students' families, and other members of the school community. Don't let yourself get isolated; this is an occupational hazard for many leaders. Lean on the power of "us" in the school community. Remember that you share a forceful connection with all the people around you: they are the ones who—like you—work or live with, know, and love your young adolescent students. Keep your relationships with these people strong and trusting. You are not alone in your mission; they are "with" you. Boost and champion one another for mutual uplifting. Learn together. Laugh together.

TAKE CARE OF YOURSELF.

You spend much of your life at school or concerned with school matters. Some of your self-care comes from within that setting, as I've suggested above. When you are in strong connection with your students, colleagues, and others in your school community, you'll have less stress, higher morale, increased stamina, and more job satisfaction. These good relationships are a boost to your well-being.

Take care of your physical self. I know it's hard for many of us to do this, what with our breakneck schedules in and beyond school. You'll be a better leader when you attend to your health. I don't need to elaborate on all the benefits. I will say that nothing relieves stress, nourishes my brain and spirit, and energizes me like exercise. Caring for yourself also means attending to your attitudes, motivations, and habits. Don't get trapped in rigid patterns or negative outlooks. Try to let go of old hurts, hostilities, or problems. Don't hold hard stuff inside. Share it. Deal with it. Carefully protect time for a life outside of school. Fuel your well-being by being present with those you love and who feed your whole being.

KEEP BELIEVING.

Approach your leadership with tenacious optimism. Keep looking forward. Believe in the future. There are new ventures, new students and families, new colleagues, new possibilities, new chapters for you and your colleagues. No matter what city, what neighborhood, what the condition of your school, what political issues surround you, believe that things can be better. Believe in the human spirit—in yours and in those you work with—that you can adapt, struggle, bear things you think are unbearable, survive, thrive, and rejoice together. Pass on this belief to your students, colleagues, and students' families, **not by what you say, but by how you lead**. Remember what my principal friend Dr. Vonda Beaty said: "Our scholars and teachers need a lift, not a lecture."

You have gifts, power, and courage that you have not yet used. You have the capacity to continue learning, dreaming, imagining, and soaring. It's all there, available to you, in your heart, head, and hands. You are built for this!

ENDNOTES

1. Kamath, S. (2019). *Cultivating self-awareness to move learning forward.* Education Dive. https://www.k12dive.com/spons/cultivating-self-awareness-to-move-learning-forward/565498/
2. Goleman, D. (2006). *Emotional intelligence: Why it can matter more than IQ.* Bantam.
3. Caprara, G. V., Barbaranelli, C., Steca, P., & Malone, P. S. (2006). Teachers' self-efficacy beliefs as determinates of job satisfaction and students' academic achievement: A study at the school level. *Journal of School Psychology, 44*(6), 473–490.
4. Kauffman, J. M., & Wong, K. L. (1991). Effective teachers of students with behavioral disorders: Are generic teaching skills enough? *Behavioral Disorders, 16*(3), 225–237.
5. Silvia, P. J., & O'Brien, M. E. (2004). Self-awareness and constructive functioning: Revisiting "the human dilemma." *Journal of Social and Clinical Psychology, 23*, 475–489.
6. Sutton, A., Williams, H. M., & Allinson, C. W. (2015). A longitudinal, mixed-method evaluation of self-awareness training in the workplace. *European Journal of Training and Development, 39*, 610–627.
7. Ridley, D. S., Schutz, P. A., Glanz, R. S., & Weinstein, C. E. (1992). Self-regulated learning: The interactive influence of metacognitive awareness and goal setting. *The Journal of Experimental Education, 60*, 293–306.
8. Silvia, P. J., & O'Brien, M. E. (2004). Self-awareness and constructive functioning: Revisiting "the human dilemma." *Journal of Social and Clinical Psychology, 23*, 475–489.
9. Sutton, A. (2016). Measuring the effects of self-awareness. *European Journal of Psychology, 12*(4), 645–658.
10. Bandura, A. (1997). *Self-efficacy: The exercise of control.* W Freeman/Times Books/ Henry Holt & Co.
11. Bishop, P. A., & Harrison, L. M. (2021). *The successful middle school: This we believe* (pp. 55–64). Association for Middle Level Education.
12. *King James Standard Version Bible.* (2023). Prov. 18:21.
13. Pope, A. (2018, July 12). *Shaq Reebok commercial 1993.* [Video]. YouTube. https://www.youtube.com/watch?v=taKQHlEAeNE

14. Bishop, P. A., & Harrison, L. M. (2021). *The successful middle school: This we believe* (p. 9). Association for Middle Level Education.
15. Sinek, S. (2009). *How great leaders inspire action*. [Video, 3:10-3:17]. YouTube. https://www.ted.com/talks/simon_sinek_how_great_leaders_inspire_action/transcript
16. Sinek, S. (2009). *How great leaders inspire action*. [Video, 3:02-3:49]. YouTube.
17. https://www.ted.com/talks/simon_sinek_how_great_leaders_inspire_action/transcript
18. Sinek, S. (2009). *How great leaders inspire action*. [Video, 15:00-6:00]. YouTube. https://www.ted.com/talks/simon_sinek_how_great_leaders_inspire_action/transcript
19. NPR. (2023, January 16). *Read Martin Luther King Jr.'s Speech 'I have a dream' speech in its entirety*. [Audio]. National Public Radio. https://www.npr.org/2010/01/18/122701268/i-have-a-dream-speech-in-its-entirety
20. Peters, K., & Haslam, A. (2018, August 6). Research: To be a good leader, start by being a good follower. *Harvard Business Review* (para. 3.). https://hbr.org/2018/08/research-to-be-a-good-leader-start-by-being-a-good-follower
21. Haslam, S. A., Reicher, S. D., & Platow, M. J. (2011). *The new psychology of leadership: Identity, influence, and power*. Psychology Press.
22. Peters, K., & Haslam, A. (2018, August 6). Research: To be a good leader, start by being a good follower. *Harvard Business Review* (para. 11). https://hbr.org/2018/08/research-to-be-a-good-leader-start-by-being-a-good-follower
23. Peters, K., & Haslam, A. (2018, August 6). Research: To be a good leader, start by being a good follower. *Harvard Business Review* (paras. 4–5). https://hbr.org/2018/08/research-to-be-a-good-leader-start-by-being-a-good-follower
24. Bishop, P. A., & Harrison, L. M. (2021). *The successful middle school: This we believe* (p. 9). Association for Middle Level Education.
25. *King James Standard Version Bible*. (2023). Ex. 18:12–27.
26. *King James Standard Version Bible*. (2023). Ex. 18:16, 18.
27. Council of Chief State School Officers. (2015). *Model Principal Supervisor Professional Standards 2015* (pp. 14–15). CCSSO.
28. McKay, B. (2018, November 12). *Leadership lessons from the pastor of one of America's most innovative churches*. Art of Manliness Podcast. [Audio]. https://www.artofmanliness.com/career-wealth/leadership/pastor-craig-groeschel-interview/

ENDNOTES

29. Siegel, D. J., & Bryson, T. P. (2018). *The yes brain: How to cultivate courage, curiosity, and resilience in your child.* Bantam.
30. Merriam-Webster. (n.d.). Courage. In *Merriam-Webster.com dictionary*. Retrieved September 17, 2023 from https://www.merriam-webster.com/dictionary/courage?src=search-dict-box
31. Haughey, D. (2014). *A brief history of SMART goals.* Project SMART. https://www.projectsmart.co.uk/brief-history-of-smart-goals.php
32. Leithwood, K., Louis, K. S., Anderson, S. E., & Wahlstrom, K. L. (2004). *How leadership influences student learning, executive summary.* The Wallace Foundation. Available at https://www.wallacefoundation.org/knowledge-center/pages/how-leadership-influences-student-learning.aspx
33. Louis, K. S., Leithwood, K., Wahlstrom, K. L., & Anderson, S. E. (2010). *Investigating the links to improved student learning: Final report of research findings.* The Wallace Foundation. Available at https://www.wallacefoundation.org/knowledge-center/pages/investigating-the-links-to-improved-student-learning.aspx
34. Leithwood, K., Louis, K. S., Anderson, S. E., & Wahlstrom, K. L. (2004). *How leadership influences student learning, executive summary.* The Wallace Foundation. Available at https://www.wallacefoundation.org/knowledge-center/pages/how-leadership-influences-student-learning.aspx
35. Grissom J. A., Egalite, A. J., & Lindsay, C. A. (2021). *How principals affect students and schools: A systematic synthesis of two decades of research.* The Wallace Foundation. Available at http://www.wallacefoundation.org/principalsynthesis
36. Cascade Team. (2022). *51 strategy statistics and 3 key lessons to help you succeed.* Cascade. https://www.cascade.app/blog/51-strategy-statistics
37. Jackson, T. (2023, April 14). *50+ eye-opening strategic planning statistics 2022.* ClearPoint Strategy. https://www.clearpointstrategy.com/blog/strategic-planning-statistics
38. Kaplan, R. S., & Horton, D. P. (1996). *The balanced scorecard: Translating strategy into action.* Harvard Business Press.
39. School Superintendents Association. (2015, May 5). *The balanced scorecard* (para. 7). AASA. https://www.aasa.org/resources/resource/the-balanced-scorecard
40. School Superintendents Association. (2015, May 5). *The balanced scorecard* (paras. 8–11). AASA. https://www.aasa.org/resources/resource/the-balanced-scorecard
41. McChesney, C., Covey, S., & Huling, J. (2021). *The 4 disciplines of execution: Achieving your wildly important goals.* Simon & Schuster.

42. Neuman, S. B. (2016). Code red: The danger of data-driven instruction. *Educational Leadership*, (para. 1). https://www.ascd.org/el/articles/code-red-the-danger-of-data-driven-instruction
43. Neuman, S. B. (2016). Code red: The danger of data-driven instruction. *Educational Leadership*, (para. 25). https://www.ascd.org/el/articles/code-red-the-danger-of-data-driven-instruction
44. Neuman, S. B. (2016). Code red: The danger of data-driven instruction. *Educational Leadership*, (paras. 26–32). https://www.ascd.org/el/articles/code-red-the-danger-of-data-driven-instruction
45. Bishop, P. A., & Harrison, L. M. (2021). *The successful middle school: This we believe* (p. 46). Association for Middle Level Education.
46. Routeledge. (2023, January 16). *A guide to visible learning and resources.* Routeledge blog. https://www.routledge.com/blog/article/what-is-visible-learning
47. Visible Learning (2023). *Collective teacher efficacy (CTE) according to John Hattie.* Visible Learning Website. https://visible-learning.org/2018/03/collective-teacher-efficacy-hattie/
48. Routeledge. (2023, January 16). *A guide to visible learning and resources.* Routeledge blog. https://www.routledge.com/blog/article/what-is-visible-learning
49. Adams, J. (2023). *The 7 habits of highly effective instructional leaders.* AMLE.org. para. 2). https://www.amle.org/the-7-habits-of-highly-effective-instructional-leaders/
50. McChesney, C., Covey, S., & Huling, J. (2021). *The 4 disciplines of execution: Achieving your wildly important goals.* Simon & Schuster.
51. McChesney, C., Covey, S., & Huling, J. (2021). *The 4 disciplines of execution: Achieving your wildly important goals* (p. 19). Simon & Schuster.
52. McChesney, C., Covey, S., & Huling, J. (2021). *The 4 disciplines of execution: Achieving your wildly important goals* (pp. 21–22). Simon & Schuster.
53. McChesney, C., Covey, S., & Huling, J. (2021). *The 4 disciplines of execution: Achieving your wildly important goals* (pp. 18–21). Simon & Schuster.
54. McChesney, C., Covey, S., & Huling, J. (2021). *The 4 disciplines of execution: Achieving your wildly important goals* (pp. 18-21). Simon & Schuster.
55. Bishop, P. A., & Harrison, L. M. (2021). *The successful middle school: This we believe* (p. 26). Association for Middle Level Education.
56. Bruce, M., Bridgeland, J. M., Fox, J. H., & Balfanz, R. (2011). *On Track for Success: The Use of Early Warning Indicator and Intervention Systems to Build a Grad Nation.* Civic Enterprises. Available at https://files.eric.ed.gov/fulltext/ED526421.pdf

ENDNOTES

57. Dynarski, M., Clarke, L., Cobb, B., Finn, J., Rumberger, R., & Smink, J. (2008). *Dropout prevention: A practice guide (NCEE #2008-4025).* U.S. Department of Education, Institute of Education Sciences, National Center for Education Evaluation and Regional Assistance. Available at https://ies.ed.gov/ncee/wwc/Docs/PracticeGuide/dp_pg_090308.pdf
58. Osher, D., Sprague, J., Weissber, R. P., Axelrod, J., Keenana, S., Kendziora, K., & Sins, J. E. (2007). Promoting social, emotional, and academic growth in contemporary schools. *Best Practices in School Psychology (4)*1, 1–16.
59. Strategic Data Project. (2012) *Are students who are off track to graduate in the ninth grade able to get back on track?* Center for Education Policy Research at Harvard University. https://sdp.cepr.harvard.edu/files/cepr-sdp/files/sdp-spi-v2-off-track-infographic.pdf
60. Fisher, D., & Frey, N. (2014, January). Using teacher learning walks to improve instruction. *Instructional Leader* (pp. 58–61).
61. Bishop, P. A., & Harrison, L. M. (2021). *The successful middle school: This we believe* (p. 9). Association for Middle Level Education.